# JANUA LINGUARUM

## STUDIA MEMORIAE
## NICOLAI VAN WIJK DEDICATA

*edenda curat*

C. H. VAN SCHOONEVELD

*Indiana University*

*Series Minor, 124*

# PROBLEMS IN THE CONSTRUCTION OF A THEORY OF NATURAL LANGUAGE

*by*

## PHILIP TARTAGLIA

*State University College at Potsdam*

1972

MOUTON

THE HAGUE · PARIS

P
106
T28

Printed in Belgium by NICI, Printers, Ghent.

64485

# ACKNOWLEDGEMENT

I wish to thank Professor Kai Nielsen for his valuable suggestions and encouragement in the writing of this book. Also, I gratefully acknowledge my indebtedness to a number of books from which I learned the basics of logic and linguistics and from which I have drawn in the following pages. Among these are : Church's *An Introduction to Mathematical Logic* (Princeton University Press, 1956), Gleason's *An Introduction to Descriptive Linguistics* (Holt, Rinehart and Winston, 1961), Harris' *Methods in Structural Linguistics* (University of Chicago Press, 1951), and Nagel's *The Structure of Science* (Harcourt, Brace and World, 1961).

# TABLE OF CONTENTS

Details of language — Ordinary language — Clarity — Words as tools — Different conceptual schemata — Excuses — Systematic aids — Logical grammar — Comprehensive science of language.

Ordinary use of an expression — Use and usage — Unwritten laws — Category — Category-mistake — Logical geography of concepts — Logical cross-bearings of concepts.

Uninterpreted calculus — Requirement of effectiveness — Interpretation — Soundness — Syntax and Semantics — Object-language and meta-language — Carnap's formal semantics — State-description — Meaning postualtes — Pragmatics — Semantic rules — Synonymy — Analyticity.

Description of natural language — Stipulation — Distortion of natural language — The ideal model — Unsystematic nature of natural language — Consistency and elegance.

Correspondence rules — Primitive semantic terms — Pure mathematics — Relevance to natural language — Carnap's formal semantics — Empirical behavioristic procedures for formal semantic notions — Intensionality — Intuitive controls — Appeal to the linguistic intuition.

Descriptive linguistics — Historical linguistics — Comparative linguistics.

Language and dialect — Collective data — Elements as logical symbols — Phonology — Morphology — Semantics.

Intuitive and nonintuitive explanations — Phonetic difference — Phonemic difference — Minimal contrasting pair —

Phonemic relativity to particular languages — Nonintuitive characterization of phoneme — Complementary distribution — Contrastive distribution — Phonetic transcription — Allophones — Kinds of phonemes in English.

Intuitive and nonintuitive explanation — A higher level of linguistic element — Recurrent partials — Smallest meaningful recurring phoneme sequences — Kinds of morphemes — Allomorphs — Infixes — Affixes — Phonological conditioning — Morphological conditioning — Morphemic segments — Free variation — Tentative morphemes — Morphemes.

Derivation and inflection — Traditional description — Distributional relations — Paradigmatic classes — Syntactic classes — Inflectional suffixes — Derivational affixes.

Immediate constituent grammars — Structural similarity — Construction — Constituent — Immediate constituent — Comparing samples — Method of substitution — Freedom of occurrence.

Goals — Traditional grammar — Conditions of adequacy — Abstract grammar — Models for grammar — Frequency model — Finite state Markov process model — Phrase structure model — Immediate constituent grammar — Transformational grammar — Obligatory transformations — Optional transformations — Success in grammar — Grammar and meaning.

Absolute meaning — Platonic idea — Essence — Mental image — Reference — Synonymy — Linguistic context — Extra-linguistic context — Goal of semantics — Scope of semantics — Components of a semantic theory — Dictionary — Projection rules — Semantic interpretation.

Practical and nonintuitive — Kind of synonymy — Criterion for synonymy — Definition — Interchangeability — Stimulus meaning — Stimulus synonymy — Sentence synonymy — Goodman's criterion for synonymy.

difference — Common relevant semantic difference —
Dictionary entry.

Inadequacy of principle of conventionality — Relevant
conditions — Irrelevant conditions — Degree of generality
— Vagueness of 'condition' — Inadequacy of the principle
of composition — Appeal to linguistic intuition — Status of
intuitive insights — Conditions generally associated with an
utterance.

Conflict with experience — Re-evaluation of statements —
The Lexicographer's problem in terms of the analytic-synthetic distinction — Incompatibility with lexicographer's
problem — Exact synonymy — Fuzzy boundaries.

Isolated hypotheses — Systematic principles — The nature
of light — Newton's optics versus Huygens' optics —
Refutation of postulates of physics.

Kinetic energy — Revision of principles — Conventionality
in science — The language of science and natural language.

Hofstadter's attack upon holism — The systematic view,
not the holistic view — Stipulation by the theory — A single
dictionary — Grice and Strawson's criterion for statement
synonymy — Appeal to linguistic intuition.

What Quine claims to show — What Quine in fact shows —
The insolubility of the lexicographer's problem.

A plea to our semantic intuition — Family circle of interdefinable expressions — Informal explanation — Sentence
significance and synonymy — Putnam's criteria — Generally
accepted criterion for the use of a term — Circular
definitions — Too strong a condition of adequacy — Mates's

empirical criterion for analycity — The appeal to intuition
— The observation of behavior — Fuzziness.

# LIST OF FIGURES

# I

## INTRODUCTION

In recent years there has been much talk about a theory of natural language. First we heard such talk from ideal-language philosophers, then from ordinary-language philosophers, and most recently from structural linguists. The fact that concern about a theory of natural language has been shown by men of such different academic backgrounds as Ryle and Chomsky indicates that a theory of natural language is not the preoccupation of a small group of specialists. The question of the possibility of the construction of a theory of natural language, as well as questions concerning the actual construction of such a theory, are live questions today. The successful construction of such a theory would be of considerable importance to such disciplines as philosophy (as we shall show) and linguistics as well as to such a practical enterprise as machine translation. It is interesting to note that a number of trends in this century have combined to provide the groundwork for a theory of natural language and to make the construction of such a theory something more than a hopeful dream. Among these trends have been the linguistic revolution in philosophy, certain achievements in modern mathematics, and the development of structural (descriptive) linguistics as a genuine science.

Before we go any further we must make quite clear what we mean by 'theory of natural language'. The definition of 'theory of natural language' which we choose, of course, is determined by what we expect from such a theory; that is, the definition is determined by the goal we set for such a theory. The goal of a theory of natural language is the explication of the mechanism by which fluent speakers of a language are able to produce and understand the meaningful utterances of the given language.[1] Involved in this goal are the following: A theory of natural language must be able to predict which utterances will be acceptable to fluent speakers as meaningful sentences and which will not. A theory of natural language must be able to predict of an acceptable utterance that it will be interpreted in one way rather than another or that it will be interpreted in several ways.

From the goal of a theory of natural language we begin to note the essential features of such a theory. A theory of natural language is a descriptive device. Such a theory describes the actual verbal behavior of fluent speakers as well as how fluent speakers interpret this behavior. A theory of natural language is a predictive device. It predicts in a practical nonintuitive manner those meaningful utterances which might be produced or understood by a fluent speaker. For any given utterance, it predicts in a nonintuitive manner whether or not it will be understood, whether or not it will be understood in more than one way, and the different ways in which it will be understood. A theory of natural language is a falsifiable device. There always remains the possibility of the falsification of a theory of natural language by means of empirical matters regarding fluent speakers. A theory of natural language is a nonintuitive device. Since it is the linguistic intuition of fluent speakers which the theory must explicate, it should be obvious that, upon pain of vicious circularity, the theory must not rely upon such intuition. (Though this point seems rather elementary, it has often been overlooked.) Though linguistic intuition cannot be appealed to in the actual working of the theory, linguistic intuition plays a role in the empirical control upon the theory. *The bachelor is dead* can be understood in a number of ways depending upon the senses of the constituent

---

[1] For a more detailed discussion of the goals of a theory of language see Noam Chomsky, *Syntactic Structures* (The Hague: Mouton and Co., 1957), Chapters 1, 2, 4.

words. A theory of natural language must be able to predict (by strictly nonintuitive means) the different ways in which this utterance may be interpreted. Though our linguistic intuition is an empirical check upon the theory, our linguistic intuition cannot be part of the theory itself. Thus we see that a theory of natural language is a genuine scientific theory (vs. speculative or vacuous theory) whose aim is the explication of the linguistic intuition of fluent speakers, and consequently which cannot appeal to the linguistic intuition of fluent speakers, whether the investigator's or his subject's.

We place some further restrictions upon the type of theory of natural language in which we shall be concerned. We shall be concerned only with theories which do not attempt to take matters of extra-linguistic setting or context into consideration. The justification for our choosing such a type of theory for our concern will have to wait till later. Further, we shall be concerned only with a type of theory which has a 'dictionary' as part of its semantic component. (We shall use the word 'dictionary' in a strictly technical sense which we shall make clear later.) Our conclusions concerning the construction of a theory of natural language only pertain to a theory which contains such a dictionary.

Above we have already used the terms 'intuition' and 'nonintuitive', and we shall go on to use the term 'intuition', 'intuitive', and 'nonintuitive' many times in the chapters which follow. Because there is a certain amount of ambiguity associated with these terms, it is important that there be no misunderstanding as to what we mean by them. By 'intuition' we do not mean 'a mysterious avenue of knowledge'. For example, we do not use 'intuitive' as it would normally be understood in the sentence *Women are more intuitive than men.* When we speak of our linguistic intuition we mean our unanalyzed habits of language. When we say that we have an intuitive notion of grammaticalness we mean that we habitually and without reflection distinguish some utterances as grammatical and others as ungrammatical. When we say that *porpoise* and *dolphin* are intuitively synonymous we mean that we habitually and without reflection take them to be synonymous. Quine, in protesting that his use of 'intuitive' has been misconstrued, writes : "By an intuitive account I mean one in which terms are used in habitual ways without reflecting on how they might be defined or what presuppositions they might conceal."[2]

In the context of language theory the word 'formal' often is used ambiguously. Sometimes it is used in the sense of 'in abstraction from meaning', 'free from considerations of meaning', or 'syntactical', while at other times it is used in the sense of 'nonintuitive'. In this book we shall always use 'formal' in the former sense. In many a universe of discourse 'formal' and 'nonintuitive' are co-extensional but not in the universe of discourse concerning language theory. For example, by appealing to our linguistic intuition of grammatical structure we might give an intuitive formal account of some portion of grammar. Such an account would be intuitive because it appealed to one's linguistic intuition, yet it would be formal because it was free from considerations of meaning. To use 'formal' and 'nonintuitive' interchangeably, as is often done, can only lead to confusion.

Descriptive linguists and logicians prefer to work with sentences and 'readings of sentences' rather than with statements. The reason for this is that 'statement', having a richer and more controversial philosophical history, is often used in more than one way. We, however, shall find it necessary to speak of statements; therefore, it is imperative that we stipulate just what we shall mean by 'statement'.

Consider the sentence *The bachelor was hungry*. Further, assume that *bachelor* is the only ambiguous word in this sentence. The four possible meanings for *bachelor* are :

1. A young knight serving under the standard of another knight.
2. One who possesses the first or lowest academic degree.
3. A man who has never been married.
4. A young fur seal when without a mate during the breeding season.

[2] W.V. Quine, *Word and Object* (Cambridge : M.I.T. Press, 1960), footnote, p. 36.

Now taking *bachelor* in each of these four senses we can obtain four different readings for the sentence *The bachelor was hungry*. Let us call these, respectively : Readings (1), (2), (3), (4).

We shall say that each reading expresses one and only one statement. In other words, we shall use 'statement' in such a way that a statement is completely determined by a reading of a sentence. Some philosophers use 'statement' to mean 'that which is expressed by a reading of a sentence on a particular occasion and for a particular purpose'. According to such a use of 'statement', Reading (1) (*The young knight serving under the standard of another knight was hungry*) could express two different statements depending upon the context of its use. We preclude, by stipulation, such a possibility. A reading of a sentence makes one and only one statement. As we shall show in a later chapter, a theory of natural language which takes extra-linguistic context into consideration is not feasible. Therefore the descriptive linguist is forced to work with the notion of statement as here stipulated. He cannot possibly work with a notion of statement which is dependent upon extra-linguistic context.

The problems we set for ourselves in this book are the following : To what extent do so-called theories of natural language ('theory of natural language' and similar expressions are often used loosely in philosophical literature) represent attempts to construct genuine scientific theories of natural language ? What achievements have been made in the construction of such a theory, and what difficulties have been encountered ? To what extent are these difficulties merely technical difficulties requiring only further study for solution, and to what extent are these difficulties logical difficulties due to the very nature of natural language ?

The critical aims of this book are the following : We shall attempt to show that the so-called language theories of both ordinary-language philosophers and ideal-language philosophers are not genuine scientific theories. We shall attempt to show that behavioristic theories of natural language of the type offered by Skinner have met with total failure. We shall attempt to show that though structural linguists have made very impressive progress in certain aspects of language theory, they have failed to solve certain crucial problems in semantics. We shall try to show that the early success achieved by structural linguists in language theory, rather than being reason for optimism concerning the solution of their remaining problems, actually is reason for pessimism concerning the solution of these problems. Lastly, we shall try to show that not only have structural linguists met with repeated failure concerning crucial problems, but also that these problems are in principle insoluble because of the very nature of natural language.

Let us at this point briefly mention what we shall attempt to do in each of the chapters which follow. In Chapter II we make an abstract analysis of scientific theories. This we do for two reasons. First, certain of our critical remarks concerning ideal-language philosophy depend upon a thorough understanding of the abstract nature of scientific theories. Second, we want to show quite clearly that the type of theory structural linguists are attempting to construct is genuinely scientific; that is, we want to show that the type of theory structural linguists are attempting to construct conforms to the abstract requirements of scientific theories.

In Chapter III we show that ordinary-language philosophers have not provided us with a descriptive theory of natural language, and in Chapter IV we show that ideal-language philosophers have not provided us with such a theory.

Our concern with the structural linguists' theories of natural language (a major concern of this book) begins with Chapter V. This chapter serves more or less as an introduction to the problems and methods of structural linguists in the fields of phonology and morphology. In Chapter VI, after getting into the fields of grammar and semantics, we attempts to show that the achievements of structural linguists in grammar should not make them optimistic concerning their semantic task. In this chapter we also discuss a number of the difficulties encountered in the attempts to solve relatively elementary semantic problems. In

Chapters VII and VIII we show how Katz and Fodor, and Ziff, respectively, fail in their attempts to provide us with the semantic portion of a descriptive theory of natural language. In Chapter IX we present a fairly well accepted view of natural language which is incompatible with the solution of the problems of semantics. In Chapter X we defend our critical remarks against arguments appearing in the recent literature. In order to make our survey of attempted language theories complete, in Chapter XI we consider Skinner's attempt at functional analysis. Though Skinner's functional analysis is essentially different in aim from the other language theories which we discuss in this book, it can be considered as an attempt to provide some sort of a theory of natural language. In Chapter XII we bring together our conclusions.

At this point it seems natural to ask : Of what philosophical value would a theory of natural language be ? There are those who would answer that a theory of natural language would be of use to the ordinary-language philosopher, for it could provide him with such information as what can and cannot be said in natural language, which sentences are ambiguous, which sentences are paraphrases of other sentences, etc. We do NOT make such a claim. The ordinary-language philosopher does not need a theory for he, as a fluent speaker of his language, knows what can and cannot be said in natural language, which sentences are ambiguous, which sentences are paraphrases of other sentences, etc. As we have already noted, a theory of natural language attempts to duplicate, nonintuitively, the linguistic intuition of fluent speakers concerning such matters as grammaticalness, meaningfulness, ambiguity, and analyticity. The linguistic intuition of fluent speakers concerning such matters has logical priority over the nonintuitive explication of such linguistic intuition. First comes the intuition and then comes the nonintuitive device. If a fluent speaker required a theory of natural language to tell him whether or not a given sentence was ambiguous, there could be no theory; for the adequacy of a theory of natural language is itself determined by the linguistic intuition (including that concerning ambiguity) of fluent speakers. Before I can judge the adequacy of a nonintuitive explication of ambiguity, I must intuitively be able to recognize cases of ambiguity; otherwise there would be nothing to explicate.

Where then does the philosophical value of a theory of natural language lie ? It lies simply and clearly in the explication of intuitive concepts relevant to philosophy. I would gain considerable insight into a matter traditionally considered in the realm of philosophy if I could nonintuitively explicate my intuitions of synonymy, analyticity, or significance. Logic, since Aristotle, has been considered a part of philosophy. Language theory should be considered merely as an expanded logic. The nonintuitive explication of intuitive concepts of traditional concern to philosophy, is justification enough for a theory of natural language. Herein lies the philosophical value of such a theory.

# II

# A LOGICAL ANALYSIS OF SCIENTIFIC THEORIES

Though we certainly do not want to get bogged down in scientific methodology, it is necessary that we make a few preliminary remarks about the nature of scientific theories. This is necessary for two reasons. First, we want to make it quite clear that the sort of theory of natural language attempted by linguists qualifies as a genuine scientific theory. Second, certain criticisms of the ideal-language approach to language theory can be fully understood only after certain essential features of scientific theories have been established.

For the purposes of this book it is not necessary that we get involved in the controversy over the cognitive status of scientific theories or the nature of theoretical objects. We are interested in analyzing scientific theories only from a very special logically abstract point of view. It makes no difference to the argument of this book whether scientific theories are no more than instruments or more than instruments. All that we must establish in that they are at least instruments. It should be remembered that an instrumentalistic interpretation of scientific theories is not at all incompatible with a realistic interpretation of scientific theories. To say that scientific theories are instruments is not to say that they are no more than instruments. In what follows it may seem that we are advocating an exclusively instrumentalistic conception of scientific theories. We are not. For our purposes it is only necessary that we establish the instrumental role of theories. Scientific theories may be more than just instruments, but they are at least instruments. We are only concerned to make some points about scientific theories as instruments.

### SCIENTIFIC THEORIES AS INSTRUMENTS

From a certain point of view, a scientific theory can be considered a device (function) which, by means of statements concerning abstract entities, systematizes observed phenomena and from such phenomena predicts new phenomena. Using a different mode of speech we might say : A scientific theory is a device which, by means of statements involving abstract primitive terms, relates observational statements and from such statements predicts other observational statements. Going a step further, since a scientific theory is a predictive device, its validation consists in testing its predictive power.

The logical character (from our abstract point of view) of scientific theories is nicely brought out in Nagel's "Symbolism and Science",[1] an article in which he deals with the various kinds of symbols found in science. A descriptive symbol, according to Nagel, is a symbol which, regardless of how its use may have been learned, can be applied by its users to "matters falling within some controlled observation or sets of observations". An auxiliary symbol is a symbol "whose primary function is to serve as a connective between other symbols — and ultimately between descriptive symbols — and whose role in the total system of symbols is not affected by the circumstance that there may be no rules or habits associated with it which govern its application to anything that may be manifest to observation".[2] Auxiliary symbols provide logical relations between descriptive symbols, which prior to the introduction of auxiliary symbols were logically isolated from each other. Descriptive symbols, thus, are given a

---

[1] E. Nagel, "Symbolism and Science", *Logic without Metaphysics* (Free Press, 1956). First pub. in *Symbolism and Values* (Harper, 1954).
[2] *Ibid.*, p. 117.

significance beyond that which they had prior to the introduction of auxiliary symbols.

Nagel goes on to contend that scientific theories and their constituent symbols are auxiliary symbols. Scientific theories are instruments for establishing linkages between descriptive symbols. A scientific theory is an instrument which logically connects two sets of descriptive symbols in such a manner that if a member of the first set correctly characterizes a given phenomenon then a corresponding member of the second set also correctly characterizes some other phenomenon. "In short, the function of a theory is that of an auxiliary symbol, with the further provision that it is an auxiliary symbol which must enable us to predict."[3]

In explicating the nature of scientific theories it is helpful to compare them with experimental laws — statements which, though similar to scientific theories, are significantly different. Each descriptive (nonlogical) constant in an experimental law is associated with at least one overt experimental procedure. The procedure associated with a given nonlogical constant thereby fixes (even if only partially) the meaning of the given constant. Because the meanings of the nonlogical constants in experimental laws are determined independently of the experimental laws themselves, it is possible to obtain direct evidence for given experimental laws. Consider the experimental law : Metals expand when heated. Each descriptive constant is associated with some experimental procedure. There are definite procedures, independent of this law, for determining whether or not a given substance is metal; there are definite procedures, independent of this law, for determining whether or not something has expanded; there are definite procedures, independent of this law, for determining whether or not something has been heated. Because of this, direct evidence can be obtained for the above experimental law.

Contrasting with what is true of descriptive (nonlogical) constants in experimental laws is the fact that not all the descriptive (nonlogical) constants in a scientific theory are associated with

[3]    *Ibid.*, p. 126.

at least one overt experimental procedure. Most, if not all, of the descriptive (nonlogical) constants — that is, most, if not all, of the primitive descriptive terms — are defined only implicitly by means of the postulates in which they occur or are given meaning only indirectly by means of the uses to which the theory eventually may be put. The various sets of meanings which may be assigned to the descriptive (nonlogical) constants of a theory when it is put to some use, are restricted to those sets of meanings which satisfy the structural relations specified by the formal postulates. Since not all of the nonlogical constants in a theory are defined independently of the postulates in which they occur — that is, since not all of the nonlogical constants are associated with definite experimental procedures — it is not possible to obtain direct evidence for a scientific theory. In fact there can be no question of evidence until the theory is 'applied'.

## COMPONENTS OF SCIENTIFIC THEORIES

Now that we have made a preliminary comparison of theory and law we are ready to make a more detailed analysis of theory. Nagel in *The Structure of Science*[4] distinguishes three components of a scientific theory: First, there is an abstract calculus (uninterpreted calculus) which 'implicitly defines' the primitive notions of the theory and thus provides the logical skeleton of the theory. Second, there is a model or interpretation for the abstract calculus which provides the calculus with a familiar conceptual or visualizable interpretation. (Such a model or interpretation, however, does not necessarily relate the theory to an empirical subject matter — as is often but erroneously thought.) Third, there is a set of rules which relates the elements of the theory to experimental procedures and thus assigns an empirical content to the abstract calculus.

Let us first consider the abstract calculus of a scientific theory.

[4]   E. Nagel, *The Structure of Science* (New York : Harcourt, Brace and World, 1961), p. 90.

The abstract calculus is no more than a symbolic system whose nonlogical symbols have no meaning other than the abstract relational 'meaning' supplied by the logical relations among the nonlogical symbols. The abstract nonlogical constants of an abstract calculus are only 'implicitly defined' by the postulates in which they occur; that is, they have no meaning other than the structural 'meaning' they receive by virtue of their place in the postulate system. It is not incorrect to say that the abstract calculus of a scientific theory is a symbolic system whose nonlogical symbols are merely markings on paper devoid of meaning except for that purely syntactical 'meaning' provided by the logical symbols relating the nonlogical symbols. Since the postulates of a given abstract calculus are not statements but only statement forms, they assert nothing whatsoever. From the postulates of the abstract calculus other statement forms are derived by the rules of deduction. These statement forms are as 'meaningless' as the postulates from which they are derived. By now it should be clear that the only genuine meanings involved in the abstract calculus of a scientific theory are logical meanings (meanings which belong to logic proper such as the interpretations given to the symbols '$\supset$', '$\vee$', '$(\exists x)$', etc.) either in the form of logical symbols connecting the nonlogical symbols or in the form of rules of deduction which permit inferences from statement forms to statement forms.

Customarily, the postulates of a scientific theory are embedded in a model or interpretation. Theories are not usually stated solely in terms of abstract postulates — that is, abstract calculi are usually not presented totally uninterpreted — but rather are stated in terms of familiar conceptual or visualizable notions. Such a practice is followed in order to facilitate the understanding of the abstract notions of the theory and in order to take advantage of the suggestive powers of the model — suggestive powers concerning fresh lines of inquiry. Though interpretations and models are considered most valuable, it must be remembered that the nonlogical terms of the postulates are defined (implicitly) solely by the postulates themselves and not in the least by the particular conceptual or visual interpretation which may be given to the nonlogical constants. Though a scientific theory usually is presented in the form of a model or interpretation, the theory still requires to be applied to an empirical subject matter. The model of a theory does not replace the need for connecting the abstract nonlogical constants of the abstract calculus with concrete matters of experiment. (The only exception to this is when the model is of such a nature that in addition to its usual heuristic function, it also relates the abstract calculus to experimental procedures. However, that a model plays this dual role is not usually the case and certainly cannot be assumed.) Models or interpretations though of practical and heuristic importance are eliminable in principle. Contrarily, abstract calculi and rules relating the calculi to experimental matters are indispensable to theories.

In order to complete our explication of the abstract calculus component and the model component of a scientific theory, let us consider an example of a scientific theory. Nagel provides us with such an example — a sketch of Bohr's atomic theory.

It [Bohr's atomic theory] assumes that there are atoms, each of which is composed of a relatively heavy nucleus carrying a positive electric charge and a number of negatively charged electrons with smaller mass moving in approximately elliptic orbits with the nucleus at one of the foci. The number of electrons circulating around the nucleus varies with the chemical elements. The theory further assumes that there are only a discrete set of permissable orbits for the electrons, and that the diameters of the orbits are proportional to $h^2n^2$, where $h$ is Planck's constant (the value of the indivisible quantum of energy postulated in Max Planck's theory of radiation) and $n$ is an integer. Moreover, the electromagnetic energy of an electron in an orbit depends on the diameter of the orbit. However, as long as an electron remains in any one orbit, its energy is constant and the atom emits no radiation. On the other hand, an electron may "jump" from an orbit with a higher energy level to an orbit with a lower energy level; and when it does so, the atom emits an electromagnetic radiation, whose wave length is a function of these energy differences.[5]

[5]   *Ibid.*, p. 94.

As with most scientific theories, Bohr's atomic theory is presented by way of a model, a model depicting a rather easily visualizable state of affairs — particles moving in elliptical orbits around other particles and occasionally jumping from one orbit to another. Though the model facilitates the handling of the abstract notions in the theory, it is the set of abstract postulates and not the model which defines (implicitly) the abstract notions such as electron and electron jump. Though the model presents electrons as particles — small bits of matter having the usual characteristics of such — 'electron' has no meaning other than that assigned to it by the abstract postulates. The usual meanings associated with the familiar notions in the model can not be automatically assigned to the abstract terms of the calculus. Bohr's atomic theory is no more and no less than the logical relations which hold among the abstract concepts as stated by the abstract postulates. Further, it should be recognized that though the model of Bohr's theory provides us with a visual representation of the theory, the model in no way relates the theory to experimental procedures and thus in no way gives it an empirical content. A model must not be confused with correpondence rules — which we shall next consider.

Correspondence rules — the third component of a scientific theory, if the theory is to be anything more than a game — relate the abstract calculus of a theory to concrete materials of observation and experiment, and in so doing, assign empirical content to the theory. A correspondence rule institutes a relation, sometimes called an epistemic correlation, between an abstract notion and an experimental notion. Northrop writes :

An epistemic correlation is a relation joining an unobserved component of anything designated by a concept by postulation [an abstract notion] to its directly inspected component denoted by a concept by intuition [experimental notion]. Such relations are two-termed relations. This means, also, that an epistemic correlation joins the aesthetic component of a thing to its theoretic component.[6]

[6]   F. Northrop, *The Logic of the Sciences and the Humanities* (New York : Meridian, 1959), p. 119.

It is by means of epistemic correlations that unobservable entities and relations designated by concepts by postulation take on an operational meaning and thereby become capable of being put to experimental test. Thus it is the relation of epistemic correlation which makes the operational meaning of a theoretical concept of science possible and which makes the operational definitions of scientific concepts important.[7]

Let us consider our example of a scientific theory, Bohr's atomic theory, in order to see how correspondence rules relate the abstract calculus to experimental procedures. The abstract notions in Bohr's theory, such as electron jump, are defined (implicitly) only by the abstract postulates of the theory and thus do not directly apply to experimental procedures. It is the job of the correspondence rules to connect the abstract notions to definite experimental notions. As for the abstract notion of electron jump, this is done in the following manner. A correspondence rule associates an electron jump from one orbit to another with the wave length of a light ray emitted by an atom. The wave length of the light ray emitted by the atom is, in turn, associated with a line in the spectrum of an element. Thus, we have a connection between the notion of an electron jump and a definite experimental notion — a line in the spectrum of an element. Once the connection is made between the abstract and experimental notions the theory can be used to deduce statements about observational matters, and observational matters can serve to confirm or disconfirm the theory relative to a given application. In other words, once correspondence rules are instituted, the theory can be put to work and questions of adequacy, with regard to a particular application, become relevant.

In passing it should be noted that, although some nonlogical constants in a theory must be linked with experimental procedures, not every nonlogical constant need be linked with an experimental procedure. Scientific theories, by retaining some abstract notions which have no empirical application, remain flexible in the sense that the theory may be extended to cover new areas of inquiry. New areas can be covered by introducing additional

[7]    *Ibid.*, pp. 122-123.

correspondence rules for those abstract notions not yet linked with experimental procedures. However, if a theory is to have empirical content — if a theory is to apply to empirical matters and if questions of adequacy are to be in order — at least some of the abstract notions must be correlated with experimental procedures by correspondence rules. Further, if individual abstract notions in the theory are to be empirically significant they must be linked with experimental procedures by correspondence rules.

# III

## LANGUAGE THEORY AND
## ORDINARY-LANGUAGE PHILOSOPHY

Our primary concern in this chapter is to ascertain whether or not ordinary-language philosophers have supplied us with a theory of natural language, or any part of one, meeting the requirements outlined in Chapter I. We shall not be concerned with attacking or defending the method of ordinary-language philosophy. Nor shall we be concerned with the question of whether or not a systematic theory of natural language is a prerequisite for doing ordinary-language philosophy. We take as more or less representative of ordinary-language philosophers: Wittgenstein, Austin, and Ryle. Our procedure shall be to give brief accounts of those parts of their thought which might be construed as relevant to developing a theory of natural language. Then we shall look to see whether or not they have, in any way, contributed to the construction of a theory of natural language. We begin with Wittgenstein.

### WITTGENSTEIN

It is not our purpose to examine thoroughly the Wittgensteinian revolution in philosophy nor to indiscriminately review Wittgenstein's methodological ideas. Since those ideas of Wittgenstein which are relevant to our discussion are not found in any compact section of his writing, we are forced to select relevant comments where we can. We shall restrict ourselves to the later Wittgenstein, and more specifically to his *Philosophical Investigations.*[1]

[1] Ludwig Wittgenstein, *Philosophical Investigations* (New York : Macmillan, 1953).

We noted earlier in our discussion concerning the requirements of a theory of natural language, that such a theory is a purely descriptive device. A theory of natural language seeks only to describe — and not to improve upon in any way — natural language, in the sense of reproducing the mechanism by which fluent speakers make and understand meaningful utterances of the language. This notion of the description of language is stressed throughout the later Wittgenstein. According to him philosophy explains nothing, it only describes. In order to overcome philosophical disorder concerning such matters as knowledge, sensation, and intention, we have no recourse but to describe exactly our usage of the words employed in speaking about such matters. "We must do away with all *explanation*, and description alone must take its place. And this description gets its light, that is to say its purpose — from the philosophical problems."[2] There is nothing beyond exact description in philosophy; there is nothing to explain, simply because there is nothing which is hidden. "Philosophy simply puts everything before us, and neither explains nor deduces anything. — Since everything lies open to view there is nothing to explain."[3]

Wittgenstein maintains that it is not the job of the philosopher to improve upon language. "... It is clear that every sentence in our language 'is in order as it is'. That is to say, we are not *striving after* an ideal, as if our ordinary vague sentences had not yet got a quite unexceptionable sense, and a perfect language awaited construction by us."[4] Wittgenstein takes very seriously the maxim that philosophers, in dealing with the problems of philosophy, must not tamper with natural language as they find it. "Philosophy may in no way interfere with the actual use of language; it can in the end only describe it."[5] The problems of philosophy will be solved by examining language as it is found in everyday intercourse, no matter how gross or vague. The prob-

---

[2] *Ibid.*, sec. 109.
[3] *Ibid.*, sec. 126.
[4] *Ibid.*, sec. 98.
[5] *Ibid.*, sec. 124.

lems will not be solved by attempting to concentrate our intellectual powers upon extremely fine points of thought as if the solution to our philosophical problems lay hidden from us and required that we clear away the misleading mundane language responsible for the problems. "Here it is difficult as it were to keep our heads up, — to see that we must stick to the subjects of our every-day thinking, and not go astray and imagine that we have to describe extreme subtleties... ."[6] We must examine language when it is doing its daily work and not when it is idling, that is, not when it is wrenched from its natural commonplace setting. "When philosophers use a word — 'knowledge', 'being', 'object', 'I', 'proposition', 'name' — and try to grasp the *essence* of the thing, one must always ask oneself : is the word ever actually used in this way in the language-game which is its original home ?"[7]

A theory of natural language must reflect all of the various functions of language. A theory of natural language cannot assume that language functions in only one way or that language has some primary function. The touchstone in constructing a theory of natural language must always be the fluent speaker and not the specialist. Wittgenstein's remarks concerning the task of the philosopher are in harmony with these ideas. He, in discussing a certain paradox which arises concerning sensation, writes : "The paradox disappears only if we make a radical break with the idea that language always functions in one way, always serves the same purpose : to convey thoughts — which may be about houses, pains, good and evil, or anything else you please."[8] Wittgenstein would not only want to broaden our conception of language so as to include more than just the descriptive function of language, but it seems that he would draw no definite boundary for meaningful utterances. At any rate, he would make the boundary relative to purpose.

---

[6] *Ibid.*, sec. 106.
[7] *Ibid.*, sec. 116.
[8] *Ibid.*, sec. 304.

To say "This combination of words makes no sense" excludes it from the sphere of language and thereby bounds the domain of language. But when one draws a boundary it may be for various kinds of reason. If I surround an area with a fence or a line or otherwise, the purpose may be to prevent someone from getting in or out; but it may also be part of a game and the players be supposed, say, to jump over the boundary; or it may show where the property of one man ends and that of another begins; and so on. So if I draw a boundary line that is not yet to say what I am drawing it for.[9]

We noted above the difference and relation between our intuitive knowledge of language and a formal nonintuitive theory of language. We are able to make and understand meaningful utterances of our language even though we are not able to describe the mechanism whereby we do this. Wittgenstein has made the similar point that though we know how to use certain words, we are unable to see in detail the connections between such words and others. "The aspects of things that are most important for us are hidden because of their simplicity and familiarity. (One is unable to notice something — because it is always before one's eyes.)"[10] Though we know how to use certain words we do not know how to describe their use. "The problems are solved, not by giving new information, but by arranging what we have always known."[11]

Those advocating the construction of a theory of natural language presuppose that natural language is systematic, that it is capable of formalization, that it is governed by rules. Wittgenstein, in speaking of language, makes use of some quasi-technical terms which might tempt one to think that he views language as governed by rules. One such term is 'grammar'. "Grammar does not tell us how language must be constructed in order to fulfil its purpose, in order to have such-and-such an effect on human beings. It only describes and in no way explains the use of

---

[9] *Ibid.*, sec. 499.
[10] *Ibid.*, sec. 129.
[11] *Ibid.*, sec. 109.

signs."[12] He not only speaks of grammar, but also distinguishes two types of grammar.

In the use of words one might distinguish 'surface grammar' from 'depth grammar'. What immediately impresses itself upon us about the use of a word is the way it is used in the construction of the sentence, the part of its use — one might say — that can be taken in by the ear. — And now compare the depth grammar, say of the word "to mean" with what its surface grammar would lead us to suspect.[13]

Still another favorite term is 'rule of grammar'. "The rules of grammar may be called 'arbitrary', if that is to mean that the aim of the grammar is nothing but that of the language."[14]

Finally, the expression 'language game' has been contributed to philosophical terminology by Wittgenstein.

The criteria which we accept for 'fitting', 'being able to', 'understanding', are much more complicated than might appear at first sight. That is, the game with these words, their employment in the linguistic intercourse that is carried on by their means, is more involved — the role of these words in our language other — than we are tempted to think.[15]

Although it might at first appear that Wittgenstein sees language and the role to be played by philosophy in much the same way as those who call for the construction of a systematic theory of natural language, it becomes rather clear that his comments concerning rules of grammar etc. must not be taken too literally.

A rule stands there like a sign-post. — Does the sign-post leave no doubt open about the way I have to go? ... But where is it said which way I am to follow it, whether in the direction of its finger or (e.g.) in the opposite one? — And if there were, not a single sign-post, but a chain of adjacent ones or of chalk marks on the ground — is there only *one* way of interpreting them?[16]

Although he claims that in order to solve philosophical prob-

---

[12]  *Ibid.*, sec. 496.
[13]  *Ibid.*, sec. 664.
[14]  *Ibid.*, sec. 497.
[15]  *Ibid.*, sec. 182.
[16]  *Ibid.*, sec. 85.

lems we must acquire a broad grasp of certain regions of usage and that we must come to know the many interconnections among the usages of certain expressions, he does not advocate a comprehensive systematization of natural language nor does he give us a mechanical method for doing philosophy. The philosopher's task is to gather and significantly arrange reminders for a given philosophical purpose. "The work of the philosopher consists in assembling reminders for a particular purpose."[17]

The task of the philosopher is to invent intermediate cases for philosophical purposes.

A main source of our failure to understand is that we do not *command a clear view* of the use of our words. — Our grammar is lacking in this sort of perspicuity. A perspicuous representation produces, just that understanding which consists in 'seeing connexions'. Hence the importance of finding and inventing, *intermediate cases*.[18]

The philosopher's task is not a passive one. He cannot sit back and let a systematic network of rules — assuming that he had such a network — solve his problems for him. The philosopher must be active, inventive, and imaginative. "The real foundations of his enquiry do not strike a man at all."[19]

Finally, an example of Wittgenstein's methods might throw some light on his views concerning philosophy and language. He writes :

"When I teach someone the formation of the series .... I surely mean him to write .... at the hundredth place." Quite right; you mean it. And evidently without necessarily even thinking of it. This shows you how different the grammar of the verb "to mean" is from that of "to think". And nothing is more wrong-headed than calling meaning a mental activity![20]

Though Wittgenstein, with his position on the descriptive nature of philosophy, the many functions of language, and the

[17]    *Ibid.*, sec. 127.
[18]    *Ibid.*, sec. 122.
[19]    *Ibid.*, sec. 129.
[20]    *Ibid.*, sec. 693.

relation between linguistic intuition and a theory of natural language, shares some views with those who advocate the construction of such a theory, he does not share their views about the more fundamental questions concerning such a theory. It is clear that Wittgenstein has not given us a theory of natural language or any part of one. It is also clear that he does not call for the construction of such a theory. In fact it appears from his comments on philosophical method that he believes that the philosopher must proceed by methods other than constructing and consulting a theory of natural language. Whether he believes that the construction of such a theory is not possible or that, if possible, such a theory could not replace the active and creative activity of the philosopher, is not clear.

## AUSTIN

Austin's approach to ordinary-language philosophy is somewhat more linguistic than Wittgenstein's. He exhibits a certain fascination with the details of language. "Much, of course, of the amusement, and of the instruction, comes in drawing the coverts of the microglot, in hounding down the minutiae... ."[21] At times solutions to perplexing philosophical problems are offered in the form of fine grammatical points. Let me illustrate. The ordinary-language statement, *I know what he is feeling* often is offered as support for the position that we are able to know that which another person is feeling. Austin argues that in the above statement *what* functions as an interrogative conjunction and not as a relative conjunction equivalent to 'that which'. Therefore, the sentence, *I know what he is feeling* must be understood as "I know that such-and-such is being felt by him' and not as 'I know that which he is feeling'. Here Austin not only uses grammar to make a point, but he uses traditional classroom grammar rather than grammar in the broader philosophical sense.

[21]  J. L. Austin, "A Plea for Excuses", *Ordinary Language*, ed. V. C. Chappell (Prentice-Hall, 1964), p. 41. First pub. in *PAS* (1956).

Though most commentators on Austin agree with the above point, that his approach to philosophy is more linguistic than Wittgenstein's, no one has given an illuminating account of this method. For the most part Austin practices his method rather than talks about it; however, he has left us with a few methodological remarks which are helpful in attempting to come to grips with his philosophical methods. At this point, let us attempt to do just this.

First let us consider his attitude toward ordinary language. Ordinary language, according to Austin, embodies a set of practical and tested distinctions which should not be abandoned without good reason :

... our common stock of words embodies all the distinctions men have found worth drawing, and the connexions they have found worth making, in the lifetimes of many generations: these surely are likely to be more numerous, more sound, since they have stood up to the long test of the survival of the fittest, and more subtle, at least in all ordinary and reasonably practical matters, than any that you or I are likely to think up in our arm-chairs of an afternoon — the most favoured alternative method.[22]

Yet, he maintains (reminiscent of Wittgenstein), our words are not always crystal clear, and there is always the danger that we shall fall into philosophical traps set by our own words. A striving for clarity in the use of ordinary language is a safeguard against the pitfalls of language.

... words are our tools, and, as a minimum, we should use clean tools: we should know what we mean and what we do not, and we must forearm ourselves against the traps that language sets us.[23]

Going further, he maintains (contrary to Wittgenstein) that clarity is not enough. Sometimes our ways of saying things are inadequate; sometimes the distinctions and connections we make could be improved upon. Words are not the things they are about; words are tools and thus their use is justified pragmatically.

[22] *Ibid.*, p. 46.
[23] *Ibid.*

... words are not (except in their own little corner) facts or things: we need therefore to prise them off the world, to hold them apart from and against it, so that we can realize their inadequacies and arbitrariness, and can relook at the world without blinkers.[24]

Austin does not urge a comprehensive and systematic study of all the words in our language. It is "preferable to investigate a field where ordinary language is rich and subtle" as it is in the matters of excuses, facts, pretending, etc., but not in the matter of time. Further, it is preferable to investigate a field which is not "too much trodden into bogs or tracks by traditional philosophy", for in such a case even our everyday words "become infected with the jargon of extinct theories". "If only we could forget for a while the beautiful and get down instead to the dainty and the dumpy."[25]

Austin allows that not everyone has the same conceptual schema. A consequence of our having different conceptual schemata is that we see the world differently and hence disagree about what we would say in certain situations.

If our usages disagree, then you use 'X' where I use 'Y', or more probably (and more intriguingly) your conceptual system is different from mine, though very likely it is at least equally consistent and serviceable: in short, we can find *why* we disagree — you choose to classify in one way, I in another.[26]

This, however, we should not bemoan, for it is precisely at those points where our usages disagree, at those points where our conceptual schemata differ, that we have most to learn.

A disagreement as to what we should say is not to be shied off, but to be pounced upon: for the explanation of it can hardly fail to be illuminating.[27]

Perhaps the best way to get an insight into the method of analysis used by Austin is to look to the procedure he suggests for

[24]  *Ibid.*
[25]  *Ibid.*, p. 47.
[26]  *Ibid.*, p. 48.
[27]  *Ibid.*

investigating excuses. In general our object, according to Austin, is to imagine the different kinds of situations in which excuses are made and then to examine the expressions which are used to make excuses in such situations. The combination of a lively imagination and an ample experience of dereliction will go far in the investigation of excuses. However, it is always good to have system in our method. For excuses there are three systematic aids : the dictionary, the law, and psychology.

In working with a dictionary, one can begin by looking up those words which are obviously relevant to excuses. In the explanation of the meanings of such words one will come upon other words germane to excuses. These words are then looked up. Austin assures us that if we use this method, rather than obtaining an ever increasing number of words germane to excuses, the family circle of such words begins to close until we come upon only repetitions of words we have already looked up.

The law provides us with another systematic aid although it must be used cautiously. If we keep in mind that the law relies heavily upon precedent and that it likes to pigeonhole things, we can learn much from the wealth of cases, pleas, and analyses it offers.

With psychology, the third systematic aid to the investigation of excuses, Austin includes anthropology and animal behavior. Though with psychology we should have even more trepidation than with the law, there is considerable to be offered by psychology. There should be no contempt for the 'jargon of psychology' when it limits itself to supplementing ordinary language and not replacing it. There are some explanations of behavior which have been noticed and classified in psychology although overlooked in ordinary language. Here is where the value of psychology lies for philosophy.

These three systematic aids together with a good imagination should start us upon an understanding of excuses. High upon our priority list should be explanatory definitions (as contrasted with definitions having no explanatory power such as abbreviative definitions) of the words germane to excuses.

... it is not enough to show how clever we are by showing how obscure everything is. Clarity, too, I know, has been said to be not enough: but perhaps it will be time to go into that when we are within measurable distance of achieving clarity on some matter.[28]

Directly relevant to the matter of a systematic theory of natural language are a few of Austin's remarks about grammar and a science of language. Austin has real doubts that there is an ultimate boundary between the 'logical grammar' of the philosopher and the grammar of the linguist or grammarian.

There are constant references in contemporary philosophy, which notoriously is much concerned with language, to a 'logical grammar' and a 'logical syntax' as though these were things distinct from ordinary grammarian's grammar and syntax: and certainly they do seem, whatever exactly they may be, different from traditional grammar. But grammar today is itself in a state of flux.... Do we know, then, that there will prove to be any ultimate boundary between 'logical grammar' and a revised and enlarged *Grammar*?[29]

Austin leaves open the possibility that someday a comprehensive science of language will absorb a certain portion of what now is considered philosophy, this portion being logical grammar or logical syntax "whatever exactly they may be". But he goes on to add that though philosophy may throw off some portion of itself, as it has before in its history, it will not thus exhaust itself.

Is it not possible that the next century may see the birth, through the joint labours of philosophers, grammarians, and numerous other students of language, of a true and comprehensive *science of language*? Then we shall have rid ourselves of one more part of philosophy (there will still be plenty left) in the only way we ever can get rid of philosophy, by kicking it upstairs.[30]

Surely Austin's urging that we strive for clarity in our use of ordinary language is compatible with the project of constructing a systematic theory of natural language. Further, his doubts about

---

[28]   *Ibid.*, p. 52.
[29]   J.L. Austin, "Ifs and Cans", *Philosophical Papers*, ed. Urmson and Warnock (Oxford UP, 1961), pp. 179-180. First pub. in *PBA* (1956).
[30]   *Ibid.*, p. 180.

there being an ultimate boundary between the logical grammar of the philosopher and the grammar of the linguist indicates that he is not unsympathetic with a least some of the enterprises of linguists in their attempts at constructing a theory of natural language. Lastly, his leaving open the possibility that someday a comprehensive science of language will absorb an indefinite portion of what is now considered philosophy, indicates that he does not rule out some sort of a theory of natural language for some future date. However, no matter how sympathetic he may seem toward the project of linguists in their attempts to construct a systematic theory of natural language, it is quite clear from his method that he has neither given us the elements of a theory of natural language nor attempted to do so.

Whereas a theory of natural language, of the type we are concerned with, is a comprehensive theory, Austin urges us to investigate those fields in which ordinary language is rich and subtle, and not too trodden into bogs by traditional philosophy. Though the initial investigation of special fields is not incompatible with an ultimately comprehensive theory, Austin gives no indication that the initial investigation of special fields is to be followed up by an investigation of the remaining fields. Rather, his method seems to take him from special fields of ordinary language to matters outside ordinary language, such as the law and psychology. His method does not involve an initial comprehensive investigation of ordinary language as does the method advocated by linguists.

We shall see in a later chapter that the lexicographer's problem, just one of the problems involved in a theory of natural language, depends for its solution upon there being a single conceptual schema for a given natural language. Austin, in allowing different conceptual schemata, conceives of natural language as a much looser sort of thing than structural linguists do. The fact that he allows different conceptual schemata may even indicate that the "comprehensive science of language" which he envisions is quite different in nature from the type of language theory we are dealing with in this book.

It is quite clear that Austin does not attempt to provide us with nonintuitive procedures for determining what can and cannot be said in ordinary language. His appeal to one's imagination, a fundamental aspect of the method he advocates, is clearly an intuitive approach to the investigation of language. Further, his suggestion that we make use of a conventional dictionary, a dictionary compiled intuitively, clearly indicates that he is not concerned with the lexicographer's problem of compiling a dictionary strictly by means of nonintuitive procedures. Austin's method of ordinary-language analysis may be characterized roughly as piecemeal and intuitive; while the kind of language theory we are concerned with in this investigation may be characterized as comprehensive and nonintuitive.

## RYLE

Next let us turn to Ryle. He, in attempting to make clear what he means by the phrase 'the ordinary use of the expression ....', makes several comments which are relevant to the project of constructing a theory of natural language. In discussing the above phrase, Ryle informs us that the operative word is 'use'. By placing the stress upon 'use' one is reminded that we are interested in only what is done with an expression, or for that matter any other expression which can do the same thing. Hume was not concerned about the word 'cause'; he was concerned about the use of 'cause'. Concern about the use of 'cause' is the same as concern about the use of '*Ursache*'.

Ryle, in order to make clear what he means by the expression 'using words' offers the expressions 'managing words', 'handling words', and 'employing words' as equivalents. We can go on to speak of the misusing, mismanaging, mishandling, and misemploying of words. We can do something wrongly with words precisely because there are "rules to keep or break, codes to observe or flout". By not noting the force of the prefix 'mis', which can be meaningfully applied to 'using', 'managing', etc., it is easy to lose sight of the underlying rules which govern natural language. "Among the things that we learn in the process of learning to use linguistic expressions are what we may vaguely call 'rules of logic'; for example, that though Mother and Father can both be tall, they cannot both be taller than one another; or that though uncles can be rich or poor, fat or thin, they cannot be male or female, but only male."[31]

Ryle also warns us against confusing 'use' with 'usage'. A usage is a custom, practice, or fashion. It does not make sense to speak of a misusage or miscustom, etc. "Describing the mode of employment of an expression does not require and is not usually helped by information about the prevalence or unprevalence of this way of employing it.... . What is wanted is, perhaps, the extraction of the logical rules implicitly governing a concept, i.e., a way of operating with an expression (or any other expression that does the same work)."[32] Keeping to the theme of rules but for the moment reverting to the terminology of meaning rather than use, Ryle writes : "If I know the meaning of a word or phrase I know something like a body of unwritten rules, or something like an unwritten code or general recipe."[33]

In order to understand more clearly what Ryle means by 'unwritten rules' or 'general recipe' we must leave his discussion of use and take up his discussion of category and category-mistake. In "Categories"[34] Ryle supplies us with the following method for showing that two expressions differ in category. Consider the sentence-frame ... *is in bed.* In this sentence-frame we can insert *Jones* or *Socrates* without arriving at an absurdity. But we cannot insert *Saturday* without an absurdity resulting. This is sufficient to show that *Jones* belongs to a different category from *Saturday* and that *Socrates* belongs to a different category from *Saturday*. It does not, however, show that *Jones* and *Socrates*

[31] Gilbert Ryle, "Ordinary Language", *Ordinary Language,* ed. V.C. Chappell (Prentice-Hall, 1964), p. 29. First pub. in *PR* (1953).
[32] *Ibid.,* p. 33.
[33] *Ibid.,* p. 35.
[34] Gilbert Ryle, "Categories", *Proceedings of the Aristotelian Society,* 1937.

belong to the same category, for there might be a sentence-frame in which *Jones* could be inserted without absurdity but not *Socrates*, or vice versa.

Smart in "A Note on Categories"[35] comments that if furniture words do not form a category, we may well ask what words do. Yet *The seat of the ... is hard* is not rendered absurd by filling in *chair* or *bench* but is rendered absurd by filling in *table* or *bed*. Smart notes further that most logicians regard the names of integers as of the same logical type (category), yet it is easy to show that according to Ryle's test no two integers belong to the same category. For any two different integers $x$ and $y$, con-sider the sentence-frame $\frac{3}{x-()} = \frac{1}{2}$. Filling in the parenthesis with $y$ would not result in an absurdity, while filling in the paren-thesis with $x$ would. From this we see that Ryle's method for showing that two expressions differ in categroy has the effect of relegating to different categories expressions which obviously belong to the same category, and perhaps relegating each ex-pression to a different category. At any rate, Ryle has not in "Categories"[36] supplied us with a characterization of 'category' which could be of use in constructing a theory of natural lan-guage.

Ryle again takes up the notion of category, and introduces the notion of category-mistake, in his *The Concept of Mind*.[37] These two notions are used by Ryle in solving a number of philosophical problems. In the solution of these problems, it often appears that the notions of category and category-mistake are used as if they constituted a portion of a theory of natural language. Sometimes, one is tempted to think that the category method for solving philosophical problems is offered as a more or less mechanical procedure whereby we look to see whether or not certain rules concerning categories have been followed. Words belong to cat-

---

[35] J.J.C. Smart, "A Note on Categories", *British Journal of the Philoso-phy of Science*, 1953.
[36] Ryle, "Categories", *op. cit.*
[37] Gilbert Ryle, *The Concept of Mind* (New York: Barnes and Noble, 1949).

egories, we are told, so in determining whether a given statement is meaningful or not, all that we have to do is determine whether or not any category-mistakes have been committed — as if we had the categories and rules listed before us and merely had to go through a mechanical procedure of checking.

Though Ryle at no time gives us a suitable definition of 'category', or 'category-mistake' or even a clear partial characterization of these two notions, let us try, from Ryle's comments and examples, to get some sort of determinate notion of 'category' and subsequently of 'category-mistake'. Ryle writes :

> Many people can talk sense with concepts but cannot talk sense about them; they know by practice how to operate with concepts, anyhow inside familiar fields, but they cannot state the logical regulations governing their use... .
>
> For certain purposes it is necessary to determine the logical cross-bearings of the concepts which we know quite well how to apply.
> . . . . . . . . . . . . . . . . . . . . . . . . . . . . . . . .
> To determine the logical geography of concepts is to reveal the logic of the propositions in which they are wielded, that is to say, to show with what other propositions they are consistent and inconsistent, what propositions follow from them and from what propositions they follow. The logical type or category to which a concept belongs is the set of ways in which it is logically legitimate to operate with it.[38]

Such expressions as "logical regulations governing the use of concepts", "logical cross-bearings of concepts", "logical geography of concepts", and "logic of propositions" help us precious little. And to speak of the "logical geography of concepts" in terms of the consistency and entailment of propositions is clearly misleading, since it at least is clear that categories deal with linguistic elements smaller than propositions and that if matters of category are relevant to the consistency and entailment of propositions it is only derivatively so. The last sentence in the above quotation at least gives us some idea of what is involved in the notion of category; however, the expression "set of ways" is much too vague to be of help to us.

Our only recourse is to turn to Ryle's examples involving cate-

[38] *Ibid.*, pp. 7-8.

gories and category-mistakes: If a person visiting Oxford is shown a number of colleges, libraries, museums, and administrative offices, and then proceeds to say that he also wants to see the university, he is committing a category-mistake. *Colleges, libraries, museums,* and *administrative offices* belong to one category while *university* belongs to another category. Concerning the person making the above category-mistake Ryle writes : "He was mistakenly allocating the University to the same category as that to which the other institutions belong."[39] Ryle also gives the following example : If a child, while looking at a march-past of a division, sees the squadrons, batteries, and battalions, and then proceeds to ask when the division is going to march by, he is committing a category-mistake. *Squadrons, batteries,* and *battalions* belong to one category; *division* to another.

Now by considering these examples and by exercising our imagination as well as drawing upon our knowledge of semantic theories constructed by linguists, we can arrive at the following characterizations of the notions of category and category-mistake. A category is a set of terms whose members can be meaningfully combined with the members of the same set or different sets in certain restricted ways. A category-mistake is the combining of members of categories in ways not permitted. Now let us try to determine what is involved in such characterizations of category and category-mistake and to what extent they can be used in a theory of natural language.

The words *colleges, libraries,* etc. belong to one category. We might call this category the set of terms designating parts of a complex educational institution. *University* belongs to another category : the set of terms designating institutional wholes. Now it is perfectly permissible to say *I saw the colleges, but I could not find the administrative offices,* for these terms *(colleges* and *administrative offices)* belong to a category which permits its members to be combined in the above fashion. However, we are committing a category-mistake if we say *I saw the colleges, libraries, etc., but I couldn't fiind the university,* for *university*

[39]   *Ibid.,* p. 16.

belongs to another category, the members of which are not permitted to be combined in the above way with the members of
the category having *colleges,* etc. as members.

*Battalions, batteries,* and *squadrons* belong to one category,
let us say, to the set of terms designating parts of a division.
*Division* belongs to another category, let us say, to the set of
terms designating complex military units higher than battalions.
Members of the first category are not permitted to be combined
in certain ways with members of the second category. Because of
this it is not meaningful to say that the division was engaged but
not the battalions.

It should be evident that categories alone do not determine
what words can be meaningfully combined. It is always a matter
of categories and a set of rules governing the combination of
terms from the same or different categories. In other words, if
we are to put the notions of category and category-mistake to
practical use we must not only know to what categories words
belong but we must also have a set of rules governing what combinations of words are permitted among categories. It is for this
reason that I included in my characterization of category the
very important phrase 'in certain restricted ways'. In claiming
that a category-mistake has been committed is is not enough to
show that the relevant terms belong to different categories. Let
us look at an example : We are not using language correctly
when we say *I saw the colleges, libraries, etc., but not the university.* However we are using language correctly when we say *A
university consists of colleges, libraries, etc.* Now if one wanted
to explain why the first is a category-mistake while the second is
not, rules of combination would have to be specified. An explanation in terms of categories and rules might be something
like the following : In any sentence if one term belongs to the
category consisting of terms designating parts of a complex educational institution and another term belongs to the category
consisting of terms designating complex educational institutions,
then these two terms cannot be meaningfully combined by *and,
but, and not,* or *but not.* However in any sentence if one term

belongs to the first category just mentioned, and another term belongs to the second category just mentioned, then if the latter term functions as subject and the former term functions as object, these two terms can be meaningfully combined by the phrase *consists of.*

Though in order to put the notions of category and category-mistake to practical use, a body of rules is required, Ryle does not supply us with such a body. He, however, does offer us one rule. It should be evident that before any rule for combining the members of categories can be given, the categories must be made determinate. Ryle gives his rule while leaving the categories totally indeterminate. He writes : "Where two terms belong to the same category, it is proper to construct conjunctive propositions embodying them."[40] This rule, however, is much too simple to be of any practical use, as can be seen from the following examples : *Fish* and *dandelion* both belong to the same category, the set of terms designating living things. We can construct the meaningful conjunctive proposition embodying them, *Fish need oxygen and dandelions need nitrogen.* But, contrary to Ryle's rule, we can also commit a category-mistake by constructing the conjunctive proposition, *I see the backbone of the fish but I don't see the backbone of the dandelion.* Ryle's rule is of no practical value whatsoever.

Of course a defender of Ryle might say that Ryle's rule holds, for we must consider *fish* and *dandelion* to be in the same category — the set of terms designating living things — for the first conjunctive proposition, but in different categories — *fish* in the set of terms designating animals with backbones, and *dandelion* in the set of terms designating plants — for the second conjunctive proposition. The trouble with this defense is that unless Ryle gives us a procedure — a nonintuitive practical procedure — for determining which of the many categories to which *fish* belongs we should take as the relevant category and which of the many categories to which *dandelion* belongs we should take as the relevant category in a given proposition, we have no

40  *Ibid.,* p. 22.

way of applying his rule. Surely, Ryle does not want to account for the meaningfulness or meaninglessness of a preposition in terms of categories and then to account for the categories in terms of the meaningfulness or meaninglessness of the given proposition. Yet this is exactly what would be done if one attempted to fix the appropriate category of *fish* and the appropriate category of *dandelion,* above, by appealing to our linguistic intuition of the sentence being considered. Ryle's single rule is radically incomplete, not only in the trivial sense that it is just one rule of countless rules required, but in the more significant sense that it cannot be applied unless a nonintuitive procedure is supplied for determining which is the relevant category on which it is to operate. It cannot be too greatly stressed that if a theory of language, or part of one, is to avoid vicious circularity it must not appeal to a speaker's intuition of language. For it is precisely the speaker's intuition of language which the theory must explicate.

By considering examples such as ours involving *fish* and *dandelion,* we see that a term does not belong exclusively to one category. Each term belongs to many different categories. A term belongs to all those different categories determined by definitions more comprehensive than the given term's definition. Given any two terms a category can be found to which both belong and two different categories can be found to which each belongs independently. Depending upon what in a given context is significant in respect to the meanings of the terms, we can place the terms in the same or in different categories.

It should not be thought that we are chiding Ryle for not supplying an adequate definition for 'category' or practical rules to operate upon categories, for it is hardly likely that Ryle ever attempted to supply us with such. I believe that he, rather than attempting to provide us with a practical method — in the form of a definition of 'category' and a body or rules — for doing philosophy, was using such terms as 'category', 'category-mistake', and 'rules' to stress that criteria for meaningfulness must be based upon correct usage. Saying that a category-mistake has been committed is not so much an explanation as to why a sentence does not make sense as it is a directive to look and see why correct usage does not permit a certain combination of words. Reference must always be made to how words are used in language. To say that a category-mistake has been committed is to say that language has been abused. Is is to say that language is not being used correctly. It is not the case that words can be meaningfully combined because they belong to the same category. On the contrary, it is because they can be meaningfully combined that they belong to the same category. Usage comes before the classification of usage. Category and category-mistake are rather superfluous concepts which often blur the issue rather than clarify it. At most, these concepts are a convenient shorthand. But as with all shorthands, it is imperative that we do not lose sight of the full formula.

We see that Ryle, also, has not supplied us with any part of a theory of natural language. The question arises: Have ordinary-language philosophers contributed anything to the construction of a theory of natural language ? In the efforts of ordinary-language philosophers to characterize the use of philosophically interesting words, they have touched upon matters which are in the domain of the dictionary component of a theory of natural language. However, they have not supplied us with a method for assigning even the simplest semantic properties to words. For example, they have not supplied us with a method for determining when two different expressions have the same use or a method for determining when a word is ambiguous — two of the most elementary projects for a theory of the semantics of natural language. If ordinary-language philosophers have contributed anything to the construction of a theory of natural language, the contribution is in the form of specific intuitive insights concerning the use of expressions which a lexicographer may someday make use of in constructing a dictionary for a theory of natural language. At any rate, we can safely say that ordinary-language philosophers have not provided us with any part of a formal nonintuitive systematic theory of natural language !

# IV

## LANGUAGE THEORY AND
## IDEAL-LANGUAGE PHILOSOPHY

In the past few decades we have heard considerable talk about theories of language (natural or otherwise) from ideal-language philosophers. Therefore it is appropriate that we, in our efforts to determine whether any descriptive theories of natural language exist, turn to those theories provided by ideal-language philosophers. In this chapter we shall attempt to determine whether or not ideal-language philosophers have provided us with a theory of natural language — or even the groundwork for such a theory. However, before doing this we must first examine, in some detail, the nature of formalized languages (variously called ideal languages or artificial languages) and look at examples of formalized languages. We must also note what is said about these formalized languages in the syntax and semantics of such languages.

### FORMALIZED LANGUAGES

A formalized language, in the tradition of ideal-language philosophy, is a meaningful language, formalized; that is, it consists of both an uninterpreted formal part and an interpretation. In setting up a formalized language, we first set up the purely formal part of the language, which is called uninterpreted calculus. This calculus is set up in abstraction from all considerations of meaning.

First let us consider the setting up of the uninterpreted calculus.

We begin by listing the primitive symbols of the calculus. These primitive symbols are indivisible in the double sense that, within the calculus, we make no use of any part of these symbols, and that, given a series of primitive symbols, each primitive symbol can be read in only one way. The possibility is thus precluded that, for example, the right part of one symbol be grouped (in reading) with the left part of the symbol to its immediate right. A formula of the calculus is a finite linear sequence of primitive symbols. A well-formed formula (*wff*) is a formula of the calculus which satisfies certain specified rules of construction. Certain well-formed formulas (*wffs*) are designated as axioms, and primitive rules of inferences are set up. A primitive rule of inference is a procedural rule by which we are permitted to add a certain *wff* to a sequence of *wffs,* provided that certain *wffs* already appear in the sequence. A finite sequence of *wffs* constitutes a proof if each *wff* either is an axiom or is inferred by a primitive rule of inference from *wffs* standing above it in the sequence of *wffs.* A proof is a proof of the last *wff* in the sequence of *wffs.* Since by deleting *wffs* from the bottom of a sequence of *wffs,* we do not affect the proof consisting of the undeleted *wffs,* we see that a proof exists for each of the *wffs* in a given proof of a *wff.* A theorem of the uninterpreted calculus is a *wff* for which a proof exists.

Requirements of effectiveness are placed upon certain parts of the uninterpreted calculus. An effective method of procedure amounts to a method of computation or calculation which is purely mechanical in the sense that a machine could be built to do the computations. The requirements of effectiveness placed upon our system are the following: There must be an effective method whereby, given a symbol, it can always be determined whether or not the symbol is a primitive symbol. There must be an effective method whereby, given a formula, it can always be determined whether or not the formula is well-formed. Analogously, the notions of axiom and primitive rule of inference must be effective. With the above requirements of effectiveness satisfied, it follows that the notion of proof is effective in the following sense : Whenever a finite sequence of *wffs* is given it can always be determined whether or not the sequence is a proof. The notion of theorem is not effective; or rather, the effectiveness of the notion of theorem does not follow from the demands of effectiveness which we have imposed above, though for some particular calculus it may turn out that, because of the specific nature of the calculus, the notion of theorem is effective.

Requirements of effectiveness are imposed upon our uninterpreted calculus in order to guarantee that, upon interpretation, the calculus have certain minimal features for being a useful language. Consider for a moment a case in which the notion of *wff* is not effective. Confronted with a finite linear sequence of primitive symbols, we might not be able to determine whether or not the sequence was well-formed; and thus, upon interpretation, we would not even known whether or not an assertion had been made. For similar reasons we make the other demands of effectiveness, and these demands taken together have the consequence, as noted above, of making the notion of proof effective. The requirement of effectiveness for the notion of proof is necessary because it is essential to a proof that, upon interpretation, it convey final conviction for the conclusion, for anyone accepting the premisses. Now, were the notion of proof in the uninterpreted calculus non-effective, upon interpreting the calculus, one might find oneself in a situation in which though accepting the premisses of an argument one could still be in doubt concerning the conclusion, because one might not be sure whether or not a proof had been given.

Thus far we have considered the setting up of the uninterpreted calculus. In order to transform this into a formalized language we must give an interpretation of the calculus. At this point in our development the notion of meaning (as ordinarily understood) first appears. The interpretation is given by means of semantical rules which assign a value or a range of values to each proper primitive symbol (to each constant or variable), and prescribes how the value or range of values for any *wff* is to be computed from the values or ranges of values assigned to the constituent proper primitive symbols.

Restrictions of a general sort are imposed upon the interpretation. The values of *wffs* prescribed by the semantic rules must always be truth-values; that is, upon interpretation a *wff* either denotes a truth-value or has always truth-values as values. (Here we are following Church's semantic theory. As we shall see below, Carnap considers truth-values as properties of sentences rather than as denotations of sentences. Some readers may balk at the application of truth or falsity to sentences rather than to 'readings of sentences' or statements. However, it should be kept in mind that both Church and Carnap deal only with unambiguous sentences. Therefore to say that a sentence [an unambiguous sentence] is true amounts to the same as saying that the statement expressed by the sentence is true.)

Each axiom must either denote truth or have always the value, truth. If the premisses of an immediate inference either denote truth or have always the value, truth, then the same must be true of the conclusion. If the preceding two requirements are met then the interpretation is sound. The requirement of soundness is imposed upon the interpretation, since the proof of a theorem should justify its assertion. Unsound interpretations are to be rejected since we have no use for an interpretation which produces a formalized language containing false statements.

As a sound interpretation of a particular formulation of the classical propositional calculus, in which the primitive symbols are '[', '⊃',']', '∼', and an infinite list of propositional variables, we have, following Church :

(a) The variables are variables having the range *t* and *f*. ['*t*' is the abbreviation for 'the truth-value truth' and '*f*' is the abbreviation for 'the truth-value falsehood'.]

(b) A *wff* consisting of a variable *a* ['*a*' is a syntactical variable whose range is the propositional variables of our calculus] standing alone has the value *t* for the value *t* of *a*, and the value *f* for the value *f* of *a*.

(c) For a given assignment of values to the variables of *A* [*A* is a syntactical variable whose range is the *wffs* of our calculus], the value of $\sim A$ is $f$ if the value of $A$ is $t$; and the value of $\sim A$ is $t$ if the value of $A$ is $f$.

(d) For a given assignment of values to the variables of $A$ and $B$ [$B$ also is a syntactical variable whose range is the *wffs* of our calculus], the value of $[A \supset B]$ is $t$ if either the value of $B$ is $t$ or the value of $A$ is $f$; and the value of $[A \supset B]$ is $f$ if the value of $B$ is $f$ and at the same time the value of $A$ is $t$.[1]

Rule (a) assigns a range of values to the propositional variables (the only proper primitive symbols of our calculus). The remaining rules show how the value or range of values for any *wff* is to be computed from the values or ranges of values assigned to the propositional variables. The soundness of this interpretation, of course, cannot be demonstrated from what we have here, for the axioms and the rules of inference have not been given. We have quoted the above rules of interpretation primarily to illustrate the two different types of rules, one type assigning values and the other prescribing a method of computation.

The difference between the uninterpreted calculus and the formalized language (the interpreted calculus) cannot be too greatly stressed. The difference is the difference between a meaningless game and a meaningful language. In connection with this it should be pointed out that, in a proof of a theorem of the uninterpreted calculus, no reference to the interpretation is permitted. For example, though is may be obvious that every statement implies itself, this intuitive linguistic fact cannot be used in the proof [$p \supset p$]. Also in connection with the difference between the uninterpreted calculus and the interpreted calculus we might note the following distinction between syntax and semantics. The syntax of a formalized language consists of everything which can be said about the purely formal part of the language, that is, about the uninterpreted calculus. Proof, for example, is a purely syntactical notion. The semantics of a formalized language, on the other hand, consists of that which is intelligible

---

[1] Alonzo Church, *Introduction to Mathematical Logic* (Princeton : Princeton University Press, 1956), Vol. I, p. 120.

only after an interpretation has been placed upon the calculus. For example, truth, soundness, and analyticity are semantical notions.

Before we go on to examine the semantics of a formalized language in greater detail, we must say a word about the difference between object-language and meta-language. The object-language is the language being talked about and in our case, therefore, is the language being formalized. The meta-language is the language which we use to talk about the object-language and in our case, therefore, is the language within which we formalize the object-language. Syntax and semantics have the object-language as subject matter but are carried out within the meta-language.

In order to give an interpretation of an uninterpreted calculus, as object-language, and in order to carry on other matters of semantics, it is necessary that the meta-language within which the semantics is developed, have certain features. First, since we must be able to talk about all the expressions of the object-language, we must have within the meta-language a way of naming all the expressions in the object-language. This is usually accomplished by having in the meta-language names for all the primitive symbols of the object-language together with some sort of a device for naming the spacial relation between any two primitive symbols. For example, let $P$ be the name of $p$ and let $Q$ be the name of $q$, and let $\perp$ be the name of the spacial relation of something's being immediately above something else. Then, given the object-language expression $\frac{p}{q}$, its name in the meta-language would be $P \perp Q$. Second, since the meta-language must, in assigning an interpretation to the object-language, deal with the very same things with which the object-language deals, the meta-language must be able to say anything which the object-language can say. This is usually expressed by saying that the meta-language must contain a translation (in its own terms) of all the permissible expressions of the object-language. Thus far we see that the meta-language must be able to talk about the expressions of the object-language and to talk about that which the object language talks. Thirdly and finally, the meta-language must be able to relate the expressions of the object-language to that about which the object-language talks. This is done by introducing into the meta-language some specifically semantic terms — terms which upon interpretation of the uninterpreted calculus deal with matters of meaning.

In order to illustrate the nature of the semantic theories of ideal-language philosophers we shall sketch two different but related ways in which Carnap attempts to explicate analyticity. In the first semantic analysis we shall examine, Carnap attempts to give a formal definition of 'analyticity' in terms of the concept of state-description as amended by Carnap himself. The amendment of Carnap's original semantic theory — forced upon him by certain difficulties — makes use of the notion of 'meaning postulates', a notion which Carnap ascribes to Kemeny. Carnap's definition of 'analyticity' in terms of the notion of state-description can be looked upon as an attempt to give a formal definition of Leibniz' notion of necessary truth. Leibniz recognized two different kinds of truths : necessary and contingent. A necessary truth is a truth which holds in all possible worlds, while a contingent truth is a truth which holds in the actual world but not in all possible worlds. Carnap provides us with a concept, state-description, which allows us to formalize the notion of 'a possible world' with respect to a given language. The notion of 'a possible world' with respect to a given language is reduced to the more precise notion of a state of affairs concerning the individuals within the domain of the given language.

Before we continue with Carnap's semantic analysis we must place a restriction upon the nature of the language with respect to which the concept of state-description can be used. The language must have an individual constant designating each individual in the intended domain. This amounts to saying that the domain of the language can have no more than an enumerable (countable) infinity of individuals. Let us assume that we have a language meeting the above requirement and further that the language has as primitive logical operations : negation, alternation, and universal quantification. An atomic sentence of this language is defined as an expression consisting of an $n$-ary predicate constant followed by $n$ individual constants. We are now prepared to define a state-description of our language. A state-description of our language (a formalized language) is a class of sentences of our language which for every atomic sentence of our language contains either the given atomic sentence or its negation, but not both the given atomic sentence and its negation.

Next we must define the notion of a sentence's holding in a given state-description. A sentence holds in a given state-description of our language if and only if the given sentence is a sentence of our language and one of the following conditions holds : (a) the given sentence is an atomic sentence and it belongs to the given state-description (a class of sentences), (b) the given sentence is the negation of another sentence of our language, and this other sentence does not hold in the given state-description, (c) the given sentence is an alternation of two sentences, one of which holds in the given state-description, (d) the given sentence is a universal quantification of an expression of our language which holds in the given state-description for the entire domain of the free variables of the given expression.

We have used the formal notion of 'holding' which on the surface is free from matters of interpretation; however the notion of 'holding' only takes on its full significance when an intended interpretation of the uninterpreted calculus is considered. Then we note the following. Saying that a given sentence holds in a given state-description is saying, in the light of an intended interpretation, that the given sentence (statement) would be true if the given state-description were true. (A given state-description, of course, is true when all of its member sentences [statements] are true.) Since every sentence either holds or does not hold in a given state-description, the truth of a given state-description uniquely determines the truth value of every sentence (statement) in our language. Thus, coming back to Leibniz, we might say that every state-description of our language determines a possible world with respect to our language. However, Carnap had to withdraw from this original identification of a state-description with a possible world, the reason for which we shall now note.

Once an interpretation is given to our language it may turn out that some of the state-descriptions, as defined above, involve contradictions and therefore describe no possible world. Contradictions will necessarily crop up if our language contains extra-logical synonym-pairs such as *bachelor* and *unmarried man.* Another way of putting this is saying that contradictions will necessarily crop up if the atomic sentences of our language are not mutually independent. If our language contains both the atomic sentences *John is a bachelor* and *John is unmarried* then there will be some state-description which will contain the sentences *John is a bachelor* and *John is not unmarried.* Such a state-description, of course, would involve a contradiction and thus represent no possible world.

Carnap gets around this difficulty by means of the notion of meaning postulate. Whenever an intended interpretation of the predicate constants of our language involve predicates which are not independent, such as *is a bachelor* and *is an unmarried man,* the logical dependencies of these predicate constants are to be indicated by means of certain rules called meaning postulates. For example, if *B* is a predicate constant which is to be interpreted *is a bachelor* and *U is* a predicate constant which is to be interpreted *is an unmarried man* then one of our meaning postulates must be $(x)[[B(x) \lor \sim U(x)] \land [\sim B(x) \lor U(x)]]$. Under the interpretation of *B* and *U* which we are considering this meaning postulate sets down the rule that if something is a bachelor it is also an unmarried man, and if something is an unmarried man it is also a bachelor. Concerning meaning postulates Kemeny writes: "These serve for extra-logical terms analogously to the way that the logical axioms serve for logical constants."[2] Of all the state-descriptions of a language containing the predicate constants *B* and *U,* interpreted as indicated above, the

[2] John Kemeny, "Analyticity versus Fuzziness", *Synthese* (March, 1963), p. 62.

only such state-descriptions which represent possible worlds — that is, which do not involve contradictions — are those in which the above meaning postulate holds. More generally, the only state-descriptions of a given language which represent possible worlds are those state-descriptions in which the meaning postulates — constructed in the light of an intended interpretation — hold. Given a language, those state-descriptions in which the meaning postulates hold are called admissible state-descriptions.

It should be evident that there are certain sentences in our language which hold in all admissible state descriptions. We see that by condition (b) above, for any given sentence $A$ in our language and any given admissible state-description $S$, either $A$ holds or $\sim A$ holds. Further, by condition (c) above, the alternation $A \vee \sim A$ holds in $S$. Since both $A$ and $S$ are arbitrary elements, $A \vee \sim A$ holds in all possible worlds. Now we come to the culmination of our semantic theory — the definition of 'analyticity'. A sentence of our language is analytic if the sentence holds in all those state-descriptions of our language in which the meaning postulates of our language hold. This is to say that a sentence of our language is analytic if the sentence holds in all the admissible state-descriptions of our language.

Next, let us look at a sketch of another semantic analysis of analyticity by Carnap.[3] This second analysis has the added feature of concerning itself with the relation between a natural language and an ideal (or artificial) language. Carnap begins by describing a natural language as a system of habits "serving mainly for the purposes of communication and of co-ordination of activities among the members of a group". Though language has many different uses such as commanding, questioning, exclaiming, etc., he will be concerned solely with the use of language for making assertions. Following Morris, he distinguishes three components in a situation involving language. These components are brought out in the following example :

[3]   Rudolf Carnap, "Foundations of Logic and Mathematics", *The Structure of Language*, ed. Jerry Fodor and Jerrold Katz (Englewood Cliffs : Prentice-Hall, 1964), pp. 419-436. First pub. in *IEUS*, vol. I.

... (1) the action, state, and environment of a man who speaks or hears, say, the German word *blau*; (2) the word *blau* as an element of the German language (meant here as a specified acoustic or visual design which is the common property of the many sounds produced at different times, which may be called the tokens of that design); (3) a certain property of things, viz., the color blue, to which this man — and German speaking people in general — intends to refer (one usually says, "the man means the color by the word", or "the word means the color for these people", or "... within this language").[4]

The components in the order examplified above are : pragmatics (according to Carnap "the basis of all linguistic research"), syntax and semantics. ('Semantics' as understood by Carnap shall turn out, as we shall see, to be what is usually called 'formal semantics' — that is, the semantics of formalized languages — and should be distinguished from 'semantics' in the sense of the semantics of a natural language, which has some similarities to Carnap's pragmatics. The context should make it clear as to which sense of 'semantics' we intend.)

In order to deal more concretely with these three components, Carnap offers an example of a natural language, *B* ("very poor and very simple in its structure"), which he goes on to analyze pragmatically, semantically, and syntactically. (We shall omit the syntactic analysis.) First, let us note the pragmatics of *B*. Since pragmatics is an empirical discipline we begin our pragmatic investigation of *B* by noting which words the speakers of *B* use, which forms of sentences they use, what the words and sentences are about, the situation in which the words and sentences are used, etc. In other words we "investigate the role of the language in various social situations". Carnap asks us to assume that our pragmatic investigation of natural language *B* has resulted in the following data :

PRAGM. 1: Whenever the people utter a sentence of the form "... *ist kalt*", where "..." is the name of a thing, they intend to assert that the thing in question is cold.
PRAGM. 2a: A certain lake in that country, which has no name in

⁴ *Ibid.*, p. 421.

English, is usually called *titisee*. When using this name, the people often think of plenty of fish and good meals.

PRAGM. 2b: On certain holidays the lake is called *rumber*; when using this name, the people often think — even during good weather — of the dangers of storms on the lake.

PRAGM. 3: The word *nicht* is used in sentences of the form "*nicht* ...", where "..." is a sentence. If the sentence "..." serves to express the assertion that such and such is the case, the whole sentence "*nicht* ..." is acknowledged as a correct assertion if such and such is not the case.[5]

Now we turn to the semantic analysis of B. We begin by restricting our attention to one aspect of the facts concerning B; that is, we restrict our attention to one portion of the data which we have collected by observing speakers of B. The portion of the facts concerning B which we focus upon now consists of the relations between the expressions of B and their *designata*. We are told that on the basis of the facts concerning the relations between the expressions of B and their *designata* we lay down a system of rules establishing these relations — a system of semantic rules. No sooner does Carnap tell us that our semantics must answer to the facts we have established by empirical investigation of the language, B, than he tells us that the facts do not determine whether the use of a certain expression is right or wrong.

A question of right or wrong must always refer to a system of rules. Strictly speaking, the rules which we shall lay down are not rules of the factually given language B; they rather constitute a language system corresponding to B which we will call the *semantical system B-S*. The language B belongs to the world of facts; it has many properties, some of which we have found, while others are unknown to us. The language system *B-S*, on the other hand, is something constructed by us; it has all and only those properties which we establish by the rules.[6]

Carnap then goes on to assure us that the artificial or ideal language *B-S* is not arbitrarily constructed but rather is constructed

[5]  *Ibid.*, p. 422.
[6]  *Ibid.*, pp. 422-423.

with one eye upon the facts and thus is to a certain degree in accordance with *B*.

The semantic rules which Carnap gives for *B-S* are somewhat different — though not different in the job they perform, as we shall note — from the semantic rules of the classical propositional calculus which we looked at above. *B-S*, being a higher order language, contains individual constants and predicate constants. Let us note, here, just a portion of the semantic rules which he provides for *B-S* :

RULES *B-SD*. *Designata of descriptive signs*:

*SD* 1. The *names* designate things, and especially
    (*a*) each of the thing-names *titisee* and *rumber* designates the lake at such and such a longitude and latitude... .

*SD* 2. The *predicates* designate properties of things, and especially
    (*a*) *kalt* designates the property of being cold;
    (*b*) *blau* designates the property of being blue... .

RULES *B-SL*. *Truth conditions* for the sentences of *B-S*. These rules involve the *logical signs*. We call them the *L*-semantical rules of *B-S*:

*SL* 1. *ist*, form *F*1. A sentence of the form '...$_n$ *ist* - - -$_p$' is true if and only if the thing designated by '...$_n$' has the property designated by '- - -$_p$'.

*SL* 2. *nicht*, form *F*2. A sentence of the form '*nicht* ...$_s$' is true if and only if the sentence '...$_s$' is not true.

*SL* 3. *wenn* and *so*, form *F*3. A sentence of the form '*wenn* ...$_s$, *so* - - -$_s$' is true if and only if '...$_s$' is not true or '- - -$_s$' is true.[7]

Rules *B-SD* assign values to the nonlogical primitive terms of *B-S* just as, in our earlier example from Church, (*a*) assigns values to the nonlogical primitive terms of the classical propositional calculus. Rule *SL* 1, in conjunction with rules *B-SD*, assigns truth values to the atomic sentences of *B-S* just as (*b*) assigns truth values to the atomic sentences of the classical propositional calculus. *SL* 2 and the remaining semantic rules given by Carnap, by referring ultimately to the atomic sentences provided with

[7]  *Ibid.*, p. 424.

truth values by *SL* 1, assign values to all the nonatomic sentences of *B-S* just as (*c*) and (*d*) do for the classical propositional calculus.

We are reminded by Carnap that every semantic term is relative to a semantic system; that is, every semantic term must be defined in terms of the semantic rules. Before looking at Carnap's semantic analysis of analyticity let us take a brief look at his semantic analysis of synonymy. Two expressions are semantically synonymous if they have the same *designatum* according to the semantic rules. According to the semantic rule *SD* 1 (*a*), the names *titisee* and *rumber* are semantically synonymous in *B-S*. However *titisee* and *rumber* are not pragmatically synonymous in *B*, as a brief reference to the statement of the pragmatic data for *B* (see above) will indicate. Carnap explains this by saying that because the transition from pragmatics to semantics is an abstraction, "some properties drop out of consideration and hence some distinctions disappear." For reasons analogous to those given above for the semantic synonymy of *titisee* and *rumber*, the sentences *Titisee is kalt* and *Rumber is kalt* are semantically synonymous though they are not pragmatically synonymous.

Now we are ready for Carnap's semantic definition of 'analyticity'. A sentence in *B-S* is analytic if it is true in such a way that the semantic rules of *B-S* alone are sufficient to establish its truth. More generally, a sentence in a given language is analytic if it is true in such a way that the semantic rules alone are enough to establish its truth. In *B-S*, the sentence *Wenn titisee ist kalt, so titisee ist kalt* is analytic, because its truth can be established by the semantic rules alone, namely by *SD* 1 (*a*), *SD* 2 (*a*), *SL* 1, and *SL* 3. It should be noted at this point, that just as two sentences may be semantically synonymous but pragmatically nonsynonymous, so a sentence may be semantically analytic but pragmatically synthetic — the reason being that, semantics being an abstraction from pragmatics, some considerations drop out in making the transition.

## DESCRIPTIVE, LEGISLATIVE, AND IDEAL CLAIMS FOR IDEAL-LANGUAGES

Now that we have looked at some examples of what ideal-language philosophers are doing, we are ready to pose the main question of this chapter. We are not asking whether or not the construction of ideal languages is of any value. We are not asking whether or not the construction of ideal-languages is of any use in the solving of philosophical problems. Our sole question is this : Have ideal-language philosophers provided us with a genuine scientific theory of natural language, or even the groundwork for such a theory ? That some ideal-language philosophers may not have attempted to provide a theory of natural language, we are willing to concede. However, we are not willing to concede that ideal-language philosophers, in general, were never interested in questions about natural language and that they never felt that their ideal languages should be responsible to natural language. Not only were ideal languages actually constructed to deal with philosophical problems stemming from natural language but, as will be brought out below, most ideal-language philosophers felt that their formalizations had to be responsible to some portions of natural language and that their work consisted of a formal reconstruction of natural language. Without lingering further on the motives of ideal-language philosophers, let us look to see whether or not any of them have left us with a genuine theory of natural language.

Though all formalists (ideal-language philosophers) construct artificial languages and then go on to talk about these languages and natural language, there is some variance among formalists, and often within the writings of the same formalist, concerning the relation between the artificial language and natural language. At times the descriptive nature of artificial languages is stressed, at other times the ideal nature of artificial languages is stressed, and still at other times the legislative nature is stressed. Since our primary concern here is to determine whether or not formalists have given us a scientific theory of natural language, we shall evaluate the descriptive, ideal, and legislative claims made concerning ideal-languages — these claims having a direct bearing upon whether or not ideal languages qualify as scientific theories. First let us take up the descriptive and legislative claims for ideal languages; later we shall deal with the claim that ideal languages are idealizations of natural language.

Though Carnap often emphasizes the ideal or legislative nature of artificial languages he sometimes seems to emphasize the descriptive nature. Note the general impression of the following :

> We now proceed to restrict our attention to a special aspect of the facts concerning the language B which we have found by observations of the speaking activities within the groups who speak that language. We study the relations between the expressions of B and their designata. On the basis of these facts we are going to lay down a system of rules establishing those relations. We call them *semantical rules*.[8]

The second from the last sentence could easily have come from a descriptive linguist. There are those formalists who while talking about the clarity and precision of artificial languages, as opposed to the vagueness and imprecision of natural language, still want to emphasize the essentially descriptive nature of artificial languages. Concerning artificial languages Rogers writes :

> There is about them, and results based upon the use of them, a kind of definiteness which it is impossible to obtain when one is working with an ordinary language. And because, though formalized, such languages have much in common with ordinary languages, and can be made successively to approximate such languages in power of expression, semantic analyses carried out with respect to formalized languages are of interest not only to students of such languages, but also to those who are especially interested in the semantics of ordinary, unformalized languages.[9]

Though probably most ideal-language philosophers would not want to emphasize the descriptive nature of ideal languages over the legislative or ideal, it cannot be denied that such philosophers,

---

[8]   *Ibid.*, p. 422.
[9]   Robert Rogers, "A Survey of Formal Semantics", *Synthese* (March, 1963), p. 18.

especially when their work is being attacked as irrelevant to natural language and philosophy, slip into an emphasis upon the descriptive nature of ideal languages.

Although we are not here concerned with the approach of ideal-language philosophers to problems of philosophy, their approach to such problems clearly speaks out for the legislative nature of their artificial language. This legislative nature is made quite explicit by some formalists. Carnap, as we have seen in a quotation above, explicitly states that the semantic rules which are laid down in connection with a given natural language, are not rules of that language but are rules of another language, an artificial language "constructed by us". Professor Martin in indicating certain requisites for "clear minded philosophy" calls attention to the legislative role of ideal languages.

Because of the presence of the logical as well as of the semantical or epistemological antinomies, it seems very likely that natural language, even just its declarative, cognitive part, is inconsistent. For inconsistent L, the term 'analytic in L' seems scarcely worth bothering with. For inconsistent L, presumably every sentence of L is analytic. To talk about natural L with the kind of care and precision necessary for clear minded philosophy, without indicating how one would give an explicit, consistent formalization of it, is to forget the very first lessons which Frege, Carnap and Tarski have taught us.[10]

Kemeny takes a similar position :

Philosophers must face up to the fact that there are certain important problems that cannot be discussed except in terms of a language free of vagueness and ambiguity, and with a clearly-understood structure.[11]

It would appear to me that Philosophical studies conducted in terms of incompletely understood languages must eventually lead to chaos.[12]

Kemeny is quite explicit concerning the legislative role of ideal languages :

[10]   R.M. Martin, "On 'Analytic' ", *Philosophical Studies* 3 (1952), p. 44.
[11]   Kemeny, *op. cit.*, p. 72.
[12]   *Ibid.*, p. 75.

It is precisely in the cases of ambiguity or vagueness that the philosopher must be given the freedom to legislate.[13]

Kemeny at one point quite explicitly makes the descriptive element of ideal languages secondary to the element of fruitful legislation. Speaking about the judging of proposed explications of intuitive concepts (including semantic concepts) he writes :

Of course we would wish to know that the concept proposed corresponds reasonably with the way a term is used in ordinary language. But this cannot be an overriding consideration. After all, if a proposed concept fails this test, it only means that it is an explication of a concept other than the one originally proposed. Therefore we may argue that some other term should be used for describing it, but the explication need not necessarily be abandoned. I propose that the only legitimate criterion for the criticism of a philosophical explication is the criterion of fruitfulness... .

I suggest that the criteria for judging an explication are in part similar to the criteria by which a mathematician judges the attractiveness of an axiom system.[14]

As for those who emphasize the descriptive nature of artificial languages and would like to think of formal semantics as a theory of natural language, we can point out that the various ideal languages hardly resemble natural language and that the concepts of formal semantics have little relation to our intuitive understanding of such semantic notions as synonymy and analyticity. Below when we discuss the empirical controls upon linguistic theories we shall show why the concepts of formal semantics fail to explicate such intuitive semantic notions. For now, let us note some of the divergencies between ideal languages and natural language. Following Strawson, we first note that for every idiom of an ideal language there are many idioms of natural language which are forced into a correspondence with it. Because of the algorithmic method used with ideal languages, the reduction of the many idioms of natural language to the few of the ideal lan-

---

[13]   Ibid.
[14]   Ibid.

guage is a necessity. The price paid for algorithmic purposes, however, is a great one; the ideal language is greatly impoverished. One need only look back upon the examples we have given of ideal languages and compare the logical connectives there with the connectives which one might find in legal or diplomatic language. There is no doubt that in the reduction of the many idioms of natural language to the few of a formalized language, much is lost. Not only is natural language distorted in the reduction, but even those logical connectives which are taken over into ideal languages are squared up and thus do not wholly conform with natural language use. Take the simple case of *or*. In English, a natural language, *or* is sometimes used inclusively and sometimes exclusively. Similar divergencies occur with the quantifiers *all* and *some*.

In natural language there are what Quine calls truth value gaps, which are not found in ideal languages. Take, for example, the following English conditional : *If it rains I shall stay inside the house*. Ordinarily, this statement would not be considered true or false, but rather the consequent would be considered to be conditionally true or false given the antecedent. In an ideal language this conditional would have to be either true or false. Next consider the statement (involving a singular description) : *The present king of France is bald*. In natural language if the object which the singular description purports to describe does not exist the question of the truth of the statement containing the singular description does not arise. The question of the truth of the statement *The present king of France is bald* just does not come up. However it does in ideal languages, where no truth value gaps are allowed; and Russell found it necessary to elaborate a special semantic theory to deal with the problems arising from this distortion of natural language.

Even the theory of reference found in the theories of formal semantics do not adequately describe the way we refer to things in natural language. As we have seen in our examples of the semantic interpretation of an uninterpreted calculus, semantic rules provide *designata* for the individual and predicate constants, as well as domains for individual and predicate variables. Such an oversimplified theory of reference, however, is not capable of dealing with some rather elementary problems which arise in natural language. Th:s is so because whether or not reference is being made to something, often is determined by syntactic and semantic considerations which the theory of reference does not take into account. Consider, for example, the ambiguous sentence: *I struck the boy with the bat.* An adequate theory of reference would have made provisions for a reading of this sentence in which the boy with the bat is referred to and another reading in which just the boy is referred to. The theory of reference found in formal semantics is not equipped to give such readings. By now it should be clear that ideal languages are significantly different from natural languages and, following from this, that any semantic theory which accurately describes an ideal language does not accurately describe a natural language.

With the ideal-language philosopher who stresses the legislative nature of ideal language and does not claim to be giving us a descriptive theory of natural language, we have no quarrel. To legislate is not to describe, and to the extent that the linguistic theories of ideal-language philosophers legislate, these linguistic theories are not genuine scientific theories of natural language.

Closely related to the notion of the descriptive nature of artificial languages is the notion of the ideal nature of such languages. In fact the descriptive and ideal aspects of an artificial language can be only fully understood in terms of each other. All systematic and comprehensive theories must to some extent represent an ideal to which the subject matter being described only approximates. Ideal-language philosophers being at home in science and mathematics — where the ideal nature of scientific theories and mathematical systems is well known — have never ceased pointing out to their critics, especially those critics who charge them with not being true to natural language in their theoretical descriptions, that their artificial languages represent ideals and therefore cannot be expected to account for every last detail of natural language. Carnap points out that the flaws in natural language preclude the feasibility of constructing a truly descriptive theory of natural language.

In consequence of the unsystematic and logically imperfect structure of the natural word-languages (such as German or Latin), the statement of their formal rules of formation and transformation would be so complicated that it would hardly be feasible in practice. And the same difficulty would arise in the case of the artificial word-languages (such as Esperanto); for, even though they avoid certain logical imperfections which characterize the natural word-languages, they must, of necessity, be still very complicated from the logical point of view owing to the fact that they are conversational languages, and hence still dependent upon the natural languages.[15]

Carnap goes on to claim that ideal languages are indeed relevant to natural language, because they are ideals of language and thus are as relevant to their empirical subject matter as any ideal theory is to its empirical subject matter. He then goes on to reiterate the thesis that a genuinely descriptive theory of natural language is not feasible.

The method of syntax which will be developed in the following pages will not only prove useful in the logical analysis of scientific theories — it will also help in the logical analysis of the word-languages. Although here, for reasons indicated above, we shall be dealing with symbolic languages, the syntactical concepts and rules — not in detail but in their general character — may also be applied to the analysis of the incredibly complicated word-languages. The direct analysis of these, which has been prevalent hitherto, must inevitably fail, just as a physicist would be frustrated were he from the outset to attempt to relate his laws to natural things — trees, stones, and so on. In the first place, the physicist relates his laws to the simplest of constructed forms; to a thin straight lever, to a simple pendulum, to punctiform masses, etc. Then, with the help of the laws relating to these constructed forms, he is later in a position to analyze into suitable elements the complicated behavior of real bodies, and thus to control them.... In the same way, the syntactical property of a particular word-language, such as English, or of particular classes of word-languages, or of a particular sub-language of a word-

---

[15]   Rudolf Carnap, *The Logical Syntax of Language* (Paterson : Littlefield, Adams and Co., 1959), p. 2.

language, is best represented and investigated by comparison with a constructed language which serves as a system of reference.[16]

Alonzo Church speaks of ideal languages as norms to which natural language is an empirical approximation.

> Let us take it as our purpose to provide an abstract theory of the actual use of language for human communication — not a factual or historical report of what has been observed to take place, but a norm to which we may regard every-day linguistic behavior as an imprecise approximation, in the same way that, e.g., elementary (applied) geometry is a norm to which we may regard as imprecise approximations the practical activity of the land-surveyor in laying out a plot of ground or of the construction foreman in seeing that building plans are followed. We must demand of such a theory that it have a place for all observably informative kinds of communication — including such notoriously troublesome cases as belief statements, modal statements, conditions contrary to fact — or at least that it provide a (theoretically) workable substitute for them.[17]

Bar-Hillel in attacking Moore's ordinary-language approach to philosophical problems indicates that ideals are just as important to the analysis of language as they are in science. He writes :

> Moore's method of approaching these tasks is just as Sisyphian as a physicist's who should start to "analyse" the facts of free fall, without constructing or imagining artificial ("ideal") conditions (vacuum, etc.) in the manner of Galilei.[18]

With regard to the above quotations — with their comparisons of ideal languages to ideal models in science — questions of empirical controls upon the ideal theories are in order as well as questions about the ideal nature of theories. However, at this point we shall restrict our attention to matters concerning the ideal nature of theories and save for later the matter of empirical controls.

[16]   *Ibid.*, p. 8.
[17]   Alonzo Church, "The Need for Abstract Entities in Semantic Analysis", *Proceedings of the American Academy of Arts and Science*, 80 (1951), pp. 100-101.
[18]   Yehoshua Bar-Hillel, "Analysis of 'Correct' Language", *Mind* (1946), p. 339.

According to Carnap, Bar-Hillel and other ideal-language philosophers, natural language is so unsystematic and irregular that
any analysis which attempted to do justice to the details of natural
language — that is, to a considerably greater extent than formalists have done — would be doomed to failure. The impli-
cation is that their ideal languages come close to describing all
that is coherent and systematic in natural language. From this,
together with the great simplicity and descriptive poverty of their
ideal languages, we should conclude that most of natural language is unsystematic and incoherent. (Below we shall make
some comparisons between the complexity of natural language
and the simplicity of ideal languages.) But this conclusion is
hardly acceptable. First we note that there is *prima facie* evidence
against the supposition that natural language is overwhelmingly
unsystematic and irregular. Children at a very young age and in
a very short time learn to speak fluently. Not only do they make
impressive progress in being able to construct novel grammatical
and semantically correct sentences, but the very nature of their
mistakes seems to indicate that they are learning their language
systematically. At any rate if natural language were as irregular
and unsystematic as some ideal-language philosophers would have
us believe, it is hardly likely that children could master it at
such an early age.

Our main argument against the supposition of ideal-language
philosophers, that most of natural language is unsystematic, is
taken from Katz and Fodor.[19] The inability of a theory to describe
in detail the complexities of a natural language may be due either
to the unsystematic nature of the natural language or to the
weakness of the theory. The failure of ideal-language philosophers
to capture the richness of natural language does not imply that
this richness cannot be captured by a systematic theory; it only
implies that they have not been able to do so. To assume at the
outset that a given subject matter is unsystematic seems to be
bad methodology. It is customary in science to assume that the

[19]  Jerrold Katz and Jerry Fodor, "What's Wrong with the Philosophy of
Language ?" *Inquiry*, 5 (1962), pp. 197-237.

subject matter is highly systematic, for this is no other than the assumption — so basic to science — that the phenomena being investigated are governed by general law. Then, if after many attempts to theoretically account for the complexities of a subject matter, there is no success, it would be in order to consider that the subject matter was not systematic. Even then an open mind should be kept.

The supposition as to the grossly unsystematic nature of natural language might be excusable if it were not for the work of descriptive linguists. As we shall see in subsequent chapters, descriptive linguists, especially in grammar, have succeeded in exhibiting much of the 'complex' structure of natural language. In the light of the impressive achievements of descriptive linguists in systematically accounting for the details of natural language — to an extent which makes ideal languages look extremely feeble as descriptive devices — it constitutes a gross misreading of theoretical progress in linguistics to claim that natural language is too irregular and unsystematic to be theoretically described in greater detail than ideal languages do.

By acting upon the assumption that natural language is systematic — governed by general law — one constructs a theory which accounts for as much linguistic detail as possible. By making the theory responsible for the actual details of natural language we have some sort of standard for evaluating competing theories. Ideal-language philosophers by disregarding the details of natural language have in practice replaced the standard of accounting for the details of natural language, by the standards of consistency and elegance. These may be proper standards for systems of pure mathematics but certainly not for descriptive theories. Ideal-language philosophers, by not making their theories answerable to the details of natural language, have virtually supplied us with arbitrarily constructed 'ideal languages' whose usefulness certainly does not lie along descriptive lines.

If the above quotation from Church is interpreted so as to keep prominent the essentially descriptive nature of abstract theories of language, it seems quite reasonable as a program for a theory of natural language. In fact, with such an interpretation it comes close to what might be said by a descriptive linguist. Even descriptive linguists realize that a theory of natural language cannot account for every last detail of natural language and that all theories must be to some extent ideal. Harris writes concerning this matter :

It is widely recognized that forbidding complexities would attend any attempt to construct in one science a detailed description and investigation of all the regularities of a language.[20]

We readily concede that all scientific theories — and especially natural language theories — must to some extent be ideal and to that extent be nondescriptive. It is for this reason that the above quotation from Church appears to be so reasonable and in accord with the practice of science. Unfortunately however, though ideal-language philosophers eloquently defend the ideal nature of their artificial languages in the name of good scientific methodology, in practice they become carried away with the ideal aspect of their theories and severely neglect the descriptive aspect. In scientific theories there is a delicate balance between the descriptive and the ideal. To aim too far in the direction of the descriptive, results in making the theory's goal too high and its structure too complex. To aim too far in the direction of the ideal, results in a theory notable for its simplicity and elegance but largely irrelevant to the actual structure of natural language.

We have already pointed out some of the divergencies between ideal languages and natural languages. A systematic study of ideal languages would show that every phase of an ideal language has significant divergencies from natural language. However, even this is not the main complaint against ideal languages as descriptive devices. More significant than the divergencies between ideal and natural language at those points where they deal with similar matters, are the gross omissions by ideal languages of many significant features of natural language. For anyone who is not con-

[20] Zellig Harris, *Structural Linguistics* (Chicago : University of Chicago Press, 1951), p. 16.

vinced that ideal languages are largely irrelevant to the description of natural language there is a simple way to convince him. Reread the section devoted to the nature of ideal (formalized) languages and the section devoted to the semantic interpretation of an uninterpreted calculus, while periodically asking the question : Is this the description of a language even remotely related to the language which I ordinarily speak ?

A fruitful comparison is that between the syntax of ideal languages and the syntax of natural languages provided by descriptive linguists. We shall not examine the grammatical devices created by descriptive linguists until a later chapter. However, I believe it is safe to say that when we examine the immediate constituent grammars and transformational grammars of descriptive linguists we shall be impressed by how well they handle the grammatical details of natural language. Contrarily, when we examine the syntax of ideal languages we are amazed at how little they have to do with the syntax of natural language.


EMPIRICAL  CONTROLS  UPON  IDEAL-LANGUAGE  THEORIES

We now come to the crucial question of empirical controls upon the semantic theories of ideal-language philosophers. We have seen above that ideal-language philosophers are fond of comparing their ideal languages to idealizations in science. We are told that just as ideal gases are idealizations of physical states ideal languages are idealizations of natural language, and that just as physical idealizations are fruitful in science so linguistic idealizations should be fruitful in linguistics. Leaving aside our above criticism of the runaway ideal nature of ideal languages, let us focus upon the question of empirical controls for linguistic theories. The question we now pose is : Are there sufficient empirical controls upon the semantic theories of ideal-language philosophers for them to qualify as genuine scientific theories ?

Before attempting to answer this question let us recall our earlier comments concerning some of the features of genuine scientific theories. We said that, from a certain abstract point of view, a scientific theory can be considered a device which, by means of statements concerning abstract entities, systematizes observed phenomena and from such phenomena predicts new phenomena. We went on to note that in a scientific theory (versus an empirical law) not all the nonlogical constants are associated with at least one overt experimental procedure. Some of the non-logical constants are defined only implicitly by means of the postulates into which they enter. We distinguished three com-ponents of a scientific theory : the abstract calculus, the model or interpretation of the abstract calculus, and the correspondence rules. The abstract calculus provides the logical skeleton of the theory by implicitly defining the primitive notions of the theory. The model or interpretation provides the calculus with a familiar conceptual or visualizable interpretation. We explicitly noted that such a model or interpretation does not necessarily relate the theory to an empirical subject matter. It is the set of correspon-dence rules which relates the abstract elements of the theory to empirical procedures and thus assigns an empirical content to the abstract calculus.

In the light of such an analysis of the logical nature of scientific theories let us look to see how the semantic theories of ideal-language philosophers stack up. Though most semantic theories of ideal-language philosophers are presented informally we would have no trouble in recognizing what, in the formalization of the theory, would constitute the abstract calculus. The abstract cal-culus would contain postulates which implicitly defined the prim-itive terms of the semantic theory. Such notions as synonymy and analyticity are taken as primitive in the theory and have only that meaning which is assigned to them by the formal abstract postulates. Their meanings as primitives should not be confused with the usual meanings we assign to such notions concerning natural language. There is no doubt that the semantic theories of ideal-language philosophers satisfy the first component of a genuine scientific theory.

As for the second component — which we noted was a nonessential component even though of heuristic importance for physical theories — we need only point out the following: Even if the semantic theories of ideal-language philosophers contain the component of model or interpretation, such a component would not necessarily assign empirical content to the theory and thus would not necessarily place empirical controls upon the theory. It is the set of correspondence rules which assigns an empirical content to a scientific theory and which thus places the theory under empirical control. When we look at the semantic theories of ideal-language philosophers we find that none of them, with certain rare exceptions which we shall deal with below, contain correspondence rules connecting the abstract terms of the theory with empirical procedures. The key semantic concepts, such as synonymy and analyticity, are taken as primitives or are defined in terms of other semantic primitives, and thus are NOT linked with empirical procedures rooted in the use of natural language. The key semantic concepts are left as unanalyzed primitives. This procedure would be acceptable if the semantic theories of ideal-language philosophers were offered merely as exercises in pure mathematics, but the semantic theories are offered as much more. As Max Black puts it,

It would be idle, for instance, to complain that in *pure* semantics the crucial terms may receive no definition, being introduced perhaps by means of rules or postulates that determine only how the words are to be used in the subsequent deductive elaboration of a system defined by those very same rules; or to lament the fact that in *pure* semantics the objects under discussion are whatsoever elements may happen to satisfy the axioms — "signs" only by proleptic courtesy. For such abstractness and indefiniteness of reference are necessary in any discipline which aspires to be "pure"; the hopes of positive achievements in semantics, *qua* formal algebra of meaning, rest upon just such self-imposed limitations; and to charge it, in the mathamatical aspects of its works, with lack of empirical reference would be quite to misconstrue its purposes.

But semantics is hardly interesting enough as pure mathamatics to be pursued for its own sake; and, but for the wider claims of philosophical relevance which have been made on its behalf, the subject would have aroused little interest outside the ranks of specialists in symbolic logic.[21]

The semantic theories of ideal-language philosophers are left hanging in the realm of pure mathematics without any empirical content or controls. Further, since there are no empirical controls upon the theories there is no way of evaluating between competing theories except by the previously mentioned standards in pure mathematics of consistency and elegance.

It should not be forgotten that what we expect from a semantic theory is the clarification of semantic concepts as they apply to natural language and not as they may have been invented for an ideal language having little revelance to natural language. The questions we require a semantic theory of natural language to answer are questions like : Under what conditions are two expressions synonymous ? Under what conditions is a sentence analytic? Reference of course is being made to sentences of natural language. A semantic theory which does not have correspondence rules linking its primitive semantic concepts with empirical procedures regarding natural language cannot hope to give answers to such questions. Katz and Fodor bring out the vacuous nature of the semantic theories of ideal-language philosophers in the following :

Suppose we have three artifical languages $L_1$, $L_2$, and $L_3$ each of which is regarded as an idealization of the natural language L. Suppose, further, that the sentence S in L is taken to be analytic in $L_1$, synthetic in $L_2$, and neither in $L_3$. How do we tell which of these languages is the best idealization of L ? We must ask whether S is in fact analytic, synthetic, or neither in L. But clearly we require a theory of the semantic structure of L to answer this question. Such a theory would have to explicate the notions 'analytic in L', 'synthetic in L' etc.[22]

In order to substantiate our conclusion that the semantic theories of ideal-language philosophers are not genuine scientific theories and that the semantic notions of these 'theories' have no

[21]  Max Black, *Problems of Analysis* (Ithaca : Cornell University Press, 1954), p. 256. First pub. in *Philos. Studies* (Allen & Unwin, 1948).
[22]  Katz and Fodor, *op. cit.*, p. 204.

empirical significance — that is, are unrelated to natural language — let us recall the two examples of semantic theories which we presented : first Carnap's state-description theory and second Carnap's semantic rule theory. The first thing we note about Carnap's state-description semantic theory is that it applies to an ideal language which because of its restricted nature hardly has any resemblance to natural language whatsoever. In order to formalize the Leibnizian notion of possible world, Carnap comes up with the formal notion of state-description. A state-description of his ideal language is a class of sentences of that language, which for every atomic sentence of that language, contains the given atomic sentence or its negation but not both. The next important definition we note is that of a sentence's holding in a given state-description. This is followed by an introduction of such notions as meaning postulate and admissible state-description and finally by a formal definition of analyticity : A sentence of a given ideal language is analytic if it holds in all admissible state-descriptions of that language.

It should be clear that Carnap's presentation is kept on an entirely formal level; reference is always made to a greatly restricted ideal language and never to natural language. The key concepts such as state-description, a sentence's holding in a given state description, and analyticity, are all either implicitly defined by the postulates of the theory — that is are either taken as primitive — or are defined in terms of primitives which themselves are implicitly defined by the postulates of the theory. No effort is made to connect such formal abstract concepts with empirical procedures relating to natural language. Since no correspondence rules are introduced into Carnap's 'theory' these abstract concepts — either taken as primitives or defined in terms of primitives — have no relevance to questions of natural language. The vacuous nature of Carnap's theory can be seen if one, after studying his theory, asks : Now, regarding natural language, under what conditions is a sentence analytic ? One is as much in the dark after studying Carnap's theory as before.

Now let us recall the second of Carnap's semantic theories we looked at before. A list of semantic rules is provided for a given abstract calculus. We are reminded by Carnap that every semantic term in his semantic theory must be defined in terms of the semantic rules of the given theory since the semantic terms only have meaning relative to a given semantic system. The definition of 'analyticity' turns out to be the following: A sentence in a given language (ideal language) is analytic if it is true in such a way that the semantic rules alone of that language are sufficient to establish its truth. We recall that the semantic rules included statements like such and such a symbol designates such and such an individual and such and such a symbol designates such and such a property.

This second approach of Carnap is no better than his first as far as the empirical content of his semantic theory is concerned. In this case the key semantic concepts of his theory, such as synonymy and analyticity, are all defined in terms of a set of semantic rules which have no connection with natural language itself.[23] The formal notions of synonymy and analyticity are themselves explained in terms of the equally formal notion of semantic rules. No correspondence rules exist to connect the abstract notions of the theory with empirical procedures. The theory has no empirical controls since it says nothing about natural language. Along those lines Quine writes:

From the point of view of the problems of analyticity the notion of an artificial language with semantic rules is a *feu follet par excellence*. Semantic rules determining the analytic statements of an artificial language are of interest only in so far as we already understand the notion of analyticity; they are of no help in gaining this understanding.

Appeal to hypothetical languages of an artificially simple kind could conceivably be useful in clarifying analyticity, if the mental or behavioral or cultural factors relevant to analyticity — whatever they may be — were somehow sketched into the simplified model. But a model which takes analyticity merely as an irreducible character is unlikely to throw light on the problem of explicating analyticity.[24]

[23] For a detailed criticism along these lines see Max Black, *op. cit.*, pp. 255-290.
[24] W.V. Quine, "Two Dogmas of Empiricism", *From a Logical Point of*

Our brief look at two examples of the type of semantic theories offered by ideal-language philosophers, together with our observations concerning the correspondence rules component of scientific theories, should make it quite clear why it is that such semantic theories fail as genuine scientific theories of natural language.

Carnap, reacting against criticism along the lines we have given above, attempts in "Meaning and Synonymy in Natural Languages"[25] to save his semantic theories from vacuity by somehow co-ordinating his formal semantic notions with empirical procedures relating to natural language. To use his terminology, he attempts to give a pragmatical substructure to his semantic theories by introducing operational definitions for certain key semantic concepts, such as synonymy and analyticity. Carnap sizes up the case against him in the following way :

In the case of the semantical intension concepts there is an additional motivation for studying the corresponding pragmatical concepts. The reason is that some of the objections raised against these semantical concepts concern, not so much any particular proposed explication, but the question of the very existence of the alleged explicanda. Especially Quine's criticism does not concern the formal correctness of the definitions in pure semantics; rather, he doubts whether there are any clear and fruitful corresponding pragmatical concepts which could serve as explicanda. That is the reason why he demands that these pragmatical concepts be shown to be scientifically legitimate by stating empirical, behavioristic criteria for them. If I understand him correctly, he believes that, without this pragmatical substructure, the semantical intension concepts, even if formally correct, are arbitrary and without purpose.[26]

Then, after paying lip service to the fruitfulness of the ideal-language approach to semantics, he concedes :

The purpose of this paper is to clarify the nature of the pragmatical con-

---

*View* (Harper, 1961), p. 36. First pub. in *PR* (1951).
[25] Rudolf Carnap, "Meaning and Synonymy in Natural Languages", *Meaning and Necessity* (Chicago UP, 1960). First pub. in PSt (1955).
[26] Carnap, "Meaning and Synonymy in Natural Languages", *op. cit.*, p. 234.

cept of intension in natural languages and to outline a behavioristic, operational procedure for it.[27]

Carnap then sets out to clarify the nature of certain pragmatical concepts — that is, certain natural language counterparts to formal semantic concepts — by stating empirical, behavioristic criteria for them.

The basic concepts he chooses, in terms of which he will define such other concepts as synonymy and analyticity, is that of the intension of a term. His problem becomes : Assuming that a linguist can determine the extension of a given term (a reasonable assumption only for those terms having an extension) how can he then determine the intension of the given term. He asks us to assume that linguists have reached complete agreement concerning the extension of a term. He then notes that under such conditions it is still possible for the linguists to ascribe different intensions to the term. For example, the terms *horse* and *horse or unicorn* have different intensions though they have the same extension. Carnap's task is the stating of an empirical, behavioristic procedure which will duplicate our linguistic intuition in distinguishing between the intensions of two terms even when they have the same extension. Carnap asks and answers concerning the recourse of the linguist presented with such a problem :

But what else is there to investigate for the linguist beyond Karl's [Karl is a fluent speaker of natural language being investigated] responses concerning the application of the predicate to all the cases that can be found? The answer is, he must take into account not only the actual cases, but also possible cases.[28]

Carnap goes on to explain that the most direct way of doing this is for the investigator to use modal expressions corresponding to 'possible case'. As an alternative the investigator could describe what is possible and then ask whether the subject would apply a

---

[27]   *Ibid.*, p. 235.
[28]   *Ibid.*, p. 238.

given term to it. For example, in trying to determine the intension of *unicorn* — which has zero extension — the investigator might describe a unicorn by saying, 'a thing similar to a horse, but having only one horn in the middle of the forehead' and then ask whether the subject would apply the term *unicorn* to such a thing. It is obvious that by using such a procedure an investigator could arrive at different intensions of *unicorn* and *mentaur* although the two terms have the same extension. In concluding the statement of his method for determining the intensions of different terms, he writes :

Although I have given here only a rough indication of the empirical procedure for determining intensions, I believe that it is sufficient to make clear that it would be possible to write along the lines indicated a manual for determining intensions or, more exactly, for testing hypotheses concerning intensions. The kinds of rules in such a manual would not be essentially different from those customarily given for procedures in psychology, linguistics, and anthropology.[29]

Concepts such as synonymy and analyticity would then be defined in terms of intensionality. For example, two terms would be synonymous if and only if they had the same intension.

Now before we criticize Carnap's method for determining the intension of a term in natural language, we must make quite clear what he is attempting to do. There are certain abstract concepts in theories of formal semantics which are defined only implicitly by the abstract postulates of the theory. These concepts remain purely abstract and the theory in which they occur remains vacuous unless these abstract concepts can be correlated with their counterparts pertaining to natural language; their counterparts are called by Carnap 'pragmatical concepts'. Thus we see that behavioristic definitions are required for these pragmatical concepts concerning natural language. But how do we know when we have an adequate behavioristic definition of a pragmatical concept ? Certainly not from the semantic theory which tells us nothing of natural language. Certainly we are not free to give

<hr />

[29]    *Ibid.*, p. 240.

an arbitrary behavioristic definition for a given pragmatical concept. There must be some control, some determinant of adequacy, upon the behavioristic definition of the pragmatical concepts. We know that we have an adequate behavioristic definition of a pragmatical concept when that definition complies with our intuition of the pragmatical concept. The control upon our behavioristic definition is our linguistic intuition. For example, we know that we have an adequate behavioristic definition of 'intension' when that definition duplicates our linguistic intuition concerning the notion of intension or the meaning of a term. (The relation between definitions of linguistic concepts and the linguistic intuition of fluent speakers will become clearer when we take up the work of descriptive linguists.) An adequate definition of 'intension' would have to assign the same intension to two terms which according to our linguistic intuition had the same meaning, and would have to assign different intensions to two terms which according to our linguistic intuition had different meanings. In other words, Carnap's task is to find a behavioristic method for duplicating our linguistic intuition concerning the intension or meaning of a term. It should be obvious that if such a behavioristic definition is to be of any value it must not rely upon that which it is attempting to duplicate — the linguistic intuition of fluent speakers of the natural language. In other words, if the behavioristic definition is not to be viciously circular it must not rely upon the linguistic intuition of a fluent speaker; the definition must be nonintuitive. Carnap, therefore, must provide us with a nonintuitive behavioristic method for determining the intension of a term, a method which duplicates our intuitive understanding of the notion of intension or meaning of a term without appealing to that intuition.

The method offered by Carnap clearly appeals to the linguistic intuition of a fluent speaker and thus cannot be accepted. One cannot explicate the linguistic intuition of a fluent speaker by appealing to that intuition. According to Carnap's method, we are to ask a fluent speaker certain questions which he can only answer by drawing upon his linguistic intuition. We might as well save time and ask him to give us an intuitive definition of 'analyticity'. Just as we would not want to ask a fluent speaker to draw upon his linguistic intuition for a definition of 'analyticity', we must not ask him to draw upon his linguistic intuition as a means for providing us with a method for defining 'intension', a concept in terms of which we can go on to define 'analyticity'. Carnap's method for defining 'intension' is a complete failure. He sets out to explicate, in a nonintuitive and behavioristic way, a concept known by linguistic intuition, and he ends up appealing to that very same intuition.

Let us assume that someone succeeds where Carnap has failed. In other words, let us assume that someone succeeds in providing nonintuitive behavioristic definitions for those pragmatical concepts relating to natural language which correspond to the semantic concepts of systems of pure semantics. For example, let us assume that someone succeeds in providing such definitions for the pragmatical concepts: intension, synonymy, analyticity, etc. Would this vindicate the methods of ideal-language philosophers in their constructing of semantical theories? The providing of nonintuitive behavioristic definitions for primitive pragmatical concepts apparently would involve — as we shall come to see in our discussion of the methods of descriptive linguists — the construction of a theory of the semantic structure of natural language. Such a theory would not be a system of pure semantics as developed by ideal-language philosophers, but rather, would be a genuine descriptive theory of the structure of natural language itself. Once we have such a theory, in which nonintuitive behavioristic definitions are given for basic pragmatical concepts of natural language, it is difficult to conceive what a semantic theory developed by ideal-language philosophers could add to our understanding of the structure of natural language. Once the behavioristically defined pragmatical concepts are obtained — a task involving the development of a theory of the structure of natural language — all the work seems to be done; we would have what we started out to construct — a theory of natural language. The formal semantic theory, with its primitive terms defined within a descriptive theory of natural language, would hardly be more descriptive of the structure of natural language than the descriptive theory of natural language itself. Along these lines Katz and Fodor write :

Systems of formal semantics interconnect concepts in the theories of meaning and reference to their mutual illumination only if the primitive concepts are empirically interpreted. For example, given an operational characterization of synonymity, a system may explain analyticity in terms of the substitution of synonymous expressions in truths of logic, and entailment in terms of the analyticity of the conditional. But beyond such interconnections these systems can afford no more of a clarification of their primitives than is provided by the results of behavioral tests for their application. Thus, the question whether two expressions are synonymous might be answered by a behavioral test, but clearly a system of formal semantics contributes nothing to the clarification of this notion. If the concepts of a system of formal semantics are not otherwise empirically interpreted, then the tests themselves must provide the full account.[30]

The main question posed in this chapter was : Have ideal-language philosophers provided us with a genuine scientific theory of natural language, or even the groundwork for such a theory ? To this question we answer, No !

---

[30]   Katz and Fodor, *op. cit.*, p. 206.

V

# PHONOLOGICAL AND MORPHOLOGICAL
# FOUNDATIONS OF LANGUAGE THEORY

We include this chapter on phonology and morphology (as well
as a few comments on linguistics in general) for the following
reasons : First, much of what will be said concerning language
theory throughout the remainder of this investigation will be intelligible only with a background in phonology and morphology.
Second, we feel that it is only fair to report the impressive
progress made in these fields before we enter upon the difficulties
encountered in semantics. Third, it is necessary that we make
absolutely clear, by way of explanation and especially example,
the crucial distinction between the intuitive and nonintuitive
handling of linguistic matters. In phonology and morphology we
have the means to do this, since we can juxtapose the intuitive
explication and nonintuitive mechanism for handling the same
linguistic notion. Fourth, by indicating how linguists have
handled phonological and morphological notions nonintuitively
we indicate the general nonintuitive way in which they propose to
handle the notions of semantics. Fifth, for reasons which will
soon become apparent, we want to show how the notion of
meaning has been eliminated from the nonintuitive devices constructed in phonology and morphology.

## LINGUISTICS

Linguistics is the discipline which deals with the study of language
and languages in all their aspects. Linguistics, however, is pri-

marily concerned with the spoken language. The written language is usually only a reflection of the spoken language; the structure of the written language usually can only be understood in terms of the spoken language. Related disciplines upon which linguistics draws include human physiology, psychology, and anthropology, as well as physical acoustics and communication theory. Some of the major subdivisions of linguistics are descriptive linguistics — with which we shall be primarily concerned — historical linguistics, and comparative linguistics. Comparative linguistics deals with the relationships between languages having a common origin. Historical or diachronic linguistics deals with the changes in languages in time. Descriptive or synchronic linguistics attempts to give an exact description of the structure of languages regardless of comparative and historical considerations. Harris writes :

Descriptive linguistics, as the term has come to be used, is a particular field of inquiry which deals not with the whole of speech activities, but with the regularities in certain features of speech. These regularities are in the distributional relations among the features of speech in question, i.e. the occurrence of these features relatively to each other within utterances.[1]

Descriptive linguistics and structural linguistics are the same thing. The former designation emphasizes the notion of exact description over prescription; the latter designation emphasizes the notion of systematic structure over isolated forms.

### DESCRIPTIVE LINGUISTICS

Though descriptive linguistics is ultimately concerned with the general structure of language, descriptive-linguistic investigation must begin with the speech of a particular person or the speech of a community sharing a single dialect. (In what follows, when

[1] Zellig S. Harris, *Structural Linguistics* (Chicago : University of Chicago Press, 1961), p. 5.

we use the word 'language' in regard to a descriptive-linguistic investigation, we shall mean the speech of a particular person or the speech of a particular community sharing a dialect. When we refer to the English language or to the Hindi language, etc. we shall be referring to a particular dialect of the language.) The speech of the person or community being investigated is considered over a relatively brief period of time so as to avoid complications of historical change. The slight differences in the speech of a person or a dialectically consistent community can be handled by devices which exploit the phenomenon of free variation or by devices which take stylistic considerations into account. Any generalization which descriptive linguistics makes concerning whole languages, such as English or Hindi, or concerning families of languages or concerning language in general, is made by comparing the results of investigations carried out for particular dialects.

The collective data of descriptive linguistics consists of a sample of utterances of a given language. "An utterance is any stretch of talk, by any person, before and after which there is silence on the part of the person."[2] The notion of utterance must not be confused with that of sentence. The sample of utterances, in order to be an adequate sample, must meet certain requirements, one of which concerns size. The analysis of a sample of a given language is of interest to the investigator only if it is virtually the same as the analysis obtainable along the same lines from another sample of the given language. Therefore, as far as the size of the sample is concerned, when increasing the size of the sample does not yield different analytic results, the sample can be considered of adequate size.

The general procedure in descriptive linguistics is to set up elements (such as phonemes) and then to describe the distribution of the elements relative to each other. Each element is defined not only in terms of some features of speech in the language concerned with, but also relatively to the other elements in the

[2]    *Ibid.*, p. 14.

system of elements. Once the elements have been defined for a given language, any utterance of that language can be represented in terms of the elements. It is then possible to study, manipulate, and discover the distribution of, the elements in the utterances. The elements, because they are defined relative to each other, can be manipulated in ways which nonsystematic descriptions of the speech of a language cannot be. As a result discoveries concerning distribution are made much more feasible. Concerning systematic elements such as phonemes, Harris writes :

It is therefore more convenient to consider the elements as purely logical symbols, upon which various operations of mathematical logic can be performed. At the start of our work we translate the flow of speech into a combination of these elements, and at the end we translate the combinations of our final and fundamental elements back into the flow of speech.[3]

Descriptive linguistics can be broken down into phonology, morphology, and semantics. Phonology deals with speech sound, morphology deals with speech forms, semantics deals with meaning. Phonology can be broken down into articulatory phonetics, phonetics proper, and phonemics. Articulatory phonetics deals with the sounds usable for speech in terms of the way they are produced by the speech apparatus. Phonetics proper deals with the description and classification of speech sounds. Phonemics deals with the role played by speech sounds in the structure of language. Morphology can be broken down into morphophonemics, morphemics, and syntax. Morphophonemics deals with the phonemic structure of forms called morphemes. Morphemics deals with how morphemes enter into words. Syntax deals with the structure of longer units such as clauses and sentences. Semantics can be broken down into lexicography and the study of projection rules.

We shall further characterize semantics when we take up this topic in the next chapter. In this chapter it is our purpose to go into the subject of phonology and some aspects of morphology. In order to appreciate the bid of linguists in attempting to con-

[3]   *Ibid.*, p. 18.

struct a theory of natural language, it is necessary to understand certain key notions — such as phoneme and morpheme — in phonology and morphology and to understand how phonology and morphology (including syntax) can be developed both non-intuitively and formally. (By 'formal' we mean 'in abstraction from meaning'.) Throughout this chapter, we shall emphasize, by way of statement and example, that semantic matters do not enter into the phonological and morphological description of language. Any account which did not go into some detail concerning the achievements of linguists in phonology and morphology, could not do justice to the impressive bid being made by linguists toward a theory of natural language.

General phonetics — including both articulatory phonetics and phonetics proper — attempts to give a full description and classification of speech sounds and the mechanism of their production. Articulatory phonetics is based upon the premise that different speech sounds have different mechanisms of production. Among the different organs involved in producing speech sounds are the vocal cords, the tongue, the lips, the teeth, the pharanx, and the nasal passages. (Though 'vowel' and 'consonant' are primarily terms of phonemic description — which we shall go into below — they can be used, in a clearly derivative sense, in phonetic description. In this section on phonetics we shall do so.) Vowels are speech sounds produced in the oral passage — with the possible addition of the nasal passages — in such a way that there is little or no interference with the vibrating air by means of the tongue, lips, etc. Consonants are speech sounds in which the vibrating air passing through the oral passage is interfered with, at the point of articulation, to some extent by the lips, tongue, teeth, etc. Vowels are usually classified according to the degree of the rounding of the lips, the height of the tongue, and the advancement of the tongue. For example, the vowel sound in *cake* is produced without rounding the lips, while the vowel sound in *boot* is produced with a rounding of the lips. Consonants are usually classified according to the point of articulation. Bilabial consonants are produced with both upper and lower lips. The initial consonant sound in *mother* is a bilabial. Labiodentals are produced with the upper incisors and the lower lip. The initial consonant sound in *father* is a labiodental. For convenience, phonetic alphabets are constructed in which a particular symbol stands for a particular sound. In this book we shall not use phonetic symbols — symbols standing for particular sounds — though we shall use phonemic symbols. Phonemic symbols are symbols standing for phonemes — theoretical constructs, only partially definable in terms of speech sounds. We shall not go further into phonetics; we have included this paragraph on phonetics only because in order to understand phonemics one must have some idea of phonetics, even if only not to confuse the two.

## PHONEMES

The notion of phoneme is one of the most important building blocks in linguistics. Before formally and nonintuitively defining 'phoneme' and before giving the procedures for discovering the phonemes of a given language, let us examine the notion of phoneme in terms of our linguistic intuition. It must be kept in mind that the results of any preliminary examination of the notion of phoneme along non-formal intuitive lines cannot be considered to be a part of the formal nonintuitive theory which we shall go on to explain. Our non-formal intuitive comments should be considered merely as aids toward comprehending the formal nonintuitive theory.

In any given language the number of phonetically different sounds is rather large; however not all differences of sound are equally significant. Some sounds which differ phonetically will be 'heard' (interpreted) as 'different' sounds, while some sounds which differ phonetically will be heard as the 'same' sound. In English the *k*-like sound in *key* (the speech sound in *key* which bears most similarity to our pronounciation of the letter *k*) differs phonetically from the *t*-like sound in *tea*; these two sounds are heard as 'different' sounds by a speaker of English. The *k*-like sounds in *key, ski,* and *caw* are all phonetically different from each other; yet they are heard as the 'same' sound. Normally a person untrained in phonetics will not note that the *k*-like sounds in *key, ski,* and *caw* differ, but that they do differ can be easily shown by having the person pronounce the given words while attending to the articulation of the *k*-like sounds. It will be found that the *k*-like sounds in *key* and in *ski* are articulated further forward than the *k*-like sound in *caw.* It will also be found that the *k*-like sounds in *key* and *caw* are aspirated while the *k*-like sound of *ski* is not. To claim that we hear the *k*-like sounds in *key, ski,* and *caw* as the 'same' sound while we hear the *k*-like sound in *key* and the *t*-like sound in *tea* as 'different' sounds because the *k*-like sounds in *key, ski,* and *caw* are more similar to each other than the *k*-like sound in *key* is to the *t*-like sound in *tea,* is to be mistaken. For it can be shown that some sounds which differ relatively more are heard as the 'same' sound while other sounds which differ relatively less are heard as 'different' sounds. What then determines which speech sounds are heard as the same sound and which speech sounds are heard as different sounds ?

Consider what would happen of the *k*-like sound in *key* and the *t*-like sound in *tea* were 'heard' as the same sound. We would not be able to distinguish between *key* and *tea,* for *key* and *tea* differ only by the two sounds in question. (*Key* and *tea* constitute a minimal contrasting pair — a minimal contrasting pair being a pair of words which differ by only one speech sound.) We are forced to distinguish between these two sounds if we want to make full use of our language. Consider the fact that the *k*-like sounds in *key* and *ski* are 'heard' as the same sound. Since there are no two words which differ only by these two *k*-like sounds (that is, since there is no minimal contrasting pair for these two *k*-like sounds (we are not forced to distinguish between these two *k*-like sounds. If in English we  had a word identical with *ski* except that the *k*-like sound was aspirated, then if we wanted to distinguish between the two words we would have to distinguish between (hear as different) aspirated *k*-like sounds and unaspirated *k*-like sounds. But English does not contain such a minimal contrasting pair, so we are not forced to make the distinction. Thus we see that the *k*-like sound in *key* differs significantly from the *t*-like sound in *tea,* but the *k*-like sound in *key* does not differ significantly from the *k*-like sound in *ski.* (By the same reasoning it can be shown that none of the *k*-like sounds in *key, ski,* or *caw* differ *s*ignificantly.) The *k*-like sound in *key* and the *t*-like sound in *tea* are two different phonemes; the *k*-like sounds in *key, ski,* and *caw* are all the same phoneme. Roughly, then, a phoneme might be considered to be a set of speech sounds which are not significantly different in the sense that the member sounds must not be distinguished in order to make full use of the language.

A more accurate characterization of the notion of phoneme (for reasons which will come out below), but one which is still nonformal and intuitive, is the following : A phoneme is a minimal feature of speech by which one thing that may be said is distinguished from any other thing which might have been said.[4] It should be clear at this point that phonemes cannot be defined exclusively in terms of phonetics. Phonemes are features of the structure of language. Phonemes are abstractions from the phonetic pattern of language, abstractions which permit the linguist to describe features of language which, though obviously different, function within language as identical. "A phonemic symbol ... does not stand directly for any phonetic entity, but for a structure point in ... phonology."[5]

Above in referring to the phoneme which includes the *k*-like sounds of *key, ski,* and *caw,* we could only do so awkwardly. It is much more convenient to provide a notation for referring to the various phonemes. In order not to get the symbols for phonemes mixed up with the symbols of the written alphabet or phonetic alphabet, phonemes are designated by symbols enclosed

[4] In our discussion of descriptive linguistics a number of definitions and examples have been adapted from H.A. Gleason, *An Introduction to Descriptive Linguistics* (New York : Holt, Rinehart and Winston, 1961) by kind permission of the publishers.

[5] *Ibid.,* p. 285.

in parallel lines. The symbol /k/ designates the phoneme found initially in *key* and *caw*. The phoneme symbol /k/ must not be confused with the symbol of the written alphabet, *k*, or with any one of the symbols for the various *k*-like sounds. Among the phoneme symbols for English consonants, following Trager and Smith,[6] are the following : /s/ as occurs initially in *sill*, /t/ as occurs initially in *tea*, /θ/ as occurs initially in *thigh*, /ð/ as occurs initially in *thy*, /η/ as occurs terminally in *tang*. Among the phoneme symbols for English vowels are the folowing : /i/ as occurs in *bit*, /e/ as occurs in *bet*, /æ/ as occurs in *bat*, / ǝ/ as occurs in *but*, and /a/ as occurs in *bot*.

It should be stressed that the notion of phoneme is relative to a given language. Different languages have different sets of phonemes. A set of speech sounds comprising one phoneme in a given language may comprise two or more phonemes in another language. This is to say that speech sounds can be grouped together into different phoneme sets for different languages. Let us give an example. In English the *k*-like speech sounds in *key*, *ski*, and *caw* belong to the same phoneme, /k/. This is so because in English there are no two words which differ only by two of these *k*-like sounds. In order to make full use of English we need never distinguish between these *k*-like sounds. However, in Arabic there are two words which differ only in that one has the *k*-like sound found in *key* — a forwardly articulated *k*-like sound — and the other has the *k*-like sound found in *caw* — a backwardly articulated *k*-like sound. Therefore if a speaker of Arabic is to distinguish between these two words — the two words in question constitute a minimal contrasting pair — he must 'hear' the two *k*-like sounds as different sounds. Whereas a speaker of English includes the three *k*-like sounds in *key*, *ski*, and *caw* in a single phoneme, a speaker of Arabic includes the two *k*-like sounds in *key* and *ski* in one phoneme but the *k*-like sound in *caw* in another phoneme. For the same set of three speech sounds

[6]   G. Trager and H. Smith, *An Outline of English Structure* (Washington : American Council of Learned Societies, 1957).

the speaker of Arabic has two phonemes while an English speaker has one.

Similarly, in Hindi there are two words which differ only in that one has the *k*-like sound found in *key* — an aspirated *k*-like sound — and the other has the *k*-like sound found in *ski* — an unaspirated *k*-like sound. A speaker of Hindi, then, will 'hear' the *k*-like sound found in *key* as different from the *k*-like sound found in *ski*. For him, the *k*-like sounds in *key* and *caw* belong to one phoneme, while the *k*-like sound in *ski* belongs to another. The speaker of Hindi, then, will have two phonemes where a speaker of English has one. Further, though the speaker of Hindi and the speaker of Arabic both divide the set of *k*-like sounds in *key*, *ski*, and *caw* into two different phonemes, the divisions are not the same.

Aside from the fact that our characterization of the notion of phoneme up to now has been radically incomplete as a definition of 'phoneme', our characterization has been along nonformal intuitive lines; that is, we have relied upon our intuitive understanding of meaning. One of the nonformal intuitive notions which we have relied upon was that of wordhood — for which we have given no formal nonintuitive definition. Involved in the notion of wordhood as it was used above, is the notion of meaning — two different sequences of speech sounds, supposedly, must have different meanings to count as different words. The notion of phoneme, if it is to be part of a formal nonintuitive theory of language such as we are concerned with in this book, must not rely upon the investigator's semantic intuition. Consequently, it shall be our purpose in the next few pages to present a characterization of the notion of phoneme which, though rough and incomplete, is formal and nonintuitive.

Here we should say a word about the relation between semantics and linguistic intuition. Semantics is either intuitive or nonintuitive. Nonintuitive semantics must wait, for its development, upon the development of nonintuitive phonology and morphology. Therefore at the stage of phonology — in which we find ourselves at this point — all semantic considerations are intuitive semantic considerations. Thus we see that if linguistic intuition is precluded from phonology then semantics is precluded.

Roughly speaking, a phoneme is a set of speech sounds which are phonetically similar and which are in complementary distribution with each other. Though speech sounds can only be more or less similar and though the required amount of similarity that speech sounds must have in order to meet this condition of similarity is a systematic matter for a given language, a nonintuitive basis for judging similarity can be provided by an adequately developed phonetic analysis plus some systematic considerations concerning the given language.

Sounds are in complementary distribution (vs. contrastive distribution) when each occurs in a fixed set of phonological (vs. morphological) contexts in which none of the other speech sounds occur. We noted above that in English /k/ is aspirated in *key* but unaspirated in *ski*. Further investigation would show that /k/ is always aspirated when not preceded by /s/, but never aspirated when preceded by /s/. In other words the *k*-like speech sound in *key* and the *k*-like speech sound in *ski* each occur in fixed contexts in which neither of the other occurs. These two *k*-like speech sounds are in complementary distribution with each other — rather than contrastive distribution. In contrastive distribution there are no exclusive contexts. When two speech sounds are in contrastive distribution, we can have two words which differ only between two different speech sounds. Thus we see that the distinction between complementary distribution and contrastive distribution is the basis of the nonintuitive device which parallels the intuitive semantic insight that if two different words differ between only two sounds then the two sounds must be 'heard' as 'different' and thus marked as two different phonemes. Two speech sounds which are in complementary distribution with each other and which constitute one phoneme are allophones of the given phoneme. (Actually allophones are not individual speech sounds but classes of speech sounds in free variation. For the purposes of this book, however, we need not analyze the notion of allophone further than we have.) Consider *key, ski,* and *caw.*

The $k$-like speech sounds in each of these are similar. (Formally the similarity would have to be determined by a phonetic theory.) The $k$-like sounds have a complementary distribution. (Formally this would be determined by examining the environments in which the $k$-like sounds occur.) Therefore the $k$-like sounds in *key, ski,* and *caw* constitute a single phoneme, namely /k/. Further, each of the $k$-like speech sounds in *key, ski,* and *caw* is an allophone of the phoneme /k/.

In order to have a valid phonemic analysis of a given language it is necessary not only that the analysis be free from nonformal intuitive considerations but also that it be free from formal nonintuitive considerations of a higher level, such as morphology. It is for this reason that in the practical method for discovering the phonemes of a given language, we do not make use of such morphological notions as morpheme or sentence. We begin phonemic analysis with the notion of utterance — an utterance being a sequence of speech sounds with silence at both ends. (It should be noted that this characterization of utterance is in purely physical terms.) A sample of utterances is transcribed from the speech of a fluent speaker of the language with which we are concerned. The usual scientific requirements are placed upon the sample : The sample must be sufficiently large and must be representative of the language. It is better, especially at the beginning of the analysis, to elicit from the fluent speaker short utterances. (This of course does not imply that we shall take such utterances to be words or phrases.) Long utterances are more difficult to 'hear' correctly and to transcribe. The transcription should be made in terms of a phonetic alphabet by an investigator trained in phonetics. The investigator not only should have a keen ear for slight variations of speech sounds, but also should try to free himself as much as possible from his own phonemic system.

The phonetic transcription of utterances can depart from the phonemic structure of a given language in several ways. We shall consider only two of these ways. The phonetic transcription may be over-differentiated, in the sense that different phonetic symbols have been used for the same phoneme; the phonetic transcription may be under-differentiated, in the sense that one phonetic symbol has been used for two or more different phonemes. If the phonetic transcription is under-differentiated there is no use in continuing the analysis with the given transcription. The investigator will have to go back to the first step and listen more carefully. The ideal is for the phonetic transcription to be over-differentiated, for, as we shall see, there are rigorous methods available for correcting over-differentiation — that is, for grouping different speech sounds into their proper phonemes. For this reason the investigator should attempt to note and transcribe every conceivably different speech sound, with the hope that he does not under-differentiate and with the knowledge that if he over-differentiates, this can be corrected.

Let us now look into one method for correcting over-differentiation: the method of phonemic grouping based on complementary distribution. First, we tabulate all of the different speech sounds we find in our sample of utterances. On the basis of an antecedently developed phonetic classification, we select pairs of similar speech sounds as candidates for allophones belonging to the same phoneme. For each candidate pair we examine the distribution of each member of the pair and frame an hypothesis in phonemic terms which would account for the distribution. We then test the hypothesis by tabulating the distribution of each member and checking the tabulation against our hypothesis. If our hypothesis is confirmed we have a tentative grouping of allophones; if it is disconfirmed we reject our hypothesis and try to frame another. Though this is only one of the ways for grouping speech sounds into their proper phonemes, it gives some idea of how over-differentiation is corrected.

The above sketch of phonemic analysis is greatly over-simplified. It is not the case that first all the data is gathered and then it is evaluated and reconstructed. Rather, what is involved is a number of cycles involving the gathering of data and analysis. The conclusions for each cycle are only tentative, but with each succeeding cycle the conclusions become more reliable. The investigator must alternate between transcribing utterances and analyzing the constituent speech sounds. Tentative conclusions of analysis are taken into consideration in the transcription of the succeeding cycle. By proceeding in such a fashion the investigator is able to transform disorganized impressionistic interpretations of speech sounds into an organized phonemic system.

Let us consider some of the kinds of phonemes in English. In doing this we shall appeal to our linguistic intuition concerning contrasting pairs; however, it should be remembered that any results, concerning kinds of phonemes, we obtain intuitively can only function as suggestions for nonintuitive procedures of discovery in our nonintuitive theory. We have already considered consonants. That there are consonant phonemes is suggested by such contrasting pairs as *key* and *tea*. That there are vowel phonemes is suggested by such contrasting pairs as *bait* and *bat*. Consonants and vowels are the most obvious kinds of phonemes but not the only kinds. We said that a phoneme is a set of speech sounds. Now if we do not arbitrarily define 'speech sound' so as to include only consonant speech sounds and vowel speech sounds, and if we recall our preliminary informal definition of phoneme — a phoneme is a minimal feature of language by which one thing that may be said is distinguished from any other thing which might have been said — we will find that there are kinds of phonemes in English other than consonants and vowels.

Consider the contrasting pair *pérmit* and *permít*. If we are to keep these two words straight we must recognize the stress as a phoneme. In fact similar considerations will show that there are four different stress phonemes : $/'/, /^/, /`/$, and $/˘/$ — these have been listed in descending order of accent intensity. Notice the contrast between *bláck bîrd* and *bláckbìrd*. (As we shall see below, the fact that *bláckbìrd* is one word while *bláck bîrd* is two words is of no phonological significance.)

Consider the contrast between *night rate* and *nitrate*. It is easy to distinguish the pronunciation of these two expressions since there is a break between *night* and *rate* in *night rate* and there is no such break in *nitrate*. If we want to keep these two expressions straight we must recognize this break as a phoneme. It is called the open transition phoneme and is symbolized /⁺/. In most cases, words (as traditionally understood) are separated by /⁺/, however it would be a mistake to identify the traditional word division with /⁺/. *Slyness* is pronounced *sly⁺ness* but is only one word; *good afternoon* is pronounced without an internal /⁺/ yet consists of two words. Word divisions are largely arbitrary and only make for confusion when relied upon in phonological matters. Notice that word divisions may change without an accompanying change of pronunciation — many expressions which were once written as two words are now written as one. Still another kind of transition phoneme, which we shall mention but not go into, is the clause terminal.

It is common knowledge that pitch (tone) plays a role in Chinese, but it is not common knowledge that there is no known natural language in which pitch does not play some phonemic role. In order to become convinced that pitch is phonemic in English one need only consider the following contrasting pairs of utterances : *What are we having for dinner, mother ?* in which the pitch of *mother* remains level, and *What are we having for dinner, mother ?* in which the pitch of *mother* rises sharply at the end.

## MORPHEMES

Following the same procedure as we did with the notion of phoneme, we shall first give a nonformal intuitive characterization of the notion of morpheme — a characterization relying heavily upon our semantic intuition — and then we shall sketch a formal nonintuitive characterization of this same notion. It is important to remember that only the formal nonintuitive characterization enters into our theory of natural language. To a large extent the formal nonintuitive definition of 'morpheme' parallels the intuitive semantically based notion of morpheme, but not entirely.

The formal development of morphology presupposes an antecedently formally developed phonology. It might bear repeating here that we are dealing only with the spoken language. There•

fore in symbolizing a given morpheme (which consist of a sequence of phonemes), strictly speaking, phonemic spelling is demanded. However, since the presentation and explication of a complete phonemic alphabet would take us too deeply into a field which, for the purpose of this investigation, is overly technical and not essential, we shall symbolize our morphemes by means of the ordinary written alphabet. At all times it should be remembered that such symbolization actually stands in place of the phonemic symbolization. For example *whose* stands in place of /huwz/ and *gloomy* stands in place of /gluwmiy/.

The morpheme represents a higher level of linguistic element than the phoneme. The notion of morpheme probably can be best explained, nonformally and intuitively, in terms of recurrent partials (recurrent sequences). If we consider the forms *toys, boys, chairs, rugs, guns, doors, chains,* and *pigs* we notice the recurrent partial *s* and we intuitively realize that the meaning of *s* (plurality) is related to the forms considered. If we consider the forms *stranger, estrange,* and *strangeness* we notice the recurrent partial, *strange,* and we intuitively realize that the meaning of *strange* is related to the three forms considered. Further, we realize that no part of *strange* has any meaning which is also related to *strange* as a whole. If we consider *combination, examination, running, twine,* and *find* we notice that *in* occurs in all of them. However, we also realize that *in* contributes no common meaning to all these different forms, as *strange* does to *stranger, estrange* and *strangeness. Strange* is a morpheme in *stranger, estrange,* and *strangeness*; *s* is a morpheme in *toys, boys, chairs,* etc.; but *in* is not a morpheme in *combination, examination,* etc. For the present we might say that morphemes are the smallest meaningful recurring phoneme sequences in a language. (*Sequence* is defined so as not to preclude sequences of one or no elements.)

Morphemes must not be confused with words, syllables, or phonemes. Wordhood is determined by a largely arbitrary spelling convention. *Reconvene* is one word but three morphemes. Syllables are phonetic segments of speech (pulses of breath) and not

structural elements as morphemes are. Whereas *does* is mono-
syllabic, it consists of two morphemes; and whereas *Mississippi*
is polysyllabic it consist of only one morpheme (in English).
Though *s* in *boys* happens to be both a phoneme and a morpheme, this is not to say that the phoneme *s* is the same as the
morpheme *s*. The phoneme *s* occurs in *sheep, sleep, saw, kiss,
escape,* and *rest,* but the morpheme *s* occurs in none of these.

Let us next consider the different kinds of morphemes. The
two most general categories of morphemes are roots and affixes.
*Sleep, chair, spoon, run, script,* and *large* are examples of roots.
*Pre-, sub-, -ing, -ed, -ly* are examples of affixes. Though the formal nonintuitive definitions of 'root' and 'affix' are quite complex,
we are all more or less intuitively familiar with these two notions
from traditional language study. Roots are nuclei of longer expressions and somehow more basic than affixes; affixes are expressions affixed to roots or combinations of roots and affixes.
Affixes can be broken down into prefixes, suffixes, and infixes.
Prefixes are affixes which precede the root with which they are
associated. *Pre-, sub-, re-, in-, super-, infra-* are examples of prefixes. Suffixes are affixes which follow the root with which they
are associated. Examples of suffixes are *-ing, -ed,* and *-s.* Infixes
are affixes which are inserted into the root with which they are
associated. English has no infixes but Greek and Hebrew do.

A single morpheme usually has more than one form. Consider
the following expressions : *boys, cats, roses, oxen, geese,* and
*sheep.* We notice that one thing they have in common is that they
all are plurals —*sheep* of course is both singular and plural. We
shall show that all these forms contain the plural morpheme in
one form or other, but first let us consider just *boys, cats,* and
*roses.* From what we have already said concerning morphemes
we should be able to indentify the plural ending in these three
expressions as a morpheme, the plural morpheme. Yet if we
examine these three expressions more closely we notice that the
plural ending is pronounced differently in each of the expressions;
that is, we notice that the plural ending consists of different
sequences of phonemes in each case. Now, if we want to retain

the plural ending in *boys, cats,* and *roses* as the plural morpheme we must change our characterization of morpheme from that of a sequence of phonemes to that of a set of sequences of phonemes. In this way the plural morpheme can include all three phoneme sequences of the plural ending in *boys, cats,* and *roses.* Each of the different phoneme sequences of the plural ending in *boys, cats,* and *roses* is called an allomorph of the plural morpheme. (An allomorph is a morpheme variant which occurs in fixed environments.) Each of the different phoneme sequences of the plural ending in *boys, cats,* and *roses* is an allomorph of the plural morpheme. This quasi-technical terminology merely reflects the fact that though the endings of *boys, cats,* and *roses* are pronounced differently, they all have the same function — that of making singular forms plural.

Next, consider *oxen.* With a little thought one should realize that since the ending *en* makes *ox* into a plural, *en* is an allomorph of the plural morpheme. The plural form *sheep* is considered — for the sake of systematic simplicity — to consist of the root, *sheep* (understood singularly) plus the null suffix. The null suffix, therefore, is considered to be an allomorph of the plural morpheme. The situation is a bit more complicated for the form *geese.* We note that *geese* is the plural of *goose,* just as *boys* is the plural of *boy.* We note that the change in phonemes from *goose* to *geese* functions in some parallel fashion to the addition of the suffix *s* to *boy.* A change of phonemes such as we have from *goose* to *geese* is called a replacive. Replacives are considered to be allomorphs. More specifically, the replacive involved in going from *goose* to *geese* is an allomorph of the plural morpheme. Thus, we see that *boys, cats, roses, oxen, sheep,* and *geese,* all contain the plural morpheme though each contains a different allomorph of the plural morpheme.

Above, we said that an allomorph is a morpheme variant which occurs in fixed environments. Let us note some of these environments for the allomorphs of the plural morpheme. Of the three allomorphs of the plural morpheme in *boys, cats,* and *roses* the allomorph in *cats* occurs only after voiceless speech sounds; the allomorph in *boys* occurs only after voiced speech sounds; the allomorph in *roses* occurs only after grooved fricatives (roughly, *s*-like and *z*-like sounds). These allomorphs are said to be phonologically conditioned since the selection of the proper allomorph depends upon the phonetic character of the preceding phoneme. If we know that a given stem — a stem is a morpheme or combination of morphemes to which an affix may be added — can take the plural morpheme and that the stem phonologically conditions the plural morpheme, we can predict, from the phonetic character of the terminal phoneme of the stem, which allomorph it will take.

Again consider *oxen*. We said that *en* is an allomorph of the plural morpheme. But what is the fixed environment concerning this allomorph ? How is the allomorph conditioned ? If *en* were phonologically conditioned we should expect that the plural of *ox* would be *oxes* since *fox* and *box* are phonologically similar to *ox*. However, with the allomorph *en* in *oxen,* we have a case of morphological conditioning. More specifically, the allomorph *en* of the plural morpheme occurs only after the morpheme *ox*. Phonetics has nothing to do with this sort of conditioning. The null allomorph in *sheep* and the replacive allomorph in *geese* are, of course, also morphologically conditioned.

Now let us look at a rough sketch of a formal nonintuitive characterization of the notion of morpheme. We shall do this by outlining the procedures for morphemic analysis from the point of transcribing a sample of utterances to the point of enumerating the various morphemes. For purposes of phonemic analysis we began by transcribing a sample of utterances from the speech of a fluent speaker. The transcription was in terms of a phonetic alphabet. For purposes of morphemic analysis we transcribe a sample of utterances from the speech of a fluent speaker, however, not in terms of a phonetic alphabet but rather in terms of a phonemic alphabet. (It is understood that before entering upon a morphemic analysis for a particular language, a phonemic analysis for that language has been completed.) In what follows we shall show how the sequences of phonemes constituting the utterances of the sample are divided into segments, each segment consisting of a determinate sequence of phonemes. Each segment will be 'independent' in a sense determined by criteria which will be set up. The criteria for independence will be stated solely in terms of identical or similar distribution. The independent segments (morphemic segments) will then be grouped into various sets (morphemes) according to criteria producing the following result : Each member of a given morpheme can be substituted for any other member or is complementary with respect to environment. What takes place in morphemic analysis is that sequences of phonemes are first segmented to a degree beyond that which is morphologically useful, and then a regrouping of the segments is made in such a way that the new groups are morphologically useful. In other words, first we analyse and then we synthesize. Throughout the analysis which follows it should be noted that the notion of morpheme is not dependent upon matters of semantics but only upon matters of distribution concerning the utterances constituting the data.

We begin by stating the procedure for determining the independent phoneme sequences (morphemic segments) in particular utterances from our sample. (When we speak of a morphemic segment or an independent phoneme sequence we refer to a particular occurrence of a phoneme sequence within a given utterance. The *ing* in *running* is a different morphemic segment from the *ing* in *hunting*. Only later, shall we group these two sequence occurrence into a single set.) If a phoneme sequence is independent in a particular utterance — that is, if it is a morphemic segment — then the utterance can be matched by other utterances which do not differ from the given utterance except that the given phoneme sequence is replaced by another phoneme sequence or by the null sequence. Assume that *hunt* in *I like to go hunting* is an independent phoneme sequence. We then know that there will be phoneme sequences like *I like to go fishing* or *I like to go shooting* which do not differ from *I like to go hunting* except that *hunt* has been replaced. This condition for morphemic segment is, of course, only a necessary condition and not a sufficient condition. This condition is best restated so as to make it give the necessary and sufficient conditions for the upper limit of the number of morphemic segments in a given phoneme sequence : a phoneme sequence may consist of more than one morphemic segment if and only if one part of the phoneme sequence occurs without another part in the same total environment. For example, the phoneme sequence *hunting* in *I am going hunting* may consist of more than one morphemic segment, because one part of the phoneme sequence *ing* occurs without another part *hunt* in the same total environment in *I am going fishing*. This rule establishes the upper bound of the number of segments which a particular phoneme sequence may have. Let us call each of these segments in the upper bound, a tentative independent phoneme sequence or a tentative morphemic segment.

We next place a restriction upon the tentative morphemic segments so as to rule out some tentative morphemic segments and leave only those which we shall consider to be morphemic segments : of all the tentative morphemic segments, we shall consider as morphemic segments only those for which there are other tentative morphemic segments which have similar distributions. Assume that $A$, $B$, $C$, $D$,... are tentative morphemic segments. $A$, $B$, and $C$ will be considered to be morphemic segments if, for example, $A$, $B$, and $C$ may occur after $X$ and $Y$ but never after $Z$, that is, if $A$, $B$, and $C$ have similar distributions. Consider the phoneme sequence *boiling*. Is *boil* a morphemic segment within this phoneme sequence ? Consider *boiling* in the environment *It's boiling now*. First in order to determine whether or not *boil* is a tentative morphemic segment, we must ask the question : Can *boiling* be replaced by some other phoneme sequence which differs from *boiling* only by *boil* ? *Boiling* can be replaced by *starting*, for we can say *It's starting now*. Therefore *boil* is a tentative morphemic segment. (*Start* is likewise.) Now assume that we went through this procedure for *running, stopping*, and *climbing*, and that we concluded that *boil, start, run, stop*, and *climb* are each tentative morphemic segments. Then by noting that each can be placed into the environments *I'm _____ing now, _____ it now,* etc., and that none can be placed into the environments *I want some _____, Lift that _____,* etc., we conclude that each of *boil, start, run, stop,* and *climb* is a morphemic segment.

Let us look at a case in which a tentative morphemic segment does not qualify as a morphemic segment. Consider the phoneme sequence *notice.* Is *ice* a morphemic segment in this phoneme sequence? Consider *notice* in the environment *That's worthy of notice.* Can *notice* be replaced by some other phoneme sequence which is identical with *notice* except for *ice*? *Notice* can be replaced by *note,* for we can say *That's worthy of note.* Thus we must consider *ice* to be a tentative morphemic segment in *notice,* for it was replaced by the null sequence in the same total environment. But now if we look for other tentative morphemic segments with distributions similar to that of *ice* in *notice,* we find none. *Ice* as it occurs in *notice,* then, cannot be given the status of a morphemic segment.

The procedure for determining the morphemic segments of utterances does not require that a morphemic segment consist of an unbroken succession of phonemes; that is, a morphemic segment need not be a contiguous phoneme sequence. All that is required is that each morphemic segment be identifiable in terms of phonemes. An inventory of different kinds of morphemic segments would include contiguous phoneme sequences (by far the most common), noncontiguous phoneme sequences (phoneme sequences into which infixes may be inserted), the replacement of phoneme sequences (such as the replacement of *oo* by *ee* in going from *goose* to *geese),* and the null replacement of phoneme sequences (such as in going from singular *sheep* to plural *sheep).*

The procedure we have outlined above determines how many morphemic segments there are in a given utterance and what these morphemic segments are. In other words, the procedure defines 'morphemic segment' for a particular environment; the procedure does not define a morphemic element having various occurrences in various environments. Our morphemic analysis, therefore, has reached the point where every utterance in our sample is divided into morphemic segments. Our next task is to group various morphemic segments into the same morpheme, that is, to identify morphemic segments of one utterance with morphemic segments of another utterance or with morphemic segments of the same utterance.

We begin with free variation. If two phonemically different morphemic segments occur in identical environments in all cases, these two segments are considered to be in free variation with each other and are grouped into a single morpheme. Two different morphemic segments will occur in identical environments in all cases if and only if speakers are prepared to substitute one for the other in all cases. Consider the two different pronunciations of *apricot*. Since the two morphemic segments corresponding to the two different pronunciations will occur in identical environments in all cases — one may be substituted for the other at any time — the two morphemic segments are considered as free variants of each other and are grouped together as a single morpheme. This grouping on the basis of free variation is of great importance, for it permits a unified morphological treatment of different dialects and ideolects in which the same morphemic element is expressed in phonologically different ways. The grouping of morphemic segments on the basis of identical environments is the formal nonintuitive device for duplicating the intuitive semantic observation that though the two different pronunciations of *apricot* differ from each other no more than the pronunciations of *bat* and *bait*, the two pronunciations of *apricot* are variations of one word while *bat* and *bait* are two different words.

As for phonemically identical morphemic segments, we group them into a single tentative morpheme. Thus all the morphemic segments pronounced as in *hotel* in *Are you looking for a hotel?*, *This is a nice hotel*, and *Where is the hotel?* are grouped together into a single tentative morpheme. Likewise all the morphemic segments pronounced as in *to* in *I shall go to the store*, *I will go too*, and *Give me two, please*, are grouped into a single tentative morpheme. Now what is required is a restriction placed upon tentative morphemes which will result in assigning the different morphemic segments pronounced as in *hotel* (in the above utterances) to a single morpheme, but the different morphemic segments pronounced as in *to* (in the above utterances) to different morphemes. This restriction is imposed by matching the environments of the tentative morphemes in the following way. We first consider the distribution of one tentative morpheme and compare it with the distribution of other tentative morphemes. If one tentative morpheme has a distribution virtually identical with the distribution of another, we consider each of the two tentative morphemes to be morphemes. Assume that *hotel* and *rug* are found to be tentative morphemes. Now since *hotel* is found in *Are you looking for a hotel?*, *This is a nice hotel*, *Where is the hotel?* etc., and since *rug* has a virtually identical distribution, the tentative morpheme *hotel* is considered a morpheme and the tentative morpheme *rug* is considered a morpheme. However since no tentative morpheme can be found which has a distribution virtually identical with the distribution of the tentative morpheme pronounced *to,* this tentative morpheme does not qualify as a morpheme. This method of grouping phonemically identical morphemic segments on the basis of a camparison of distributions, is the formal nonintuitive device which duplicates our intuitive insight into the fact that *hotel,* in its various occurrences, constitutes the same word while utterances pronounced *to* do not always constitute the same word.

Phonemically different morphemes may be grouped into a single morpheme according to a procedure which we shall illustrate. Assume that the above procedure for grouping morphemic segments into morphemes has resulted in *knife* being considered a morpheme, *knive* being considered another morpheme, and *wive* still another morpheme. Now since the morpheme *knife* occurs only in one environment while the morpheme *knive* occurs only in another — that is since *knife* and *knive* have complementary distributions — the two morphemes, *knife* and *knive* are grouped into a single tentative morpheme. Similarly, since *knife* and *wive* have complementary distributions, *knife* and *wive* are grouped into a single tentative morpheme. However, since we can find environments, *I'll sharpen my* _____ *on the whetstone* and *I'll sharpen my* _____s *on the whetstone,* and since *knife* and *knive* can be substituted in the blanks respectively but not *knife* and *wive* respectively, it is concluded that *knife* and *wive* do not belong to a single morpheme while *knife* and *knive* still may — that is, it is ruled out that *knife* and *wive* belong to a single morpheme, but it is not ruled out that *knife* and *knive* belong to the same morpheme. Now, since the single morpheme *rug* (antecendently determined to be a morpheme) occurs in the environments of both *knife* and *knive* — *A knife was stolen, Several knives were stolen*; *A rug was stolen, Several rugs were stolen* — we conclude that *knife* and *knive* belong to a single morpheme. If no morpheme, such as *rug,* could be found which occurs in environments of both *knife* and *knive,* then the tentative morpheme group, *knife* and *knive,* would not qualify as a single morpheme. All this can be considered the formal nonintuitive device paralleling our intuitive insight that though *knife* and *knive* differ phonemically, they have the same meaning and are variations of the same word, though only *knife* can occur alone.

In sketching a formal nonintuitive procedure of morphemic analysis, we have largely followed Harris.[7] Harris' procedures are notably free from intuitive semantic considerations. It should not be assumed, however, that his treatment of morphemic analysis is typical. His is one of the few which defines 'morpheme' strictly structurally. Above, before sketching formal nonintuitive procedures for morphemic analysis, we gave an intuitive explanation of the notion of morpheme — an explanation dependent upon our semantic intuition. Traditional linguistics, which is yet not out of vogue today, in characterizing the notion of morpheme and in giving procedures for doing morphemic analysis, does not go beyond such semantically oriented explanations. Traditionally, little or no effort was made to develop the notion of morpheme strictly in terms of structure. In fact most of the

[7]   Harris, *op. cit.*

most recent texts concerning linguistics still give a semantic-ridden account of the morpheme and morphemic analysis. Hockett, in his well-known introductory text, writes : "Morphemes are the smallest meaningful elements in the utterances of a language."[8] Gleason, though going some way in avoiding intuitive semantic considerations and sticking to formal nonintuitive characterizations and procedures, writes :

Two elements can be considered as allomorphs of the same morpheme if: (1) they have a common meaning, (2) they are in complementary distribution, and (3) they occur in parallel formations. Note that there are three requirements. All three must be met.[9]

## PARTS OF SPEECH

We have discussed the notions of phoneme and morpheme in some detail. Now we shall continue our structural survey of language by examining the processes of derivation and inflection, and by examining the principles of arrangement of those constructions formed by derivation and inflection into larger constructions such as phrases and sentences. In order to avoid countless difficulties in our exposition, we shall make use of the concept, wordhood, without giving a formal nonintuitive definition of it. Though intuitively we have no difficulties concerning what constitutes a word, this concept is one of the most difficult in morphology to define. Roughly a word (in English) is a sequence of morphemes consisting of a root and a stress morpheme with or without derivational and inflectional affixes.

The traditional description of English grammar is in terms of eight parts of speech : nouns, pronouns, verbs, adverbs, adjectives, prepositions, conjunctions, and interjections. And the traditional classification of these parts of speech is in terms of meaning. Often these definitions in terms of meaning are vague or the

[8] C. Hockett, *A Course in Modern Linguistics* (New York : The Macmillan Co., 1958), p. 123.
[9] Gleason, *op. cit.*, p. 88.

demarcations between parts of speech are arbitrary. Nouns are defined as words which 'name' persons, places, things, qualities, actions, relationships, etc.; adjectives are defined as words which 'indicate' quality; verbs are defined as words which 'specify' actions, states, feelings, etc. Concerning these 'definitions' we note the following : Two of them make use of *etc. Quality* and *action* each occur in two of the definitions. The words *name, indicate,* and *specify* are not used in any sufficiently precise manner to be of grammatical significance. In the light of these observations we can only conclude that the definitions of parts of speech given above are totally inadequate. We must not lose sight of the fact that we are seeking nonintuitive definitions of parts of speech; that is, in defining the various parts of speech we must not rely upon our intuitions of linguistic structure. Further, since we hope that knowledge of the structure of our language will give us a basis for studying the meanings conveyed by language, it would be viciously circular to base our understanding of structure upon meaning. We must steer clear of both our intuition concerning structure and our knowledge of meanings.

The assignment of a given word to a certain part of speech does not depend upon whether it 'names', 'indicates', or 'signifies' but rather upon the distributional relations among the features of speech in question. This is the only procedure which is consistent with the definition of 'structural liguistics' given in an earlier chapter. In attempting to give definitions of parts of speech in terms of distributional relations we find that we must make use of two kinds of criteria : one kind defining paradigmatic classes and the other defining syntactic classes.

First let us consider paradigmatic classes. We find that some words fall into a small set of related forms. Further, we find that these sets fall into four patterns each of which we call a paradigm. The following examples may be taken as constituting four different paradigms, each defining a paradigmatic class :

| | | | |
|---|---|---|---|
| *boy* | *I* | *give* | *big* |
| *boys* | *me* | *gives* | *bigger* |
| | *my* | *gave* | *biggest* |
| | *mine* | *given* | |
| | | *giving* | |

Each of these four paradigms is typical of a large class of words. Any word occurring in the first paradigm may be defined as a noun; any word occuring in the second paradigm may be defined as a personal pronoun; any occurring in the third, a verb; any in the fourth, an adjective.

Next, let us consider syntactic classes. Those parts of speech which are not defined by paradigms are defined by comparable environments in utterances of our language. For this reason they are called syntactic classes. The group of words traditionally referred to as prepositions serve as an example of a syntactic class, that is, as an example of a definite class of words having charateristic syntactic uses. Very roughly, prepositions are found before nouns and at the ends of clauses with certain characteristic stress patterns.

From each of the four paradigms (considered above), noun, personal pronoun, verb, and adjective, we may abstract a set of morphemes which are affixed to the stem. For example, with the adjective paradigm we have :

adjective stem ——
adjective stem *er*
adjective stem *est*

These affixes are called inflectional suffixes. In English inflectional suffixes do not form stems. By this we mean that once such a suffix is added to a stem no further affix may be added. Inflectional suffixes may be contrasted with derivational affixes, which comprise all other affixes in English. Derivational affixes, unlike inflectional suffixes, may be used to form stems. For example, *ize* is a verb-stem-forming derivational affix (suffix). *Patronize* is a verb formed from *patron* and *ize* which may in turn serve as a verb stem by taking the additional suffix *ation* in forming *patronization*, a noun.

## GRAMMAR

In explaining the nature of immediate constituent grammars we shall first, by way of example and nonformal discussion, give an intuitive presentation of some of the key concepts involved. Following this we shall give a very brief sketch of how immediate constituent grammars are constructed along formal nonintuitive lines.

Consider the English utterance, *The old man who lives there has gone to his son's house.* First let us mark those pairs of words which intuitively seem to be most closely related.

*The old man who lives there has gone to his son's house.*

Now we notice that each marked pair may be considered to function in the utterance as a single unit. By this we mean that we may replace any of the marked pairs by a single word and get an utterance which seems to be structurally similar. For example, we might have the following replacements :

| *The* | *old man* | *who* | *lives there* | *has gone* | *to* | *his son's* | *house.* |
|-------|-----------|-------|---------------|------------|------|-------------|----------|
|       | *boy*     |       | *sings*       | *went*     |      | *John's*    |          |

Taking the marked pairs, at a given level of analysis, as units we can then proceed to mark other pairs as units on a next level and so on. The result with our original utterance is the following :

*The old man who lives there has gone to his son's house.*

At each level of analysis in the above breakdown, a single word can be found to replace a marked pair. For example *his son's* can be replaced by *John's*; *John's house* can be replaced by *Albany*; *to Albany* can be replaced by *there*.

We now go on to give rough intuitive characterizations of some of the key notions implicitly involved in the above informal analysis. A construction is a significant group of words. Probably the best way to bring out what we mean by 'construction' is to give some examples. The utterance *The old man who lives there has gone to his son's house* is a construction. In this utterance *the old man who lives there* is a construction, and *old man* is a construction. All of these constructions intuitively seem to be meaningful. On the other hand, in the same utterance, *there has* is not a construction since in the context of this utterance it does not appear to be meaningful. A single word such as *man* or *house* is not a construction since a construction must consist of more than one word.

A constituent is any word or construction which is part of a longer construction. In the utterance we are dealing with, each single word is a constituent; *his son's, his son's house, to his son's house* are also constituents. *There has* and *man who* are not constituents for they are neither single words or constructions. The utterance as a whole is not a constituent, because though it is a construction it is not part of a longer construction.

An immediate constituent is one of the constituents of which a given construction is directly formed. The immediate constituents of a given construction are the constituents of the given construction on the next level of analysis. In our example, *lives* and *there* are immediate constituents of *lives there*; *who* and *lives there* are immediate constituents of *who lives there*. But *lives there* is not an immediate constituent of *old man who lives there*.

The breakdown of constructions into immediate constituents is the fundamental operation in immediate constituent grammars. This breakdown, however, does not take place on a nonformal intuitive basis such as we have just considered. There are a number of formal nonintuitive methods for establishing the immediate constituents of a given construction. No single method is sufficient in itself, but the methods, used as complements of each other, are sufficient to break down any construction into its successive levels of immediate constituents without relying upon matters of meaning or appealing to a fluent speaker's intuition. We shall now indicate a few of the methods used.

By the method of comparing samples, we can get a foothold in immediate constituent analysis. Let us consider the construction *his son's house*. Our problem is to determine the immediate constituents of this construction. We look for a two-word construction which is comparable to *his son's house,* comparable in the sense that the two word construction may occur in similar environments. It is not enough, however, that we find just a single comparable construction; we must choose our comparable construction so that we may establish a general rule. Our results must always be general. A two-word construction which is comparable to *his son's house* is *John's house.* The same word *house* appears in both; the suffix *-'s* (of considerable structural importance) appears in both; both have similar stress patterns; the two constructions are found in similar environments. Above all, though we cannot show it here, the comparison of *his son's house* and *John's house* is typical of many others. Thus we can finally conclude that the immediate constituents of *his son's house* are *his son's* and *house*; that is, we conclude that we cut *his son's house* along the lines of *John's house.*

The above method of comparing samples is closely related to the method of substitution. When we conclude that *his son's house* and *John's house* are comparable samples we are in fact saying that *John's* may be substituted for *his son's.* We test this substitutability by collecting a large number of utterances containing *his son's* and substitute *John's* for *his son's.* If the resulting utterances are acceptable to a fluent speaker — or, more precisely, are found in our corpus of utterances — then we conclude that *John's* is substitutable for *his son's* and that the immediate constituents of *his son's house* are *his son's* and *house.*

Still another method for determining the immediate constituents of a construction is that of freedom of occurrence. Roughly speaking, that cut is best which gives immediate constituents having maximum freedom of occurrence in other utterances. For example, consider the construction *old light house*. Since *light house* has greater freedom of occurrence in other utterances than *old light*, we cut *old light house* into *old* and *light house*. Next, consider *Old Light Church*. At first blush we might cut this as we did *old light house*, however, this would not be justified by the method of freedom of occurrence. *Old Light* has a greater freedom of occurrence than *Light Church*. Whereas *Light Church* has practically no occurrence outside of *Old Light Church*, *Old Light* is found in expressions such as *Old Light theology, Old Light movement*, and *Old Light preacher*.

We have only touched upon a few of the formal nonintuitive methods used by descriptive linguists in constructing an immediate constituent grammar. Nevertheless, the general pattern of relying upon the distributional relations of features of speech and avoiding any appeal to meaning or intuition of structure has been amply exemplified. We shall go further into matters of grammar in the next chapter.

# VI

## SUCCESS IN GRAMMAR — FAILURE IN SEMANTICS

We have seen that both ordinary-language philosophers and ideal-language philosophers have not come up with a descriptive theory of natural language. Because of some recent impressive advances in structural linguistics — some of which we touched upon in the previous chapter, but especially certain achievements in grammar — linguists seem to be more confident than philosophers concerning the task of constructing a genuine theory of natural language. Some progress has been made in the construction of such a theory, priorities have been set up for further work, and some linguists look forward to the day when they will have achieved the construction of an adequate theory of natural language.[1]

As we noted earlier, the goal of linguist in their construction of a theory of natural language is the explication of the mechanism by which fluent speakers of a language are able to produce and understand the meaningful utterances of the language. We have already considered phonology and certain aspects of morphology. Next, let us turn to syntax.

### SYNTAX

The goal of linguists in their syntactical investigations is the construction of a grammar which will function as a mechanism for

---

[1] J. Katz and J. Fodor, "What's Wrong with the Philosophy of Language ?" *Inquiry* (1962), pp. 221-234.

producing, in a mechanical and nonintuitive manner, the grammatical sequences and only the grammatical sequences of the language under consideration. Traditional grammar failed to explicate a fluent speaker's knowledge of grammatical form because the speaker's linguistic abilities and intuitions themselves were necessary for applying the grammar. The type of grammar we are discussing here, being completely nonintuitive and mechanical in application, does not fall into this error.

In constructing the grammar we must have a collection of sequences which are definitely grammatical — a collection of actually observed utterances concerning which there is general agreement that they are grammatical — and also a collection of sequences which are definitely ungrammatical. These collections constitute the intuitive controls upon the grammar. These intuitive controls, however, must not be used in the application of the formal nonintuitive grammar. The formal nonintuitive grammar must duplicate (and thus explicate) the grammatical intuition of fluent speakers. The grammar must be able to generate formally and nonintuitively all of the definitely grammatical sequences and none of the definitely ungrammatical ones. As for the collection of sequences which are neither definitely grammatical nor ungrammatical, we are prepared to let the grammar itself decide concerning grammaticalness. The grammar may be considered as a mechanism which projects the finite collection of observed grammatical sequences to an infinite collection of grammatical sequences. By so doing the grammar explicates a phase of the behavior of fluent speakers who, with just the knowledge of a finite collection of grammatical sequences, are able to produce and understand totally novel grammatical sequences. It should be stressed that grammaticalness must be ultimately determined by what fluent speakers of the language under consideration would accept as grammatical. That which fluent speakers would accept as grammatical is the intuitive control placed upon the formal nonintuitive grammar.

The goal of a theory of language with respect to syntax is the following: Given two grammars, the theory must be able to select the better of the two. In other words, the theory of language must provide an evaluation procedure for the grammars.

Given two grammars the theory of language will decide which is the better according to how they meet certain conditions of adequacy. The conditions of adequacy can be divided into two groups : external conditions and internal conditions. The first external condition we have already looked at, since it is involved in the very definition of 'grammar' : A grammar must be able to generate all and only the grammatical sequences of the language. Since there are an infinity of grammatical sequences and an infinity of ungrammatical sequences, this, practically speaking, amounts to saying that a grammar must be able to generate all of the sequences in an adequate sample of grammatical sequences and none of the sequences in an adequate sample of ungrammatical sequences. Still another external condition imposed upon grammars is that a grammar should be able to explicate our intuitive understandings of certain types of sentences. For example, an adequate grammar should automatically provide more than one derivation for a syntactically ambiguous sentence. And an adequate grammar should automatically provide different derivations for sentences which are understood syntactically in different ways though superficially similar in structure.

The ultimate goal of linguists in their syntactical endeavors is a theory of linguistic form in which no reference is made to particular languages, that is, a theory of linguistic form in which language is dealt with abstractly. This ultimate goal of a theory of linguistic form should not come as a surprise, since linguists are interested in the nature of language itself as opposed to the nature of particular languages. Such a theory (actually a meta-theory) would describe an abstract grammar and give procedures for evaluating grammars. In an abstract grammar terms such as 'phoneme', 'morpheme', and 'phrase' are defined independently of any given language. The logical relation between an abstract grammar and a working grammar (a grammar for a particular language) is the same as the relation between projective geometry and any one of the metrical geometries. (In this section we are actually working within this meta theory. Rather than offering a grammar for English, we are dealing with certain meta theoretical considerations concerning grammars. These meta theoretical considerations include such matters as the goal of grammar, conditions of adequacy for grammars, and models for grammar.)

Now let us continue with conditions of adequacy for grammars. Our first internal condition for adequacy is the following : An adequate grammar must be of such a kind that the concepts and elements which it employs are special cases of the concepts and elements of the abstract grammar or linguistic theory adopted. In other words, in an adequate grammar, such key concepts as phoneme and morpheme must be deducible from more general concepts of phoneme and morpheme which are, in the abstract grammar or linguistic theory, defined independently of any particular language. The last condition for adequacy which we shall mention, but not linger with, is the internal condition of systematic simplicity. The above two external conditions together with the above two internal conditions should provide the required evaluation procedure for selecting the better of two proposed grammars. However, it is evident that we have not gone into the details of how we would go about the task of selecting the more adequate of two grammars.

Having set the goals of an adequate grammar, the next problem is to determine just what type of device is required for producing such a grammar. Suggestions have been put forth that grammaticalness in a given language is nothing more than a high order of statistical approximation to the language, and thus that our grammar should be constructed on some statistical model. A grammatical sequence in English, it is argued, is just a sequence which is likely to occur in the use of English, and an ungrammatical sequence is one which is not likely to occur. It does not take much effort to show that this view of grammar is incorrect. Both *It's a nice day for a picnic* and *Pelicans digest smelt easily* are grammatical sequences; however, the former is likely to occur in the use of English while the latter is unlikely to occur. Any model of language which bases grammaticalness upon relative frequency of occurrence in a language would be unable to account for the fact that the above sequences are equally grammatical. If English sequences of a given length were listed in the order of their likeliness to occur in English speech, the list would consist of grammatical und ungrammatical sequences in no special order. Since grammar has been shown to be a nonstatistical structure, we must look elsewhere for our model of grammar.

A more powerful model suggested for grammar — one which is not so obviously inadequate — is a finite state Markov process. (A finite state Markov process may be represented by a machine which can be in any one of a finite number of different internal states. The machine begins in the initial state, runs through a sequence of states [various different transitions between states and repetitions of states being allowed] and ends in the final state.)

A finite state grammar — a grammar constructed on the model of a finite state Markov process — is able to mechanically generate an infinite number of sequences, using a finite apparatus. This meets a minimal requirement for the type of grammar we are seeking, since we want to produce the grammatical sequences in a practical manner and since there are an infinite number of grammatical sequences. Chomsky, however, has shown[2] that if a finite state grammar produces all grammatical sequences it will also produce some ungrammatical ones, and that if it produces only grammatical sequences it will leave out some grammatical ones.

A proposed model for grammar which does not fail in the same way as a finite state Markov process model fails, is a phrase structure model. Constructing a grammar upon this model yields an immediate constituent grammar. A good portion of English which cannot be described by means of a finite state grammar can be described by means of an immediate constituent grammar.

An immediate constituent grammar consist of a finite set $\Sigma$ of initial strings and a finite set $F$ of instruction formulas having the form $X \rightarrow Y$, which is read : Rewrite $X$ as $Y$. The gram-

[2]    Noam Chomsky, *Syntactic Structures* (The Hague : Mouton and Co., 1957), chapter 3.

mar itself is symbolized by $[\Sigma, F]$. Given $[\Sigma, F]$, a derivation can be represented by a tree diagram which begins with an initial string of $\Sigma$ and each step of which is justified by an instruction formula of $F$. Let us look at the following very simple example of an immediate constituent grammar $[\Sigma, F]$, in which $\Sigma$ consists of the single initial string 'Sentence' and $F$ consists of the following instruction formulas :

(1)    Sentence $\rightarrow NP + VP$
(2)    $NP \rightarrow T + N$
(3)    $VP \rightarrow Verb + NP$
(4)    $T \rightarrow the$
(5)    $N \rightarrow man, ball, stick,$ etc.
(6)    $V \rightarrow hit, ran, fell,$ etc.

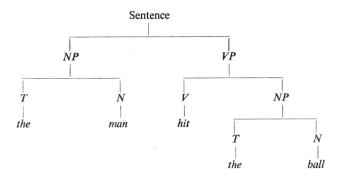

Fig. 1. A constituent structure characterization of the sentence *The man hit the ball*. (Adapted from Chomsky, *op. cit.*, p. 27.)

Given this grammar, a derivation may be represented by the tree diagram of Figure 1. This tree diagram constitutes the constitutent structure characterization of *the man hit the ball*. This derivation begins with the initial string 'Sentence'; each step is justified by one of the rules of $F$, as can be easily confirmed. This derivation generates the grammatical sentence (terminal string) *the man hit the ball*. A sequence of words of this terminal string is a constituent of type $T$ if it is possible to trace the sequence back, without remainder, to a single point of origin in the tree diagram marked $T$. The sequence *the man* can be traced back to a single point of origin marked $NP$ (noun phrase); thus, *the man* is a constituent of type $NP$. The sequence *hit the* cannot be traced back, without remainder, to a single point of origin and hence is not a constituent.

As important as immediate constituent grammars are to the grammatical analysis of natural languages, such as English, they by themselves have certain inherent limitations. Chomsky has shown[3] that a grammar based upon a phrase structure model, though not impossible, would be fundamentally inadequate on the grounds that is would be hopelessly complex, that it would require countless *ad hoc* devices, and that it would be unrevealing. Because of the shortcomings of immediate constituent grammars, they must be supplemented by a set of grammatical rules of a special type called transformations. A transformation states the structural relation between a pair of constructions. It is given in the form of a rule which applies to an input construction — a construction from an immediate constituent grammar or a prior transformation — and which in turn produces an output construction. Let us give an example of a grammatical transformation. Assume that our immediate constituent grammar has generated the terminal string *George is climbing the hill*. A grammatical transformation which might be applied to this terminal string as input construction is the following: If $S$ is a grammatical sentence of the form

$$NP_1 - is - \text{Verb} - NP_2$$

(that is to say, if $S$ is a grammatical sentence consisting of the sequence: noun phrase, *is,* verb, noun phrase) then the corresponding string of the form

$$is - NP_1 - \text{Verb} - NP_2$$

is also a grammatical sentence. Such a transformation applied

---

[3]    *Ibid.*, chapter 5.

to *George is climbing the hill* as input construction would produce the output construction *Is George climbing the hill?*

A transformational grammar has two sections. The first section consist of an immediate constituent grammar providing as terminal strings relatively simple active indicative grammatical sentences. The second section consist of a set of transformations which, operating upon the terminal strings of the immediate constituent grammar, generate more complex grammatical sentences. Some of the transformations are obligatory while others are optional. This distinction leads to a basic distinction between the sentences produced by the transformational grammar. The kernel of the language (the language defined by the transformational grammar) is the set of sentences produced when the obligatory transformations are applied to the terminal strings of the immediate constituent grammar section. Thus every sentence of the language belongs either to the kernel or is derived by means of optional transformations.

Because of descriptive linguists' success with transformational grammar, some of them look forward to the day when they will have constructed a complete theory of natural language, with both its formal grammar and formal semantics. The success linguists have had with the construction of formal nonintuitive grammars surely is ground for optimism concerning the completion and perfection of the syntactical portion of a theory of natural language. However, it seems ironic that their achievements in grammar should have made them optimistic concerning the completion of their semantical task, in fact, even the most elementary part of their semantical task — the construction of a dictionary consisting of pairs of synonymous expressions. It is ironic because the success of descriptive linguists with grammar is to a great extent due to their policy of not characterizing grammatical notions in terms of semantics.

We want to make clear at this point, if we have not already made it clear, that Chomsky's transformational grammar is completely formal. (As we said earlier, by 'formal' we mean 'in abstraction from meaning'.) In his transformational grammar there is no dependence whatsoever upon semantical notions such as significance, meaning, synonymy, and reference. In other words, in generating all and only grammatical sequences, Chomsky's transformational grammar at no time makes use of the notion of meaning. In an earlier chapter we noted that descriptive linguists defined parts of speech in purely formal ways — specifically in terms of paradigmatic or syntactical classes. We also noted that this practice is a complete departure from traditional grammar, which defined parts of speech semantically. If one looks at various attempts at constructing an adequate grammar one cannot help but note that one of the greatest hindrances to the construction of an adequate grammar was the reliance upon semantical notions.

As long as grammarians sought a foundation for grammar in semantics, only obstacles were encountered in the construction of an adequate grammar. If the appeal to semantics is taken as an appeal to a nonintuitive formal semantics, then for the present at least, grammar cannot be based upon semantics, simply because there is no nonintuitive formal semantics yet available. Furthermore, it is generally held that the formal nonintuitive semantic component of a theory of natural language must build upon the formal nonintuitive syntactic component. If the appeal to semantics is taken as an appeal to our semantic intuition — capable of formalization in the future — then most of the definitions of grammatical concepts in terms of semantical notions are plainly inadequate, as they go counter to our semantical intuition. It should be noted that even if it could be shown that grammatical concepts could be defined in terms of intuitive semantical notions, it would be of little use to a formal nonintuitive grammar unless the intuitive semantics were itself formalized. However, we need not at this point speculate concerning the formalization of our intuitive semantics, since our intuitive semantics has proven inadequate for defining grammatical concepts even informally.

We have said that most of the definitions of grammatical concepts in terms of semantical notions prove inadequate. A brief look at some attempts to define grammatical concepts in terms of semantics will make this point clear. It has been urged by some semantically oriented linguists that 'phonemic distinctness' be defined in terms of difference of meaning. It is proposed that two utterances be considered phonemically distinct if and only if they differ in meaning. Now if we make use of our semantic intuition we quickly see that 'phonemic distinctness' cannot be defined in terms of difference of meaning, since we intuitively recognize both synonyms and homonyms in our language. Synonyms such as *porpoise* and *dolphin* are phonemically distinct yet identical in meaning according to our semantic intuition; homonyms such as *top* in the sense of a toy top and *top* in the sense of the top of a mountain, are phonemically identical yet different in meaning.

Once semantics is banned from grammar the problem of phonemic distinctness is solved in a rather simple and clearcut manner. The pair test — involving merely the consistent identification of utterances — provides a quite adequate nonsemantic criterion for phonemic distinctness.[4] Similarly, attempts to define 'morphemic distinctness' in terms of difference of meaning serve only to complicate matters for linguists. As with the problem of phonemic distinctness, the problem of morphemic distinctness can be handled completely non-semantically.

Not only has semantics caused trouble with the question of morphemic distinctness, but it has also caused trouble with the definition of 'morpheme' itself. It has been proposed that morphemes be defined as the shortest sequences having independent meaning. However, this definition is quickly seen to be inadequate. The *to* in *I like to travel,* has no independent meaning according to our semantic intuition, yet we certainly would not want to classify it as a non-morpheme. The *sp* in *spit, sputter, spew, spray, spout,* and *speak* seems to have independent meaning — having to do with emanation from the mouth — according to our semantic intuition, yet we would not want to classify *sp* as a morpheme.

Perhaps the greatest hindrance to grammar by semantics was

[4]   *Ibid.,* p .96.

the proposed definition of 'grammatical sequence' as 'semantically meaningful sequence'. This definition has proved totally inadequate. Chomsky has pointed out that the two sentences *Colorless green ideas sleep furiously* and *Furiously sleep ideas green colorless'* are equally nonsensical but only the first is grammatical. Similarly, Chomsky has pointed out that *Have you a book on modern music?* and *Read you a book on modern music?* are equally meaningful yet only the first is grammatical. Thus we see that being meaningful is neither a necessary nor a sufficient condition for being grammatical. In his transformational grammar Chomsky abandons all matters of meaning and defines 'grammatical sequence' in a completely nonsemantical manner.

It is apparent that semantics brings chaos and confusion wherever it ventures. Chomsky's success with grammar — to a great part due to his rejection of the practice of defining grammatical concepts semantically — rather than being taken as a reason for hope in the task of constructing a complete theory of language, including a formal nonintuitive semantics — might be better viewed as another blow against the hopes of solving the problems of semantics and constructing a formal nonintuitive semantics.

## SEMANTICS

Before taking up the matter of the semantic component of a theory of natural language, let us quickly look at some attempts to handle the notion of 'absolute meaning'; that is, let us look at some attempts to answer the question, What are meanings? The first thing we notice is that most answers offered are actually answers to the question, What is the meaning of a term? — syncategorematic words being handled as words having no meaning in isolation. Even if at this point we disregard the difficulties offered by syncategorematic words, it should prove instructive to note the attempts to answer the more restricted question, What is the meaning of a term?

One answer which has been given to this question is that the meaning of a term is the essence or Platonic idea expressed by the term. Taking meaning as essence should not come as a surprise since meaning is what essence becomes when it is detached from the object or objects referred to by the term and attached to the term itself. The trouble of course, with defining 'meaning' in terms of essence or idea is that we are — to put it conservatively — just as much in the dark concerning the natures of essence and idea as we are of meaning. What is needed is a definition of 'meaning' in terms of something which we understand better than meaning and with which we would be able to solve such practical problems as when two meanings are the same. Defining 'meaning' in terms of essence or idea does not help us with the practical problem of the sameness of meaning, precisely because we are not clear concerning the sameness of essence or ideas. As Quine has pointed out, such a definition of 'meaning' gives the illusion of an explanation, the illusion being increased by the fact that the matter becomes vague enough to preclude a genuine solution.

Another answer given to the question, What is the meaning of a term ? is that it is the mental image for which the term stands. The trouble with this definition of 'meaning' is that the notion of mental image does not help us at all outside the realm of the familiar and commonplace. What is the mental image of an extremely large set as compared with an infinite set ? The matter becomes even worse when we attempt to determine the mental images of such words as *benign, malignant, just, courageous.*

A proposed definition of 'meaning' in which a great many linguists and philosophers have indulged consists in defining the meaning of a term as the reference of the term. The meaning of a singular term such as *Truman* would be that which is named by the term *Truman,* namely Truman himself. The meaning of a general term would be the extension of the term. This identification of meaning and reference is very tempting, because it is often clear what the extension of a term is, and there are rather clear-cut methods for comparing the extensions of different terms.

One rather simple reason for questioning the solution of the meaning problem in terms of reference or naming is that if all terms are really names then why are some terms obviously names while others seem not to be names. But rather than following up this suggestion, it will be easier to give a classic refutation. As Frege pointed out, the terms *evening star* and *morning star* refer to the same object yet they differ in meaning. We know that they differ in meaning because observational evidence was required in order to determine that they named the same object. Had they the same meaning we could have deduced that they named the same object and we would not have needed to wait for observational evidence. Thus we can conclude that the meaning of a singular term cannot be identified with the object named.

The case is similar with general terms. *Centaur* and *unicorn* obviously differ in meaning yet they have the same extension, the null set. *Man* and *language-using animal* differ in meaning yet they have the same extension. Thus we see that the meaning of a general term cannot be identified with its extension. Reference is a weaker notion than meaning. For terms having reference, sameness of reference is a necessary but not a sufficient condition for sameness of meaning.

Still another proposal is that the meaning of a term is the concept for which the term stands. Now either the concept for which a term stands is taken to be its definition or it is taken to be something similar to essence or idea. If it is taken to be the latter then we are no better off with concept than we were with essence or idea. However, if concept is taken to be definition it appears that we, at long last, begin to make some headway, for we begin to think of the meaning of an expression as some other expression. Nevertheless, as we shall soon see, the answer is not quite so simple as saying that the meaning of a term is its definition.

When the meaning of a term is asked for what is usually given is another expression having the same meaning. Linguists, therefore, rather than contending with the evasive notion of meaning and rather than continuing to search for meanings as objects, focused their attention upon one context of meaning — sameness of meaning or synonymy. The context, alike in meaning, though not exhausting the notion of meaning, is a very important context of meaning, and the isolation of this context at least gives the linguist something tangible to work with. The linguist now as lexicographer has the clear-cut task of correlating synonymous expressions — he has the task of actually listing pairs of synonymous expressions — and need no longer grope for those mysterious objects, meanings. It should be noted at this point that with the shift in interest from meaning to sameness of meaning, it is no longer necessary to restrict our discussion to terms. Syncategorematic words will appear in the lexicographer's list of mutually synonymous expressions as well as categorematic words. But before we go on to investigate the problem of synonymy let us take up the matter of the semantic component of a theory of natural language.

As we have noted above, the ultimate goal of a theory of natural language, insofar as syntax is concerned, is a theory of linguistic form in which no reference is made to particular languages — a theory of linguistic form which deals with grammar abstractly. Such a metatheory would, among other things, describe an abstract grammar and give procedures for evaluating grammars. The ultimate goal of a theory of natural language, in general, would be to deal, in an abstract manner, with both grammar and semantics. Thus a metatheory for semantics would deal with semantic universals; the semantic particulars of individual semantic theories would be subsumed under the universals of the semantic metatheory. The semantic metatheory would provide procedures for choosing between two or more individual semantic theories. In what follows, we shall be dealing with metatheoretical considerations. We shall not offer a semantic theory of a natural language, but rather we shall deal with certain abstract considerations of semantic theories. Some of the metatheoretical considerations we shall deal with are : the goal of a semantic theory, the domain of a semantic theory, the mechanism of a semantic theory, and the manner of evaluating semantic theories.

In Chapter I we said that the type of theory of natural language we would be dealing with is one which did not take into consideration matters of setting or context. At this point it seems necessary to justify our choosing such a type of theory. We must consider two different kinds of setting or context: linguistic and extra-linguistic. We shall show first that there is no need for a theory to take linguistic context into consideration, and second that it is not feasible for a theory to take extra-linguistic context into consideration.

A theory of language which takes the linguistic context of a given sentence into consideration is no more powerful than one which does not, that is, no more powerful than a theory which restricts itself to single sentences. The reason for this is simply the following: For every discourse (that is, for any given sentence together with the other sentences comprising its linguistic context) there is a single sentence consisting of all the individual sentences connected by appropriate sentential connectives. Thus we see that a theory of language need not provide for handling the linguistic context of a given sentence, since that context, together with the given sentence, can be incorporated into a single sentence upon which the theory can operate.

To include within the goal of a theory of natural language the explication of the way in which nonlinguistic setting determines how an utterance is produced and understood would simply make the theory infeasible. A theory of natural language which accounted for the way in which nonlinguistic setting determines how an utterance is produced and understood would have to represent all the knowledge fluent speakers have concerning the world.

Consider the sentences *We sell alligator belts* and *We sell money belts.* In most nonlinguistic settings the first sentence will be interpreted *We sell belts made out of alligator skin,* while the second sentence will be interpreted *We sell belts for carrying money.* If, however, a sign reading *We sell alligator belts* were hung up in a showcase displaying belts for pet alligators, the proper interpretation of the sign would be *We sell belts for alligators.* Likewise, if a sign reading *We sell money belts* were hung up in a showcase displaying belts made out of silver dollars linked together, the proper interpretation of the sign would be *We sell belts made out of money.* For a theory of natural language to choose the correct reading for *We sell alligator belts* the theory would have to represent the fact that normally alligators do not wear belts though people wear belts made out of alligator skin. For a theory of natural language to choose the correct reading for *We sell money belts* it would have to represent the fact that normally belts are not made out of money though belts are made to carry money. Now, for practically every item about the world, it is possible to construct an ambiguous sentence whose correct interpretation in context requires the representation of that item. Therefore, a theory of natural language which is to disambiguate sentences on the basis of nonlinguistic setting must represent practically every item of information about the world. Since it is infeasible to systematize virtually all the knowledge which speakers share about the world, a theory of natural language which accounts for the way in which nonlinguistic setting determines how a sentence  is produced and understood is out of the question.

A complete theory of natural language consists of both a grammatical and semantical description of the language. Since we are not concerned with matters of setting, in order to set the goal for a semantic theory we need only subtract the goal of grammar from that of a complete theory of natural language.

As we have noted earlier, the goal of a complete theory of natural language is the explication of the mechanism by which fluent speakers of a language are able to produce and understand the meaningful utterances of the language. The goal of semantics, then, can be loosely described as continuing the explication of a fluent speaker's ability to produce and understand the meaningfull utterances of the language from the point at which grammar stops. The problem which remains for us is now rather clear-cut. We must determine what is the lower bound of semantics — the upper bound of grammar. In our justification for omitting matters of setting we have already determined the upper bound of semantics — that is, what problems lie beyond the proper bounds of a theory of natural language.

Concerning sentences a semantic theory must be able to detect nonsyntactic ambiguities and to give a different reading for each possible meaning. Since the notion of syntactic ambiguity will be well-defined by an independent and antecedently developed grammar, and since the notion of ambiguity is intuitively clear, we should have no problem in determining the boundaries of nonsyntactic ambiguity. (Though in natural language the boundary between syntax and semantics is fuzzy, for convenience of classification, we stipulate a definite boundary in our nonintuitive theory. This procedure does not affect the adequacy of the theory whatsoever.) A semantic theory must be able to distinguish between semantically anomalous (deviant or irregular) sentences and semantically regular sentences in so far as the distinction does not coincide with the ungrammatical-grammatical distinction. Since the notion of grammaticalness will be well-defined by an independent and antecedently developed grammar, and since the notion of anomaly is intuitively clear, there should be no trouble here. A semantic theory must be able to decide which sentences are paraphrases of others. This clearly does not fall into the domain of grammar, since the identical grammatical structure of two sentences is neither a sufficient nor necessary condition for the two sentences being paraphrases of each other.

In grammar we required our nonintuitive device to generate all of the intuitively clear-cut cases of grammatical sequence and not to generate any of the intuitively clear-cut cases of ungrammatical sequence. We were prepared to let the device itself decide the unclear cases. Similarly, in semantics we require our nonintuitive device to generate all of the intuitively clear-cut cases of analytic statement, ambiguous statement, etc. and not to generate any of the intuitively clear-cut cases of nonanalytic statement, unambiguous statement etc., and we are ready to let the device itself decide the unclear cases.

The next metatheoretical consideration we shall take up is

that of the components of a semantic theory. Again we turn to the limitations of grammar. A grammar cannot account for the fact that two sentences with identical grammatical structure can have different meanings; a grammar cannot account for the fact that two sentences with different grammatical structures have the same meaning, that is, are paraphrases of each other. This is easily explainable if we realize that the interpretation of a sentence is partly determined by the meanings of the constituent words. It is for this reason that a 'dictionary' must be part of a semantic theory; the dictionary must assign meanings to the words and thus lay the foundation for giving an interpretation to the entire sentence. That part of semantics which deals with the construction of a dictionary is called 'lexicography'. We use the words 'dictionary' and 'lexicography' in that strictly technical sense which is relevant to a formal nonintuitive theory of natural language. By 'dictionary' we do not mean 'conventional dictionary' and by 'lexicography' we do not mean 'traditional lexicography'. We shall, in the next chapter, eleborate upon the type of dictionary we are concerned with in this book.

It should be obvious that a semantic theory must include more than a dictionary. A semantic theory consisting of only a dictionary would not be able to select for a given word of a given sentence, the 'correct' meaning or meanings from the possibly many dictionary meanings of the particular word unless the correct meaning or meanings were indicated by syntactic considerations. In other words such a semantic theory would not be able to eliminate certain meanings of a word on the basis that such meanings are precluded by the meanings of other words in the same sentence. Such a semantic theory would not be able to detect strictly semantic reductions of meaning (as when some meanings of a word are precluded by the meanings of other words), strictly semantic anomalies, nor strictly semantic paraphrases. What is needed in addition to a dictionary is a set of rules (projection rules) which, operating upon the dictionary entries of the words of a sentence, is able to take into consideration the semantic relations among the words. By so doing the rules can eliminate certain of the possible dictionary entries assigned to a word and thus reduce the possible senses of the sentence as a whole. Given the grammatical structure of a sentence, the projection rules must be able to select the allowable meanings of the words, some of the meanings assigned to the words being precluded by meanings assigned to other words. We thus see that a semantic theory must contain a dictionary for assigning possible meanings to the words of a given sentence, and a set of projection rules which, operating upon the grammatical characterization of the sentence and upon the dictionary entries of the words of the sentence, eliminates incompatible meanings and gives the correct semantic interpretation of the sentence.

### THE PROBLEM OF SYNONYMY

Let us now turn to the problem of synonymy as understood by the lexicographer. This problem is the providing of a practical nonintuitive criterion for pairs of synonymous expressions, that is, a practical nonintuitive criterion for deciding whether or not any two given expressions are synonymous. As we shall see in the next chapter, this problem is not identical with the 'dictionary problem' though the synonymy problem may be considered a part of the 'dictionary problem'. For now let us stick to the problem of synonymy as we have defined it.

The grammarian attempts to generate all and only grammatical sequences by means of some practical nonintuitive device. Similarly the lexicographer attempts to generate all and only pairs of synonymous sequences by means of some practical nonintuitive device. It is a common misconception that the grammarian's task is a strictly formal one (an abstraction from meaning) while the lexicographer's is not since the lexicographer deals with meanings while the grammarian does not. However, the lexicographer's task is just as formal as the grammarian's. The grammarian is concerned with mechanically generating, with no appeal to meaning, all and only grammatical sequences; the lexicographer is concerned with mechanically generating, with no appeal to meaning, all and only the pairs of mutually synonymous sequences.

A problem of considerable scope which must be dealt with at the start is that of deciding what sort of synonymy we are interested in. In one sense of 'synonymy' — the sense which takes as relevant emotional and aesthetic associations of an expression as well as 'logical' — no two expressions are synonymous. In another sense of 'synonymy' — the sense polar to the above sense — all expressions are synonymous. It appears rather obvious that we must not take synonymy as such a strong relation so as to preclude at the outset of our study the synonymy of any two expressions. Likewise we must not take synonymy as such a weak relation so as to preclude the usefulness of the synonymy concept in dealing with related matters of semantics such as the analytic-synthetic distinction. The fact that we need a notion of synonymy sufficiently powerful to be useful in the solution of related semantical problems, together with our intuition of synonymy, provides us with the required guides for determining the kind of synonymy we want our practical generating device to duplicate. Our actual practice below will be to take pairs of expressions which intuitively are quite definitely synonymous or nonsynonymous and look to see whether or not the particular device being considered does them justice. First we shall deal with the synonymy of short forms — words and phrases but not sentences. Later we shall deal with the synonymy of sentences as wholes.

To say that two expressions are synonymous when they have the same definition is of no help to the lexicographer, for the notion of definition as used by the lexicographer clearly depends upon the prior notion of synonymy. To suggest that a lexicographer construct his list of synonymous pairs by referring to the definitions of the expressions amounts to suggesting that the lexicographer construct his list of synonymous pairs by referring to a list of synonymous pairs. The appeal to the notion of analyticity for solving the lexicographer's problem of synonymy is likewise of little help. Although a solution of the problem of synonymy could be directly obtained from a solution of the problem of analyticity, the problem of analyticity is in as much trouble as that of synonymy.[5]

One approach to the problem of synonymy which is not obviously fated to failure is that of interchangeability. It has been proposed that two expressions be considered synonymous if and only if they can be interchanged in any sentence without affecting the truth value of the sentence. One difficulty with this which quickly comes to mind is the case in which quotation marks are used. By interchanging the intuitively synonymous expressions, *widow* and *woman who has lost her husband through death and has not remarried,* the true sentence, *'Widow' has five letters* goes over into the false sentence, *'Woman who has lost her husband through death and has not remarried' has five letters.* One might suggest at this point that if we made use of the distinction between use and mention in the statement of the interchangeability criterion (restricting ourselves to cases of use) we could get around this problem. Such a move would not help. It should be remembered that we are dealing with the spoken language and in the spoken language quotation marks do not occur; that is, there is no way of distinguishing between the use and mention of an expression.

But there is an even more serious problem with this type of interchangeability criterion. The criterion would give incorrect results for any two expressions having different meanings but the same extension. *Egg-laying biped* and *warmblooded feathered vertebrate,* though coextensional, are intuitively nonsynonymous. These two expressions, though nonsynonymous, could be interchanged in any sentence without affecting the truth value of the sentence.

Next let us consider another interchangeability criterion : Two expressions are synonymous if and only if upon their interchange in any sentence, the sentence before the interchange and the

---

[5]    For a discussion of the relation between the problem of synonymy and the analytic-synthetic problem see Quine, "Two Dogmas of Empiricism", *From a Logical Point of View* (New York : Harper and Row, 1953).

sentence after the interchange are synonymous. Of course in order to use this criterion of synonymy for the short forms with which we are here concerned, we must already have solved the problem of synonymy for sentences. Without attempting at this point to solve the problem of synonymy for sentences, let us assume that it has been solved in some sense suitable to the lexicographer. More specifically let us assume for the present that stimulus synonymy for sentences is an adequate formal non-intuitive criterion for the synonymy of sentences. We shall define 'stimulus synonymy'[6] quite explicitly as it is a notion which we shall return to below.

The affirmative stimulus meaning of a sentence for a speaker at a given time is the set of stimulations (repeatable event forms) which would prompt his assent to the sentence. For example, a rabbit hopping along in a field might be a visual stimulation which would prompt a given person at a given time to assent to the sentence *There goes a rabbit*. Another stimulation which would have the same effect might be a rabbit disappearing behind a bush. The set of all such stimulations would constitute the affirmative stimulus meaning of the sentence *There goes a rabbit*. The negative stimulus meaning of a sentence for a speaker at a given time is the set of stimulations which would prompt his dissent from the sentence. For example, a fox jumping over a log might be a stimulation which would prompt a given person at a given time to dissent from the sentence *There goes a rabbit*. The set of all such stimulations would constitute the negative stimulus meaning of the sentence *There goes a rabbit*.

The stimulus meaning of a sentence for a speaker at a given time is defined as the ordered pair of affirmative and negative stimulus meanings. Finally, two sentences are stimulus synonymous if and only if they have the same stimulus meaning for virtually all speakers at all times. This amounts to saying that two sentences are stimulus synonymous if and only if for virtually all speakers and at all times, those stimulations which would

---

[6]  For the definition and discussion regarding 'stimulus synonomy' we draw upon Quine's *Word and Object* (Cambridge : M.I.T. Press, 1960).

prompt assent to one would also prompt assent to the other, and those stimulations which would prompt dissent from one would also prompt dissent from the other. It certainly cannot be argued that by defining the synonymy of sentences in terms of stimulus synonymy we are explicating the vague by the still more vague. There is nothing vague about stimulus meaning. The stimulus meaning of a given sentence can be determined along practical and nonintuitive lines by a linguist working with fluent speakers of a language.

Now that we have defined 'stimulus synonymy' for sentences, let us get back to the problem of synonymy for short forms. Let us assume that whenever the two words *flub* and *glub* are interchanged within a sentence, the sentence before the interchange is stimulus synonymous with the sentence after the interchange. What then can we conclude concerning the synonymy of *flub* and *glub* ?

Suppose that *glub* refers to any integral part of whatever *flub* refers to. For example, if *flub* refers to a rabbit, *glub* could refer to any undetached part of a rabbit. (Here it should be understood that we are not talking about parts of meanings but rather about meanings of words referring to parts of objects.) Now two sentences differing only in one's containing *glub* for *flub* will be stimulus synonymous, for stimulus meaning is not a fine enough distinction to discriminate between words whose meanings are related in the manner of *glub* and *flub*. Whenever a speaker 'sees' a glub he also 'sees' a flub, and whenever he 'sees' a flub he also 'sees' a glub. Therefore he will be ready to assent to the sentence containing *flub* if and only if he is ready to assent to the sentence containing *glub;* and he will be ready to dissent from the sentence containing *flub* if and only if he is ready to dissent from the sentence containing *glub*. So we see that though the two interchanged words are, by hypothesis, nonsynonymous, the two sentences concerned with here are stimulus synonymous. Thus we see that even if it could be shown that stimulus synonymy were an adequate criterion for the synonymy of sentences, we still would not have solved the problem of the synonymy of short forms.

Next let us turn to the synonymy of sentences. We have defined 'stimulus synonymy' for sentences above; let us  look to see whether or not this type of synonymy — for which an effective method of determination exists — satisfies our semantical intuition. To give every possible chance to the notion of stimulus synonymy we shall overlook such sentences as, *Every periodic decimal represents a rational number* and *Yesterday's temperature was 75 degrees* for which the criterion of stimulus synonymy is obviously inadequate. Instead we shall consider sentences of direct ostension, sentences which lend themselves to treatment in terms of stimulus synonymy. Let us take the sentences, *There, is a widow* and *There, is a woman who has lost her husband through death and has not remarried.* Unfortunately, even for such sentences of direct ostension stimulus synonymy is not adequate as a criterion for synonymy. Though these two sentences are intuitively synonymous, their respective stimulus meanings would undoubtedly differ depending upon what information two different speakers had concerning the woman pointed out. One speaker might know that the indicated woman was a widow and therefore assent to the sentence, *There, is a widow.* Another speaker might not know anything about the woman and therefore neither assent to nor dissent from the sentence, *There, is a woman who has lost her husband through death and has not remarried.* Still another speaker might believe that the woman is not a widow and dissent from the same sentence.

Even if we take sentences such as, *That's azure* and *That's sky-blue* — sentences custom-made to eliminate as much as possible the relevance of knowledge and beliefs brought to the prompting situation by the speaker — there still remains the real possibility that some knowledge or belief brought to the situation will affect the answer of the speaker. One speaker, being quite certain that the prompting situation would not contain the color azure for chemical or aesthetic reasons, might 'see' the color as aqua, and therefore dissent from the sentence, *That's sky-blue.*

It is not uncommom for people to 'see' what they want to 'see'. There is no escaping the fact that we can not eliminate the possibility of information brought to the prompting situation affecting the answer of the speaker. Thus we see that even if we bend over backwards to make the case easy for stimulus meaning, it fails to provide us with a suitable criterion for synonymy of sentences.

'Stimulus meaning' was defined relative to a given speaker, and consequently it was possible that two different speakers bring different information to the prompting situation and not concur concerning the sentences offered. Now, it is evident that if two sentences are intuitively synonymous, they will be stimulus synonymous for any one speaker, for the possibility that different information being brought to the prompting situation is precluded. It turns out then that for a given speaker, stimulus synonymy is a necessary condition for synonymy, since the speaker will be ready to assent to or dissent from a given sentence if and only if he is ready to assent to or dissent from, respectively, an intuitively synonymous sentence. Is stimulus synonymy for a given speaker also a sufficient condition for synonymy ? Unfortunately, it is not. Take the intuitively nonsynonymous sentences, *There is the morning star* and *There is the evening star.* For a speaker who knows that the morning star and the evening star are one and the same, the two sentences will be stimulus synonymous.

So much for stimulus synonymy — let us go on to examine still another attempt to provide a practical nonintuitive criterion for synonymy. Chomsky remarks in a footnote : "Goodman has argued — to my mind, quite convincingly — that the notion of meaning of words can at least in part be reduced to that of reference of expressions containing these words. See N. Goodman, "On likeness of meaning", *Analysis,* vol. 10, no. 1 (1949); idem, "On some differences about meaning", *Analysis,* vol. 13, no. 4 (1953)."[7] Therefore it seems appropriate for us to look at Goodman's proposal. Goodman, in an attempt to deal with the problem

---

[7] Chomsky, *op. cit.,* p. 103.

of synonymy without reference to intensions, concepts, ideas, etc., proposes a criterion for synonymy in terms of primary and secondary physical extensions. He writes :

My proposal is that two terms are synonymous if and only if
    (a) they apply to exactly the same objects, and
    (b) each compound term constructed by combining certain words with either of the terms in question applies to exactly the same objects as the compound term constructed by combining the same words in the same way with the other of the terms in question.[8]

Though this criterion is capable of explaining the difference of meaning between *centaur* and *unicorn* by reference only to physical objects, it has the unhappy consequence that no two different words have the same meaning.

I do not intend here to get involved in the many arguments for and against Goodman's proposal. I only want to point out that though Goodman begins by seeking a practical nonintuitive criterion for synonymy — a criterion which can mechanically separate synonymous pairs from nonsynonymous pairs, a criterion of the same kind sought by the lexicographer — the consequence of his criterion, that no two different words are synonymous, renders his criterion completely useless to the lexicographer. Further, no adequate modification of Goodman's criterion for synonymy which does not have the destructive consequence of Goodman's, has been forthcoming.

Though we have not yet completed our survey of attempts at solving the synonymy problem as understood by the lexicographer, we note at this point that all such attempts examined up to now have failed.

---

[8]  N. Goodman, "On Some Differences about Meaning", *Analysis*, 13 (1953), pp. 63-64.

# VII

## KATZ AND FODOR'S SEMANTIC THEORY
## OF NATURAL LANGUAGE

### THE DICTIONARY

In the previous chapter we said that a semantic theory contains a 'dictionary' which assigns possible meanings to the words of a given sentence, and a set of projection rules which, operating upon the grammatical charaterization of the given sentence and upon the dictionary entries of the words of the given sentence, gives the correct semantic interpretation to the sentence. The giving of correct semantic interpretations by the dictionary and projection rules constitutes the empirical control upon the dictionary and projection rules. From the role that a dictionary plays in a semantic theory, we can get some idea of what a dictionary is and what the dictionary problem for semantics is.

A dictionary must somehow characterize the meaning of each word in the natural language under investigation. A dictionary consists of a collection of dictionary entries. Each entry consists of a word (lexical item) together with lexical information about the word in a prescribed form. The form of the lexical information must be such that the projection rules of the theory can operate upon the lexical information without appealing to the linguistic intuition of fluent speakers. This in broad outline is what we mean by 'dictionary'. Of course it is possible that someone construct a semantic theory which handles the problem of meaning by some device other than a dictionary and projection rules. However, no one has yet suggested the form of such a device, and it is difficult to imagine what such a device would be like.

Our comments and conclusions about dictionaries concern exclusively dictionaries as we characterized them above. Our comments and conclusions regarding semantic theories and theories of natural language concern only those theories which contain dictionaries as we characterized them above.

Katz and Fodor[1] claim to be able to provide such a dictionary and also claim to have solved the problem of the analytic-synthetic distinction (as this distinction is understood by the lexicographer) as well as a number of other related problems found in semantics. The solutions which they offer are intimately involved with a semantic theory of natural language which they sketch. In order to be able to evaluate some of the specific proposals made by Katz and Fodor concerning dictionary entries and projection rules, we must make a rather detailed examination of these proposals.

The dictionary entries of Katz and Fodor's semantic theory must be in normal form — a form which classifies the lexical information of a lexical item in a prescribed manner in order to permit the projection rules to operate upon the information. Of course the lexical information of a dictionary entry in normal form must contain all of the information required for the rules to give a correct interpretation to sentences. A dictionary entry consists of a grammatical portion, providing grammatical information for a lexical item, and a semantic portion which assigns a sense-characterization (meaning) to the lexical item which is already broken down grammatically. The syntactic and semantic breakdown of a lexical item can be represented by a tree diagram. In the breakdown we encounter first syntactic markers, then semantic markers, then distinguishers, and finally selection restrictions. Figure 2, is an example of a dictionary entry in normal form.

---

[1]   J. Katz and J. Fodor, "The Structure of a Semantic Theory", *The Structure of Language*, ed. Katz and Fodor (Englewood : Prentice-Hall, 1964). J. Katz, "Analyticity and Contradiction in Natural Language", *The Structure of Language*, ed. Katz and Fodor (Englewood : Prentice-Hall, 1964). The former first pub. in *Language* (1963).

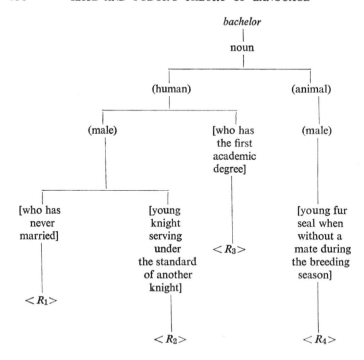

Fig. 2.  A dictionary entry for *bachelor* in normal form. (Adapted from Katz and Fodor, "The Structure of a Semantic Theory", *op. cit.*, p. 496.)

The lexical item is at the base of the trunk; the grammatical markers are unenclosed; the semantic markers are enclosed in parentheses; the distinguishers are enclosed in brackets; the selection restrictions (only symbolically represented) are enclosed within angles. Each path along one of the branches of the tree diagram represents a different sense of the lexical item. According to the above dictionary entry *bachelor* has four different senses.

The grammatical markers break down the lexical item into its grammatical categories. In our example there is only one grammatical marker; however, other lexical items might have more than one, such as, 'noun', 'verb', etc. General semantic relations within a semantic theory are expressed by semantic markers. Semantic markers mark the systematic semantic relations among the lexical items. A semantic marker in the path of a lexical item will also be found in the path of other items; the import of this is that all of these lexical items have a common semantic component in their meanings. Distinguishers mark the nonsystematic elements of meaning of a lexical item. Distinguishers handle that part of the meaning of a lexical item for which the semantic theory offers no general explanation. Whereas a semantic marker in the path of a lexical item will also be found in the path of other items, a distinguisher is unique to the dictionary. The selection restrictions, which are only symbolically represented and not spelled out in the above diagram, determine the combinations into which lexical items can enter. The nature of selection restrictions will be made clear below.

A given lexical item is ambiguous if there are two or more paths in its dictionary entry. Sentential ambiguity is a function of lexical ambiguity. A sentence which contains no ambiguous lexical item cannot be ambiguous. If a syntactically unambiguous sentence is semantically ambiguous, it must contain a semantically ambiguous lexical item. However, a semantically ambiguous lexical item in a syntactically unambiguous sentence does not guarantee that the sentence will be semantically ambiguous. This is so because the meanings of some of the lexical items may preclude a semantically ambiguous item from bearing one or more of its senses. In other words, certain lexical items may select certain senses of other items. This notion of selection is of great importance, as we shall see below, for it is instrumental in defining such key notions as anomalous sentence, semantically unambiguous sentence, and analytic sentence.

The best way to explain the notions of semantic marker, selection restriction, and selection is to look at an example of dictionary entries put to use. First let us make some intuitive observations and then let us duplicate these nonintuitively. If we are familiar with the four senses of *bachelor* we should all intuitively recognize that the sentence *The bachelor is small* is ambiguous in four ways (assuming for this discussion that none of the lexical items other than *bachelor* is ambiguous). However, we intuitively recognize that the sentence *The bachelor is honest* is ambiguous in only three ways. This we would explain by saying that the meaning of *honest* precludes its being predicated of nonhumans and thus eliminates the sense of *bachelor* in which it means 'young fur seal when without a mate during the breeding season'.

Now we want to duplicate the above insight nonintuitively. What is needed is a nonintuitive device associated with the dictionary entry for *honest* which will select only the correct senses of *bachelor*. This device is the selection restriction. A selection restriction must be attached to the path of the lexical item *honest* so that the item *honest*, in a certain combination with *bachelor*, will mechanically preclude *bachelor* from bearing one of its senses. Let us take the above dictionary entry for *bachelor* and assume that it contains no selection restriction which operates upon the sense of *honest* with which we will be concerned. Since we are assuming for this discussion that none of the lexical items other than *bachelor* is ambiguous, we shall give only one path for *honest* : *honest* → adjective → (evaluate) → (moral) → [of good character] <(human)>. The terminal information within angles in this path is a selection restriction. It should be understood as saying : This sense of *honest* can only be combined (in certain ways not specified here) with a sense of a lexical item which has the semantic marker (human) in its path. Since one sense of *bachelor* does not have the semantic marker (human) in its path, this sense is precluded by *honest*. Thus we see how the selection restrictions selects certain meanings of *bachelor* and rejects others. The sentence *The bachelor is honest* would then be judged ambiguous in three ways according to our semantic theory, a finding which tallies with our linguistic intuition. As for the sentence, *The bachelor is small,* the path of *small* (We have assumed above that *small* would have only one path) would not contain any selection restriction which would preclude one of the senses of *bachelor*.

Katz and Fodor recognize that a problem arises concerning what part of the meaning of a lexical item should be presented by semantic markers and what part should be represented by distinguishers. According to them, the intuitive discrimination concerning semantic ambiguity a fluent speaker is capable of making determines what lexical information will be represented by markers and what will be represented by distinguishers. Roughly they explain as follows :

According to the dictionary entry for *bachelor* given above, the sentence *The bachelor finally dies* would be marked as ambiguous between the senses represented by the paths : *bachelor* → noun → (human) →(male) → [who has never married]; and *bachelor* → noun → (human) → (male)→ [young knight serving under the standard of another knight]. (This is not to say that the given sentence would be marked as ambiguous only between these two senses, for it would be marked as ambiguous among other senses also). The theory would be correct, in so far as this sentence is concerned, since fluent speakers would find the sentence ambiguous between the same senses. Next consider the sentence *The old bachelor finally dies*. According to the dictionary entry given above for *bachelor,* this sentence would be marked as ambiguous between the same senses as just noted. However, a fluent speaker would not find it ambiguous between these two senses. Katz and Fodor then assure us that we can modify the dictionary entry for *bachelor* so as to accommodate the fluent speaker's intuition. We need only take the lexical information that a bachelor, in the sense represented by the second path, is young as marker information rather than distinguisher information. We would then have the two paths : *bachelor* → noun → (human) → (male) → [who has never married] : and *bachelor* → noun → (human) → (male) → (young) → [knight serving under the standard of another knight]. Now according to the dictionary entry containing these two paths, the sentence *The old bachelor finally dies* would no longer be marked as ambiguous between the senses represented by these new paths because of the incompatibiliy of *old* and the semantic marker (young). This would tally with a fluent speaker's intuition. Katz and Fodor do not carry their example of accommodation beyond this point. However, the principle they enunciate for deciding upon the classification of lexical information is clearly stated. "In the last analysis, the decision to represent a piece of lexical information by semantic markers or by distinguishers can only be justified by showing that it leads to correct interpretations for sentences."[2]

The point we want to make against Katz and Fodor is that unless every last bit of lexical information (both explicit and implicit) found in the terminal distinguishers is parceled out to individual markers (an infeasible task of course), there will always be sentences which the theory finds ambiguous but a fluent speaker does not. The proof of this is simple. Consider an arbitrary sentence which is ambiguous both theoretically and to a fluent speaker. The ambiguity must be ultimately represented in the dictionary entry of the relevant word by two paths leading to two different distinguishers. Select a piece of lexical information from one of these distinguishers and construct another sentence which will intuitively rule out this particular distinguisher because of the incompatibility between the lexical information selected from this distinguisher and the lexical information from certain other lexical items in the sencence. The result will be a sentence which according to the semantic theory is ambiguous but according to a fluent speaker is not. The crucial point is that any piece of lexical information (explicit or implicit) in a distinguisher can be chosen as the pivotal piece of information.

Let us give an example of the construction involved in this proof. If we take the sentence, *The bachelor finally dies* together with a dictionary entry representing this sentence as ambiguous between the paths : *bachelor* → noun → (human) → (male) → [who has never married]; and *bachelor* → noun → (human) → (male) → [young knight serving under the standard of another knight], we would have a case in which the sentence is ambiguous, between the senses considered, according to both the semantic theory and a fluent speaker. The piece of lexical information we select from one of the distinguishers is that a bachelor in the second sense must be young. We then construct a sentence

[2] *Ibid.*, p. 498.

which contains a lexical item incompatible with this piece of information : *The old bachelor finally dies,* and we have a sentence which is unambiguous, between the senses considered, to a fluent speaker but ambiguous according to the semantic theory. Now take the same original sentence *The bachelor finally dies* together with the same dictionary entry. This time instead of selecting the lexical information that a bachelor in the second sense must be young let us select the lexical information (implied lexical information) that a bachelor in the second sense must be reasonably healthy. We then, having this information, construct the sentence, *The congenitally blind bachelor finally dies.* This sentence would be ambiguous, between the senses considered, according to the semantic theory but unambiguous to a fluent speaker.

Let us investigate this matter a bit further. Consider the second path of the above dictionary entry for *bachelor* (*bachelor* → noun → (human) → (male) → [young knight serving under the standard of another knight]), but assume that all of the explicit lexical information in the distinguisher has been converted into marker information. We would then have something like : *bachelor* → noun → (human) → (male) → (young) → (knight) → (serving) → (under a standard) → (under the standard of another knight). Now let us take the piece of implied lexical information that a knight is a nobleman. We construct the new sentence *The common bachelor finally dies.* This sentence will be unambiguous to a fluent speaker but ambiguous according to the semantic theory. For the semantic theory to represent this sentence correctly (as unambiguous) it would have to include among the markers in the second path for *bachelor* the marker (noble) and also include the equivalent of a selection restriction attached to *common* saying that *common* can not modify a lexical item with (noble) in its path. But the marker (noble) does not appear in the path of *bachelor* we are considering. Let us put it in. We then get the path : *bachelor* → noun → (human) → (male) → (young) → (noble) → (knight) → (serving) → (under a standard) → (under the standard of another knight). This time let us take the piece of implied lexical information that a nobleman has a title. We construct the new sentence *The untitled bacheor finally dies.* This sentence will be unambiguous to a fluent speaker but ambiguous according to the semantic theory. It does not take much imagination to see that no matter how many markers are added to the appropriate paths, we could always construct a sentence which fluent speakers would find unambiguous but the theory ambiguous. As far as the dictionary entries of Katz and Fodor's semantic theory are concerned, as long as all the lexical information (including implied information) of distinguishers is not put into marker form (a task which if not impossible is certainly beyond the scope of any workable theory of language) the semantic theory will fail to give correct semantic interpretations under the conditions just outlined.

Katz and Fodor, possibly anticipating a criticism such as ours, go on to qualify their statement that decisions concerning the lexical information to be represented by semantic markers or by distinguishers can only be justified by the correctness of semantic interpretations. They add the further consideration of conceptual economy. Representing more and more information as markers rather than distinguishers will increase the complexity of the semantic theory; therefore the decision concerning what lexical information should be represented by markers and what by distinguishers should be made on the basis of which system has the greatest possible conceptual economy and the greatest possible explanatory power. "If such decisions are optimally made, there should eventually come a point when increasing the complexity of a semantic theory by adding new markers no longer yields enough of an advantage in precision and scope to warrant the increase. At this point the system of semantic markers should reflect exactly the systematic features of the semantic structure of the language."[3]

Now this is a gratuitous assumption. What guarantee do we have that there is a point at which, for the sake of conceptual economy, we can cease adding markers and at the same time

---

[3] *Ibid.*, p. 500.

have a semantic theory which meets the external requirements of generating the bulk of correct semantic interpretations ? It might very well be the case that short of constructing a tremendously complex and unwieldy system we can not even come close to generating the bulk of correct interpretations. What guarantee do we have that our minds work according to a 'mechanism' which is conceptually economical and therefore capable of duplication in a workable form ? It might be that in the field of semantics our minds work according to a 'mechanism' the form of which we are totally unfamiliar with and which cannot be duplicated by any formal nonintuitive system devised to date. Not only have we shown that Katz and Fodor have no justification for assuming that a semantic theory on their model would be adequate, but also we have shown that a semantic theory on their model would not meet the requirements for an adequate semantic theory. As we have shown above, as long as all lexical information is not represented by markers there will be a great number (too great a number to be disregarded) of rather straightforward simple sentences for which the semantic theory will give a wrong interpretation. Such a theory, it seems, would be radically inadequate and not merely imperfect. A semantic theory, on the model offered by Katz and Fodor, with a reasonable amount of conceptual economy (which amounts to letting distinguishers represent a certain amount of lexical information) will not be adequate in that it will misinterpret a great number of rather elementary sentences.

Next let us turn to the problem of evaluating the adequacy of dictionary entries and to the solution offered by Katz and Fodor. Katz and Fodor reject both the idea that a semantic theory must yield a mechanical nonintuitive procedure for constructing a dictionary and the idea that a semantic theory must yield a mechanical nonintuitive procedure for deciding whether or not a proposed dictionary entry is optimal. They recognize only the demand for a procedure for determining which of two proposed dictionary entries is the better for a given language; however, they attach a very important qualification to this demand. First, they point out that a semantic theory has two components : a diction-ary and a set of projection rules. A test of adequacy can only be for the semantic theory as a whole. Should the semantic theory fail to explicate the verbal abilities of a fluent speaker in a certain area of language, a beneficial revision might be made in either the dictionary or the set of projection rules. Second, they concede the very important point that two competing dictionary entries cannot be evaluated in isolation from the other dictionary entries. Concerning the evaluation of dictionary entries, they propose that the following question serve as the criterion : "Given projection rules and other dictionary entries that are sufficiently well estab-lished, which of the two candidate entries yields the better inter-pretations for sentences ?"[4]

Let us look more closely at this procedure for determining which of two proposed dictionary entries is the better. Since we have no method for determining a body of "sufficiently well established" dictionary entries and a set of projection rules in isolation from the candidate dictionary entries being considered, the rule given by Katz and Fodor for determining which of two candidate dictionary entries is the better, is not a procedure for choosing one of a pair of entries at all. Katz and Fodor are saying no more than that a set of projection rules and an entire dictionary must be compared with another set of projection rules and dictionary. Therefore we can never say (if we follow the procedure offered) that we have THE definition of a word. We can only say that we have a definition of a word relative to a set of projection rules and a whole body of other definitions. We thus see that, at best, Katz and Fodor have given us a procedure for determining the better of two proposed semantic theories as a whole. Even if we assume the set of projection rules, Katz and Fodor have only given us a procedure for choosing between two whole dictionaries. (We shall see later the significance of the fact that they evaluate between whole dictionaries rather than between individual dictionary entries.)

[4]  *Ibid.*, p. 502.

Chomsky rejects the demand that a linguistic theory provide a discovery procedure for grammar; that is, he rejects the demand that a linguistic theory describe a mechanical nonintuitive procedure for actually constructing a grammar. He also rejects the demand that a linguistic theory provide a decision procedure for grammar; that is, he rejects the demand that a linguistic theory describe a mechanical nonintuitive procedure for deciding whether or not a given grammar is an optimal grammar (the best possible grammar). As we noted in a previous section, Chomsky only demands of a linguistic theory that it provide us with an evaluation procedure for grammars — a procedure for determining which of two proposed grammars is the better. There are a number of reasons for believing that such a weak condition upon a linguistic theory for judging the adequacy of a grammar is sufficient for the purposes of the linguistic project. Work done in constructing grammars seems to indicate that by applying our proposed evaluation procedure for grammars, a better and better grammar will be selected. There are no good reasons for believing that by applying our evaluation procedure we will not arrive at a grammar which is adequate for generating all and only grammatical sequences. There are no good reasons for believing that a single grammar will not be found adequate. Our grammatical abilities seem to be of a kind which a transformational grammar can handle. These are some of the reasons why an evaluation procedure seems sufficient for grammar and why it does not seem necessary for a linguistic theory to supply a stronger test for the adequacy of grammars.

Katz and Fodor make the same demands upon a linguistic theory concerning the adequacy of a dictionary as Chomsky makes concerning the adequacy of a grammar. They reject demands for either a discovery procedure or decision procedure and claim that an evaluation procedure should be all that is required. (As we have already pointed out, they give a rule for determining which of two semantic theories is the better.)

In the previous chapter we were concerned with the problem of providing a nonintuitive criterion for pairs of synonymous expressions. We were in effect concerned with the providing of a discovery procedure for pairs of synonymous expressions. We did not feel that an evaluation procedure for pairs of synonymous expressions was a strong enough requirement to place upon a linguistic theory. For the same reason, we feel that an evaluation procedure for dictionaries, by itself, is not a strong enough requirement to place upon a linguistic theory. Concerning the selection of dictionaries, we would make the following requirement of a linguistic theory : Either provide a discovery procedure for dictionary entries or provide an evaluation procedure for dictionaries together with good reasons for believing that the evaluation procedure is capable of providing better and better dictionaries. In other words, we are willing to accept the demand for an evaluation procedure only if it can be shown that a dictionary is adequate for the job required of it in the semantic theory.

In the light of Katz and Fodor's rejection of the demand for a discovery procedure and their failure to show that a dictionary is adequate for the job, we must attempt to justify our demands. In the previous chapter we warned against thinking of syntax and semantics in parallel ways. It is most dangerous to think that what has been done for syntax can be done for semantics, or what is required in syntax is what is required in semantics. Here again with the problem of the adequacy of dictionaries we have an example of carrying over into semantics that which has been established for syntax. Though an evaluation procedure seems to be a strong enough requirement for grammars, it does not seem to be strong enough for dictionaries. As we have already pointed out, an evaluation procedure seems to be a strong enough requirement for grammars because it has been shown that transformational grammars can handle the problem of grammar. (Several models of grammar were discarded because they proved to be inadequate for handling the problem of grammar.) Contrary to the case with grammar, there is no good reason for believing that by applying an evaluation procedure to dictionaries better and better ones will be selected. In fact it is much more likely that before arriving at anything close to a suitable dictionary, the evaluation procedure will not be able to choose between a large number of equally inadequate dictionaries. (We shall elaborate upon this point in a later chapter when we discuss the possibility of our having more than one conceptual schema for the organization of our knowledge.) Settling for an evaluation procedure in semantics presupposes that somehow we shall be able to construct a single dictionary (which will be selected by the evaluation procedure as better than all the others to which it is compared) which will be adequate for a semantic theory. But this is just what is gravely in doubt. And since it is in doubt, before going on with our semantic theory we should make sure or at least have good reason to believe that a single dictionary will be sufficient. If we do not have good reasons for believing that a single dictionary would be adequate, we surely should not settle for an evaluation procedure for dictionaries.

Because of the inadequacy of an evaluation procedure for dictionary entries, we shall demand a discovery procedure; that is, we shall demand a practical nonintuitive procedure for constructing dictionary entries. (Of course the procedure must conform to the general restriction upon the language theory that no reference be made to extra-linguistic context.) We shall refer to the providing of such a procedure as 'the dictionary problem', 'the lexicographer's problem', or 'the problem of lexicography'. The problem of synonymy (the providing of a practical nonintuitive criterion for pairs of synonymous expressions) may be considered a part of the lexicographer's problem. Dictionary entries are pairs of synonymous expressions in a prescribed form.

## PROJECTION RULES

In order to complete our characterization of Katz and Fodor's semantic theory of natural language and get into the problem of analyticity we must first explain the notions of projection rules and semantic interpretation. Let us begin with projection rules.

The grammar of a theory of natural language provides us with a grammatical sequence (sentence) and either a constituent structure characterization or a transformation, based upon transformation rules, from a constituent structure characterization. Type 1 projection rules operate directly upon constituent structure characterizations of grammatical sentences; type 2 projection rules operate both upon semantic interpretations of sentences gotten by the use of type 1 projection rules, and upon the grammatical transformations of these sentences. In other words type 2 projection rules assign a semantic interpretation to sentences constructed by a transformational grammar on the principle that the meaning of a sentence constructed by a transformational grammar is a function of the meanings of the sentences that were operated upon by the transformation rules to produce the given sentence. Because of complexities beyond the scope of this book we will not deal further with type 2 projection rules. We shall henceforth refer to type 1 projection rules merely as projection rules.

The projection rules must associate meanings with the occurrence of lexical items in a constituent structure characterization. Each of the lexical items of a sentence in its constituent structure characterization must be correlated with just those paths from their dictionary entries which are not precluded by the syntactic considerations read from the constituent structure characterization of the sentence. The correlation is made according to the following rule : "If a path from the dictionary entry for the lexical item $m_j$ contains syntactic markers which attribute to $m_j$ the same syntactic categorization that is has in the constituent structure characterization $d_i$, then this path is assigned to the set of paths $p_j^i$ which is correlated with the occurence $m_j$ in $d_i$. Thus, the lexical item $m_1$ is associated with the set of paths $p_1^i$, $m_2$ is associated with $p_2^i$, and so on."[5]

Let us look at an example of the way in which meanings are correlated with the lexical items of a sentence. Figure 3 is a

[5]  J. Katz, "Analyticity and Contradiction in Natural Language", *The Structure of Language*, ed. Katz and Fodor (Englewood : Prentice-Hall, 1964), p. 525.

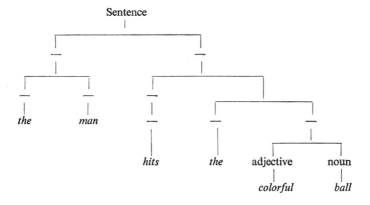

Fig. 3.  A partial constituent structure characterization of the sentence *The man hits the colorful ball.* (Adapted from Katz and Fodor, "The Structure of a Semantic Theory", *op. cit.*, p. 505.)

partial constituent structure characterization of the sentence *The man hits the colorful ball.* (The characterization is incomplete as we shall be dealing only with the phrase *colorful ball.*) From this tree diagram we can read, the grammatical information, that *colorful* is an adjective and that *ball* is a noun. We next select from the dictionary entries of *colorful* and *ball* the paths governed by the syntactic marker 'adjective' for *colorful* and 'noun' for *ball*. Let us assume that we obtain the following two paths for *colorful* : *colorful* → adjective → (color) → [abounding in variety of bright colors] <(physical object) or (social activity)>; and colorful → adjective → (evaluative) → [having distinctive character] <(aesthetic object) or (social activity)>. And let us assume that we obtain the following three paths for *ball* : *ball* → noun concrete → (social activity) → (large) → (assembly) → [for the purpose of dancing]; *ball* → noun concrete → (physical object) → [having globular shape]; and *ball* → noun concrete → (physical object) → [solid missile for projection by war engine]. Thus we associate with the lexical item *colorful* the above two paths from the dictionary entry of *colorful,* and we associate with the lexical item *ball* the above three paths from the dictionary entry of *ball.*

If the dictionary entry for *ball* had contained one path governed by 'noun' and another path governed by 'verb', we would have rejected the path governed by 'verb', since the constituent structure characterization of *The man hits the colorful ball* informs us that we must associate with *ball* only paths governed by 'noun'.

Next, other projection rules operate upon the meanings correlated with the lexical item in the above fashion and provide a characterization of the meanings of all the constituents of the sentence including the entire sentence. The characterization of the meaning of a phrase, for example, is obtained by the projection rules by combining (in certain restricted ways) the meaning characterizations of its constituent parts; the meaning characterization of the phrase then is instrumental in obtaining the meaning characterization of a larger constituent part of the sentence and finally of the whole sentence. The meaning characterization of a phrase or sentence does not merely consist of the combination of all of the meaning characterizations of its constituent parts. Some combinations will be precluded by selection restrictions attached to a path of lexical item. In this way the projection rules are able to give just those meaning characterizations for a phrase or sentence which are permitted by the semantic relations among the lexical items.

Let us continue the example we gave above. In that example there are two paths associated with *colorful* and three paths associated with *ball*. We apply our projection rules upon these paths and obtain the following combinations, which are the meaning characterizations of the phrase *colorful ball* : *colorfull* + *ball* → noun concrete → (social activity) → (large) → (assembly) → (color) → [[abounding in variety of bright colors] [for the purpose of dancing]]; *colorful* + *ball* → noun concrete → (physical object) → (color) → [[abounding in variety of bright colors] [having globular shape]]; *colorful* + *ball* → noun concrete → (physical object) → (color) → [[abounding in variety of bright colors] [solid missile for projection by war engine]]; and *colorful* + *ball* → noun concrete → (social activity) → (large) → (assembly)

→ (evaluative) → [[having distinctive character] [for the purpose of dancing]].

We quickly note that though there are six possible combinations of the meaning characterizations of *colorful* and *ball* we obtained, by means of the projection rules, only four combinations. This is because some of the combinations were precluded by selection restrictions. Specifically, *colorful* → adjective → (evaluative) → [having distinctive character] <(aesthetic object) or (social activity)> could not be combined with either *ball* → noun concrete → (physical object) → [having globular shape] or *ball* → noun concrete → (physical object) → [solid missile for projection by war engine], for this path of *colorful* has the selection restrictions <(aesthetic object) or (social activity)> which preclude combinations with paths not containing the semantic markers (aesthetic object) or (social activity).

## SEMANTIC INTERPRETATION

Let us next explain the notion of semantic interpretation. If a given sentence $S$ is syntactically ambiguous it receives more than one constituent structure characterization. We shall designate the different constituent structure characterizations of a sentence $S$ by $d_1, d_2, ..., d_n$. A sentence will be syntactically ambiguous if $n > 1$. The semantic interpretation of the constituent structure characterization, $d_i$, of $S$ is the following: (1) The constituent structure characterization, $d_i$, each lexical item found at the end of the branches of the constituent structure characterization, $d_i$, being associated with every path that can belong to it according to the dictionary entries (for the lexical items) and the projection rules. (2) The statements which follow from (1) together with the following definitions:

(D1)   $S$ is *semantically anomalous on* $d_i$ if, and only if, the set of paths associated with the node labeled $S$ in $d_i$ contains no members.

(D2)   $S$ is *semantically unambiguous on* $d_i$ if, and only if, the set of paths associated with the node labeled $S$ in $d_i$ contains exactly one member.

(D3)   S is *n-ways semantically ambiguous on* $d_i$ if, and only if, the set of paths associated with the node labeled S in $d_i$ contains exactly *n*-members $(n \geq 2)...$.[6]

Now that we have defined the notion of semantic interpretation for $d_i$ of S we must go on to define the notion of semantic interpretation of S. The semantic interpretation of S is the conjunction of all of the semantic interpretations of the different constituent structure characterizations $(d_1, d_2, ..., d_n)$ of S and all of the statements about S which follow from the definition schema : S is fully *x* if and only if S is *x* on every $d_i$. An example of a definition which is an instance of this schema is : S is fully anomalous if and only if S is anomalous on every $d_i$.

The notion of semantic interpretation which we have just explained permits us, in a purely formal and nonintuitive manner, to determine whether a sentence is anomalous or regular, ambiguous or unambiguous. However, the semantic property with which we shall be primarily concerned, because of its traditional and contemporary importance, will be that of analyticity. Katz offers a definition of analyticity which can be considered a continuation of the notion of semantic interpretation given above.

## ANALYTICITY

Traditionally it has been said that in an analytic sentence such as *Bachelors are unmarried* the predicate is contained in the subject, or perhaps less metaphorically, that the predicate does not add any further semantic information to the subject. It is precisely this intuitive notion which Katz attempts to formalize. He gives definitions of 'analytic sentence' for both copula sentences and noncopula sentences. Since the definition of 'analytic sentence' for noncopula sentences involves grammatical transformations and since our critical points will apply to noncopula sentences if

---

[6]   *Ibid.*, pp. 527-528. We shall continue this list of definitions below when we add the very important definition of 'analytic sentence'.

they apply to copula sentences, we shall deal only with the definition of 'analytic sentence' for copula sentences.

We begin by explaining a few symbols not yet encountered. The symbol $p_1$ will stand for a path from the set of paths associated with the subject of the copula sentence. The symbol $p_2$ will stand for a path from the set of paths associated with the predicate of the copula sentence. (For the sake of simplicity we have referred to subject and predicate; these notions, however, can and must be designated formally and nonintuitively.) The symbol $r_{1,2}$ stands for a reading of the entire sentence, which is the combination of $p_1$ and $p_2$. The term 'semantic element' will refer to either a semantic marker or distinguisher. Now we are prepared to give an abbreviated version of Katz's formal nonintuitive definition of 'analytic sentence for a copula sentence on $d_i$' : The copula sentence $S$ is analytic on the reading $r_{1,2}$ if and only if every semantic element in $p_2$ is also in $p_1$; $S$ is fully analytic on $d_i$ if, and only if, the set of readings assigned to $S$ in $d_i$ is not empty and, for every reading $r_{1,2}$ in this set, $S$ is analytic on $r_{1,2}$.

Katz's unabbreviated definition of 'analytic sentence for a copula sentence on $d_i$' would have involved us in notions too complicated for our purposes here. The point to keep in mind is that if our criticism of the above abbreviated definition is correct, it holds against Katz's unabbreviated definition. The essence of Katz's definition of 'analyticity' is that a sentence is analytic on a certain reading if and only if the path associated with the predicate fails to contribute semantic information to the path associated with the subject, and this is just what we have captured in the definition given above.

Katz is quick to point out that his definition of 'analyticity' is not circular (circularity being a frequent complaint against definitions of 'analyticity'). The sentence $S$ is analytic according to whether or not the semantic elements in $p_1$ and $p_2$ satisfy the relation specified in the definition of 'analytic sentence' — the definition being part of a semantic theory. The semantic theory gives us all the information concerning sentence $S$ (its semantic elements and paths) needed for applying the definition. The correctness of a semantic theory is a function of the correctness of the theory's dictionary and projection rules used in giving semantic interpretations. The correctness of the dictionary and projection rules can be decided upon independently of the question of the analyticity of $S$. The correctness of the dictionary and projection rules is determined by how well the semantic theory marks the intuitive semantic properties, such as ambiguity, anomaly, analyticity, for an infinite number of sentences other than $S$. The correctness of the dictionary and projection rules is determined by how well the semantic theory reconstructs our linguistic intuitions, concerning semantic properties, for a sample of sentences drawn from an infinity of sentences other than $S$.

We must concede to Katz that his characterization of analyticity is not circular. It would be circular if the correctness of the semantic theory were partly determined by the intuitive analyticity of $S$, but in fact, the correctness of the semantic theory does not turn on any intuitive semantic property of $S$. However, we are not ready to concede to Katz that he has given an adequate solution to the nonintuitive problem of the analytic-synthetic distinction. Let us look at the proposed definition of 'analyticity' again and see what is involved. Let us suppose that S satisfies the definition of 'analyticity'. We can then say that $S$ is analytic relative to a given semantic theory. Since the semantic theory includes a dictionary we can say that $S$ is analytic relative to a given dictionary. Thus we see that the adequacy of Katz's formal definition of 'analyticity' depends upon the adequacy of the dictionary component of his semantic theory. Therefore, if an adequate dictionary cannot be provided, there is no solution to the nonintuitive problem of the analytic-synthetic distinction.

We have shown that unless all lexical information (both explicit and implicit) is represented in terms of markers there will be semantic interpretations which are incorrect. This amounts to the following : If Katz and Fodor's dictionary is kept within the bounds of workability, there will be countless incorrect interpretations given by the semantic theory. If one considers the endless amount of implied lexical information in a distinguisher such as *woman who has lost her husband through death and has not yet remarried* one realizes that before a semantic theory, containing the dictionary proposed by Katz and Fodor, could begin to do its job, it would have gotten out of hand. Katz and Fodor simply have not provided and adequate dictionary and as a consequence have not solved the problem of the analytic-synthetic distinction.

Even if Katz and Fodor did not fail in the way just noted, they would have failed in another. As we have indicated above, the requirement of an evaluation procedure for dictionaries, without good reasons for believing that such a procedure will be capable of selecting better and better dictionaries, is not strong enough. Katz and Fodor in offering their simple evaluation procedure for dictionaries assume without good reasons that a single dictionary (together with a set of projection rules) is sufficient for duplicating the linguistic intuition of fluent speakers. And involved in this assumption is the more basic assumption that fluent speakers operate according to a single intuitive 'dictionary'. We shall go on to say in a later chapter that fluent speakers operate according to a number of intuitive 'dictionaries'.

# VIII

## ZIFF'S SEMANTIC THEORY OF NATURAL LANGUAGE

In this chapter we shall consider Ziff's *Semantic Analysis*[1] in so far as it is relevant to the construction of a theory of natural language. First let us note the aims of the book. Generally speaking Ziff attempts to supply us with a rough outline of a nonintuitive formal semantic theory, a theory having its foundation in empirical linguistics and constituting a portion of a more comprehensive theory of natural language. Actually he is almost entirely concerned with the dictionary component of a semantic theory; he does not deal with the projection rule component and only touches upon the semantic interpretation component. The rough nature of the theory offered is explicitly noted by Ziff himself : "... this entire essay is best thought of as an informal introduction to and sketch of a rigorous semantic theory."[2]

### ZIFF'S PROJECT

Ziff explicitly offers his semantic theory as an evaluation procedure for competing dictionary entries, that is, as a procedure for determining which of two candidates for the dictionary entry of a given word, is the better. "In formulating the theory presented here I have had but one objective in mind, viz. that of determining a method and a means of evaluating and choosing between

---

[1] Paul Ziff, *Semantic Analysis* (Ithaca : Cornell University Press, 1960).
[2] *Ibid.*, sec. 203.

competing analyses of words and utterances."[3] However, it becomes clear that in practice Ziff actually is offering his semantic
theory as a discovery procedure for dictionary entries, that is, as
a procedure whereby one can actually determine the dictionary
entry for a given word.

The third and final step in determining what meaning $m_i$ [a morphological element, roughly a word] has or may have in English consists
in consolidating the results of the second step, viz. in formulating the
relevant non-syntactic semantic differences between utterances of the
distributive set and the associated utterances of the contrastive set for
$m_i$ in $E$. And this means that the final step consists in formulating
a dictionary entry or something approximating to such an entry.[4]

Ziff also includes in his semantic theory a method for determining
whether or not a given word has meaning and whether two given
words have the same or different meanings. Both of these procedures follow directly from the procedure for determining dictionary entries.

Ziff makes the usual distinction between utterance type and
utterance token. This distinction parallels Carnap's distinction
between sign-design and sign-event. Roughly, an utterance token
is a particular occurrence of an utterance type. The distinction
between the two will be made whenever there is danger of confusing the two notions.

Let us look to see just how Ziff's semantic theory functions
and more specifically how dictionary entries can be generated.
Though Ziff does not refer his theory to any specific natural language we shall here refer it to English so that it will be quite
clear just how the theory operates. Ziff does refer his theory to
the corpus $E$ but adds that the letter $E$ is only supposed to suggest
"English today". The starting point of Ziff's semantic analysis,
rather than being the morphological element (roughly, word) is
the whole utterance (roughly, sentence). "... a whole utterance is
a stretch of a person's talk bounded by silence at both ends."[5]

[3]  Ibid., sec. 201.
[4]  Ibid., sec. 198.
[5]  Ibid., sec. 12.

(Below, when we are not distinguishing between whole utterances and utterance parts we shall refer to whole utterances merely as utterances.) We now specify the relevant corpus of utterance types, that is, the corpus upon which the theory operates. $E*$ designates the set of utterance types that have been or will be uttered in English regardless of whether they are uttered naturally or elicited. $E$ designates an available sample of $E*$. The semantic theory operates upon $E$. $E$ of course is a finite set, thus permitting all of its members to be operated upon by the semantic theory. It is assumed that every utterance type in the sample $E$ has been given a complete grammatical description. Further, it is assumed that if a given utterance type is ungrammatical it will be discarded and not further considered in the semantic analysis. Thus for all practical purposes $E$ consists of grammatical utterance types, broken down grammatically. Strictly speaking we should have a different name for the set $E$ minus its ungrammatical utterances, but since we want to keep to Ziff's terminology as much as possible we shall slur over this point.

## SEMANTIC REGULARITIES

Next we come to the very important notion of semantic regularity. A semantic regularity is an association between an utterance type and a condition which generally is found in situations in which the tokens of the utterance type occur. Ziff is rather confusing concerning semantic regularities because of his special and restricted use of 'statistical' and because of his introduction of the notion of deviant utterance. In order to avoid the confusion generated by his remarks, we shall interpret his comments concerning semantic regularities in the only way which would make them relevant to a genuine nonintuitive semantic theory. Semantic regularities are empirically discoverable correlations (statistical — 'statistical' here and below is used in its normal scientific sense — correlations) between the linguistic behavior of fluent speakers and conditions found in the situations in which the linguistic behavior takes place.

Semantic regularities are regularities of some sort to be found in connection with the corpus pertaining to both linguistic elements and other things, e.g. to utterances and situations, or to phrases and persons, as well as to utterances and utterances.[6]

The empirical verification of a semantic regularity is one thing and how we come to discover a semantic regularity is another. Semantic regularities are suggested by various methods involving linguistic intuition and shrewd insights; however they are verified in strictly scientific ways. Intuition of oddity or deviance concerning utterances can only function as suggestions or clues concerning regularities; to have a genuine semantic regularity a statistical regularity must actually be found between an utterance type and conditions obtaining. This is the only non-self-defeating interpretation which can be given to Ziff's notion of semantic regularity, since, if a semantic theory is to explicate our semantic intuitions, we can at no time make use of our semantic intuition in the operation of the theory. If we were to interpret Ziff's notion of semantic regularity as an association between an utterance type and a condition which generally is found in situations in which the tokens of the utterance type occur nondeviantly or without oddity — where the determination of deviance or oddity depended upon the linguistic intuition of the investigator — the notion of semantic regularity would be of no use in formulating a semantic theory.

As for the suggesting of semantic regularities, the notion of speech act is offered by Ziff as a device for getting at the conditions regularly associated with a given utterance type. Speech acts such as promising, commanding, etc. have certain conditions regularly associated with their performance. Therefore, the trick is to determine what speech act a given utterance type is performing and then to tentatively correlate the conditions, among

⁶   *Ibid.*, sec. 27.

others, associated with that speech act, with the given utterance type.

... the problem of finding tentative semantic regularities pertaining to utterances of $E$ can be dealt with in two stages. First, it is necessary to find connections between the act of uttering $u_i$ and the performance of certain other speech acts. Secondly, it is then necessary to discover the conditions under which the speech acts connected with $u_i$ in the first stage of analysis can be performed.[7]

## PRINCIPLE OF CONVENTIONALITY

According to Ziff not all regularities between utterance types and corresponding conditions are relevant to meaning, therefore he restricts the notion of semantic regularity by means of his principle of conventionality.

Generally speaking, the principle comes to this: a necessary but not a sufficient condition of a regularity being semantically relevant in the analysis of a corpus is that the speakers of the language associated with the corpus can deviate from the regularity at will.[8]

When dealing with a shared language and not an idiolect, as we are doing here, this principle in effect eliminates those conditions which are associated with all of the utterances of the language. For example, whenever the utterance *Pass the salt* is uttered vocal cords are vibrating. The principle of conventionality would rule out this correlation, since it cannot be deviated from at will. On the other hand, whenever the utterance type *Pass the salt* is uttered, there generally is present a person other than the speaker. This correlation is not ruled out by the principle of conventionality, because it can be deviated from at will : I can now, as I write this without anyone else present, say *Pass the salt*.

Ziff, in order to avoid obvious difficulties, does not directly

---

[7]  *Ibid.*, sec. 83.
[8]  *Ibid.*, sec. 57.

correlate utterance types with corresponding conditions, but rather correlates utterance types with expressions representing the corresponding conditions. A semantic regularity, then is expressed by means of a pairing of two expressions.

The statement of a regularity such as 'If 'Hello!' is uttered then generally one person is greeting one or more others.' can be construed as a statement to the effect that a pairing of the utterances (whole or part) 'Hello!' and 'one person is greeting one or more others' is in accordance with a semantic regularity to be found in connection with the corpus $E$. ... More generally, instead of saying 'If $u_i$ is uttered then such-and-such.' or 'The element $m_i$ has associated with it such-and-such.', etc., letting $w_i$ be a variable for expressions that enter into metalinguistic statements, we can speak of a pairing of $w_i$ with $u_i$ or of a pairing of $w_i$ with $m_i$.[9]

A bit of reflection should be sufficient for one to realize that not all utterance types can be correlated with conditions which are generally associated with them. Ziff offers *There is a purple gila monster on my lap blinking at me* as an example of an utterance type which most probably could not be correlated with corresponding conditions. Such an utterance is just too infrequently uttered for any statistical correlation to be found. Without going further into the subject of those utterance types for which no correlation can be found, let us just note that semantic regularities can only be directly found for a portion of $E$. Thus in summing up, we note that semantic regularities must be statistically verified, must satisfy the principle of conventionality, must be expressed in terms of the pairing of expressions, and are not to be found for all members of $E$.

It is required by Ziff's semantic theory, as we shall see below, that every utterance in $E$ be paired with an expression concerning corresponding conditions. Since statistical methods can only do this for a portion of $E$ — let us henceforth call this portion $E'$ — there must be some sort of device whereby from the correlations gotten statistically we can project correlations for the remaining portion of $E$. Further, as we shall presently see, statistical methods

[9] *Ibid.*, sec. 47.

will yield an 'incorrect' correlation for some of the utterances of
$E'$. The semantic theory, therefore, must also supply us with a
method for correcting these incorrect correlations.

### PRINCIPLE OF COMPOSITION

Let us look more closely at the problem of incorrect correlations
for some members of $E'$. Let us assume that the utterance type
*The cat is on the mat* is in $E'$. A statistical investigation of the
conditions under which this utterance is uttered would reveal
that it is generally uttered when a philosophicogrammatical discussion is under way. Intuitively we realize that this condition
is irrelevant to the meaning of the utterance and to its parts.
For this reason we call the above statistical correlation an incorrect correlation. Now the semantic theory must provide a
method for correcting this correlation. Ziff offers his principle
of composition as the method for doing this. The best way to
explain this principle is to show it in operation :

... if 'a philosophicogrammatical discussion is under way' is paired
with 'The cat is on the mat.' whereas 'some canine is on some mat' is
paired with 'The dog is on the mat.', what structural similarity there is
between 'a philosophicogrammatical discussion is under way' and 'some
canine is on some mat' can hardly be construed as a reflection of the
structural similarity between 'The cat is on the mat.' and 'The dog is
on the mat.'.[10]

However the structural similarity between *Some feline is on some
mat* and *Some canine is on some mat* can be construed as a
reflection of the structural similarity between *The cat is on the
mat* and *The dog is on the mat*. "Consequently it may be (and
in this case is) simpler to construe 'The cat is on the mat.' as
having paired with it 'some feline is on some mat'."[11] Thus we see
that the principle of composition, by means of the notion of

[10]    *Ibid.*, sec. 63.
[11]    *Ibid.*, sec. 63.

structural similarity, transforms the incorrect pairing of *The cat is on the mat* and *a philosophicogrammatical discussion is under way* into the correct pairing of *The cat is on the mat* and *Some feline is on some mat.*

The principle of composition is also used by Ziff to produce correlations for utterances which are in $E$ but not in $E'$ — utterance of $E$ for which statistical methods cannot come up with a correlation. The principle of composition, on the basis of structural similarity between a given utterance in $E$ but not in $E'$, and an utterance in $E'$ (an utterance having a statistical correlation), projects a correlation upon the given utterance. It should be clear that whether the principle of composition is operating upon an utterance which is in $E$ but not in $E'$ or upon an utterance in $E'$ for which an incorrect correlation has been found, the principle is essentially the same. Now we see that all of the members of $E$ are correlated (correctly) with expressions representing corresponding conditions.

## RELEVANT SEMANTIC DIFFERENCE

Next Ziff offers a device which operates upon utterances of $E$ and the conditions correlated with them so as to correlate parts of conditions with individual words in the utterances. The actual correlation is between a word and an expression representing a condition. Letting $m_i$ be a variable ranging over words in the utterances of $E$, let us define 'distributive set for $m_i$' and 'contrastive set for $m_i$'. The distributive set for $m_i$ is the set of utterances of $E$ in which $m_i$ occurs. The contrastive set for $m_i$ is the set of utterances of $E$ gotten by substituting $m_j$ (where $m_j$ is not identical with $m_i$) for $m_i$ in each of the utterances of the distributive set for $m_i$, with the condition that the substitution does not turn a grammatical sentence into an ungrammatical one. The meaning of $m_i$ will be specified in terms of the relative difference for $m_i$. Rather than giving the complex symbolic formulation of the notion of relative difference, we shall instead, by way of example, give an informal explanation of this notion.

Consider the distributive set for *dog* and the contrastive set for *dog*. The distributive set will contain such utterances as *This is a dog, That dog is large, Look at that dog,* etc. The contrastive set will contain such utterances as *This is a pig, That is a horse, Look at that mule,* etc., but it will not contain such utterances as *This is a quickly* or *That is a the*. Each utterance type in the distributive set or contrastive set must be correlated with all and only those conditions which generally obtain when utterance tokens of the given utterance type occur. (This is to say that all of the semantic regularities must be determined for each utterance type.) Next consider the set of ordered pairs whose first member consists of the set of conditions correlated with a given utterance of the destributive set for *dog* and whose second member consists of the set of conditions correlated with the corresponding utterance of the contrastive set for *dog*. Lastly, for each ordered pair, consider the set of those conditions which occur in the first member but do not occur in the second member. This set of conditions is the relevant semantic difference for *dog* with respect to a given ordered pair. Now if the relevant semantic differences 'do not appreciably differ' from ordered pair to ordered pair, the meaning of *dog* is obtained from the common relevant semantic difference. The common relevant semantic difference will be a set of conditions, so presumably the dictionary entry for *dog* will be obtained from expressions representing such conditions.

Although Ziff gives specific formulas for determining whether or not a given word has meaning and for determining when two words are synonymous, we need not go into that because such determinations can be easily gotten by considering the dictionary entries, if any, for the given words. If a word, occurring in the utterances of *E*, is not given a dictionary entry then presumably it has no meaning. If two different words have the same dictionary entry then the two words are synonymous.

Ziff offers the word *to* in the utterance *I want to go through Istanbul* as an example of a word which we intuitively sense has no meaning. It would be profitable to show how Ziff's semantic theory would formally handle such a word. First we consider the distributive set for *to*. This includes such utterances as *I want to eat, I like to live in Paris,* etc. Next we consider the contrastive set for *to*. The contrastive set is empty, since there is no word which can be substituted for *to* in *I want to go through Istanbul* which keeps the utterance grammatical. Thus, the relevant semantic difference for each ordered couple consists of the first member of the ordered couple, since the second member will always be the null set of conditions. But if this is so the relevant semantic difference is not approximately the same for each ordered couple. Therefore no meaning for *to* is obtained.

### CRITICAL EVALUATION

We have traced Ziff's semantic theory from the point at which semantic regularities are statistically established to the point at which dictionary entries are generated. Let us now take a more critical look at what has been proposed.

The very first thing we notice is that the principle of conventionality is totally inadequate for eliminating irrelevant conditions associated with utterances. As we noted above, the essence of the principle of conventionality, in so far as it applies to shared languages and not idiolects, is that it eliminates those conditions which hold for all utterances of a language. The reasoning behind this principle is that conditions which hold for all utterances of a language are irrelevant to the meaning of any particular utterance. Consider the utterance *Pass the salt.* The condition that vocal cords are vibrating when this is uttered is eliminated by the principle of conventionality. This is well and good, for this condition is clearly irrelevant to the meaning of *Pass the salt.* But notice that the condition that salt is present is also eliminated by the principle of conventionality, since salt is present in the human body of the speaker and a speaker is universally present when *Pass the salt* is uttered. We might amend the principle of conventionality so as to prevent it from eliminating any condition pertaining to the body of the speaker. But then the condition that vocal cords are vibrating would not be ruled out as irrelevant. Further, since I could utter any utterance while falling freely through the air, about the only condition which the principle of conventionality could eliminate — the only condition not pertaining to the body of the speaker found universally present for all utterances — would be the condition that air is present. But we would still be in trouble, for we would not be able to obtain the relevant condition that air is present for *The air today is cold.* So we see that if the principle of conventionality is not to eliminate conditions which are relevant, it cannot even eliminate one irrelevant condition. The principle is utterly useless.

We are therefore left with countless irrelevant conditions associated with each utterance. (I use 'countless' advisedly, for it is difficult to conceive of a complete enumeration of the statements concerning the conditions — both relevant and irrelevant — generally associated with a given utterance.) Consider some of the conditions which would be associated with the utterance *Pass the salt* (disregarding for the moment those conditions which are universally present with respect to the uttering of all utterances) : some food is present, some spoon is present, some table is present, some plate is present, some clothes are present, some shoes are present, carbohydrates are losing heat, gravity is attracting silver, wood is losing moisture, china is displacing air, cloth fibers are insulating something, leather is getting tougher, etc. The set of conditions, the great majority of which are irrelevant, associated with each utterance in $E$ would be so fantastically large (if finite) that at this point the theory would become impractical. It should be remembered that Ziff's theory calls for the collection of all of the relevant conditions generally associated with a given utterance. And since no adequate criterion for relevance is provided, this amounts to the collection of all the conditions.

Further, what degree of generality should be considered relevant ? Any animal — *qua animal,* letting alone *qua* ——— — can be referred to or classified according to phylum, subphylum, super-

class, class, subclass, infraclass, cohort, superorder, order, sub-
order, infraorder, superfamily, family, subfamily, tribe, subtribe,
genus, subgenus, species, and subspecies. Which category — level
of generality — is the relevant one for the statement of a particular condition ?

Not only is there difficulty due to the number of conditions
but also there is difficulty due to the vagueness of the notion of
condition. What distance and time restrictions do we place upon
conditions ? Without appealing to our linguistic intuition concerning meaning, how do we know that for the utterance *There
is a fly on my nose* we need only consider conditions relatively
close to the speaker, but for the utterance *That star is bright* we
need consider the entire universe? Since we would have to deal
with such large sets of conditions, mostly irrelevant conditions,
and since 'condition' itself is so vague, it is utopian to believe
that Ziff's theory could come up with the correct relevant differences and consequently the correct meanings. Ziff's semantic
theory must be much more selective when it comes to collecting
associated conditions. Only conditions relevant to the meaning of
*Pass the salt* should be selected. Appeal to the linguistic intuition
of the investigator concerning the meaning of *Pass the salt* in
order to obtain the relevant conditions is out of the question,
since that would render the theory empty. A theory attempting
to explicate the linguistic intuition of a speaker cannot appeal to
the linguistic intuition of a speaker. There is a striking similarity
between the inadequacy of Ziff's method for determining relevant
semantic difference and Mill's methods of agreement and difference. Both Ziff and Mill fail partly because criteria for relevant
conditions are not adequately specified.

Next let us look at the principle of composition as it is used
in correcting the 'incorrect' correlations between utterances of $E'$
and corresponding conditions. We have noted how the principle
of composition rejects the statistical correlation between *The cat
is on the mat* and *Some philosophicogrammatical discussion is
under way* and replaces it with the projected correlation between
*The cat is on the mat* and *Some feline in some mat* on the basis

of the structural similarity between *Some feline is on some mat* and *Some canine is on some mat* and the statistical correlation between *The dog is on the mat* and *Some canine is on some mat*. Intuitively we realize that the condition that some canine is on some mat, is relevant to the meaning of the utterance *The dog is on the mat* while the condition that some philosophicogrammatical discussion is going on, is irrelevant to the meaning of the utterance *The cat is on the mat*. The obvious question at this point is, what formal nonintuitive device within the theory do we have for duplicating this linguistic intuition concerning relevance ? Ziff gives no such device. Since no device is given and since linguistic intuition cannot be appealed to here, on pain of circularity, there is no reason for accepting the statistical correlation between *The dog is on the mat* and *Some canine is on some mat* as correct, while discarding the statistical correlation between *The cat is on the mat* and *Some philosophicogrammatical discussion is under way* as incorrect. In other words, without the required formal nonintuitive device, we could just as easily reject the statistical correlation between *The dog is on the mat* and *Some canine is on some mat* and replace it with the projected correlation between *The dog is on the mat* and *Some mathematical discussion is under way* on the basis of the structural similarity between *Some philosophicogrammatical discussion is under way* and *Some mathematical discussion is under way* and the statistical correlation between *The cat is on the mat* and *Some philosophicogrammatical discussion is under way*. It just does not make sense to speak of correct and incorrect correlations, without providing a formal nonintuitive device for determining which correlations are correct and which are incorrect.

Even if there were a device for determining that the correlation between *The dog is on the mat* and *Some canine is on some mat* was correct while the correlation between *The cat is on the mat* and *Some philosophicogrammatical discussion is under way* was incorrect, there would remain a crucial difficulty. Both Katz[12]

[12]    J. Katz, "Review of Semantic Analysis", *Language* (1962).

and Alston[13] point out this difficulty in their reviews of Ziff's *Semantic Analysis*. Assume that we have established a statistical correlation between *The dog is on the mat* and *Some canine is on some mat* and that we want to project a correlation for *The cat is on the mat* on the basis of the structure of *Some canine is on some mat*. According to Ziff there is a structural similarity between *Some canine is on some mat* and *Some feline is on some mat,* and on the basis of this *The cat is on the mat* is paired with *Some feline is on some mat*. But there is also a structural similarity between *Some canine is on some mat* and *Some rodent is on some mat, Some cheese is on some mat, Some stone is on some mat,* etc. The reason Ziff chooses *Some feline is on some mat* rather than *Some rodent is on some mat* or *Some cheese is on some mat,* etc., is that he has *cat* in mind and by means of his semantic intuition pairs *cat* and *feline*. But Ziff's theory offers no formal nonintuitive device, paralleling this act of intuition, for pairing *cat* and *feline,* therefore there is no reason why we should not correlate *The cat is on the mat* with *Some rodent is on some mat* or *Some cheese is on some mat*. Structural similarity does not cut finely enough to handle semantic matters. Katz puts it nicely :

This failure of composition should not be too surprising in view of the fact that we would not expect a principle stated in purely syntactical terms to make only semantically relevant associations. There is a semantic relation between *cat* and 'feline' and there is a semantic relation between *dog* and 'canine' and if the principle of composition could take such relations into account, there might be some hope for it. But it cannot take semantic relations into account because it is not so formulated and because there is no theory to determine when one term bears a certain semantic relation to another.[14]

When Ziff deals with the way the principle of composition is supposed to project correlations upon utterances which are in $E$ but not in $E'$ on the basis of statistically established correlations involving members of $E'$, he gives such a 'rough' account of the

[13]  W. Alston, "Ziff's Semantic Analysis", *Journal of Philosophy* (1962).
[14]  Katz, op. cit., pp. 65-66.

matter in terms of structural similarity that one hardly knows where to begin one's criticism.

Unfortunately I find it impossible to state the principle of composition in a precise and explicit form. Roughly speaking, it is a principle to the effect that the relevant similarity between distinct semantic correlates of $u_i$ and $u_j$ be a reflection of the relevant similarity between the two utterances.[15]

Katz passes on a point suggested to him by Chomsky which strikes the final blow against Ziff's semantic theory. The principle of composition on the basis of correlations involving utterances of $E'$ can only project correlations upon relatively few utterances outside of $E'$.

Since infinitely many utterances are extremely complex in their grammatical structure, since composition requires structural similarity between the utterances on which a projection is based and the utterance which is paired with a condition by projection, and since the utterances upon which projections are based cannot be very complex structurally (empirical regularities cannot be found in connection with utterances of very great structural complexity), the principle of composition can only cover cases of projection involving utterances with ridiculously simple grammatical structure.[16]

We have said above that we are interpreting Ziff's theory in such a way that the investigator's intuitive insights concerning semantic regularities are taken merely as clues or suggestions and are not taken as part of the formal nonintuitive theory itself. Ziff explicitly refers to intuitive insights concerning semantic regularities as clues. "There are clues to the existence of a semantic regularity. A deviaton from a semantic regularity can, as it were, be felt."[17] Despite this reference to intuitive insights as clues Ziff is not always clear concerning the official status of intuitive insights relative to his semantic theory. However, we are justified in our interpretation, since if he were making the intuitive

---

[15]   Ziff, op. cit., sec. 65.
[16]   Katz, op. cit., p. 64.
[17]   Ziff, op. cit., sec. 28.

insights of the investigator part of the formal nonintuitive theory, his theory could be easily refuted on the ground that it was circular and therefore empty. By interpreting his theory in the manner we are, we are at least making the refutation nontrivial. There is no doubt that Ziff sees his work concerning meaning as relevant to a formal nonintuitive theory, and that he is attempting to outline such a theory. He offers his book as an "informal introduction to and sketch of a rigorous semantic theory". It certainly cannot be argued that he is doing informal ordinary-language philosophy with no thought of constructing a formal theory of language.

We have noted some of the specific shortcomings of Ziff's theory. More generally now let us note some fundamental inadequacies of any theory — including Ziff's — which relies upon the notion of conditions generally associated with utterances. No semantic theory anchored in a correlation between utterances and conditions generally occuring when the utterances are uttered can distinguish between semantic equivalences and factual equivalences, without circularity. As we did in an earlier chapter, let us assume that *bird* and *warm-blooded feathered vertebrate* are synonymous while *bird* and *egg-laying biped* are factually equivalent. Given *There is a bird,* one of the conditions generally associated with this utterance would be that some warm-blooded feathered vertebrate was present. But another condition which is generally associated with *There is a bird* would be that an egg-laying biped was present. In fact it is obvious that the former condition would be found present in a situation if and only if the latter condition were found present. Assuming that the rest of Ziff's theory functioned adequately, no other result could be obtained than that *egg-laying biped* was part of the meaning of *bird*. But by hypothesis it is not; it is only a fact that birds are egg-laying bipeds. It seems quite clear that unless the notion of semantically relevant condition were specified so as to make the theory circular — semantically relevant condition might be specified in terms of our semantic intuition of *bird* and thus the condition of an egg-laying biped being present would be semantically irrelevant to any utterance containing *bird* — no theory based upon conditions can possibly distinguish between semantic and factual equivalences.

Still another fundamental inadequacy of a theory based upon conditions generally associated with an utterance is that such a theory will necessarily confuse the meaning of a word designating a whole with the meaning of a word designating an integral part of the whole. Again let us assume that *glub* actually designates an integral part of that which is designated as *flub*. Consider the utterance *There is a glub*. Any situation containing a glub will also contain a flub and vice versa, so by necessity Ziff's theory, if otherwise adequate, would not be able to distinguish between *glub* and *flub* though by hypothesis *glub* and *flub* differ in meaning.

The best that can be said for Ziff's attempt to provide us with a "sketch of a rigorous semantic theory" is that it is an impressive failure.

# IX

# A PLURALITY OF CONCEPTUAL SCHEMATA

We have shown that all attempts to solve the lexicographer's problem have failed. Now the reason for this failure might be that thus far philosophers, logicians, and linguists have not been clever enough to come up with the required practical nonintuitive procedure. On the other hand, there might be another reason. It might be the case that because of the nature of natural language and the nature of our system of beliefs, it is logically impossible to solve the lexicographer's problem.

In the history of mathematics once the solution was provided for the general quartic equation, mathematicians eagerly sought the solutions for general equations of higher degrees until a proof was given that no further solution was possible. No doubt, before this negative proof was given many mathematicians thought that the only reason for failure in finding the solutions for general equations of higher than the fourth degree was that up to that time mathematicians just had not been clever enough.

Though we are not prepared to give a proof which would be as conclusive for the problem of lexicography as the above mentioned negative proof was in mathematics, we do want to argue that due to the nature of our organization of knowledge the lexicographer's problem is insoluble. We shall present a point of view concerning the structure of the language of knowledge (a part of natural language) and our system of beliefs which is clearly incompatible with the solution of the lexicographer's problem.

QUINE'S VIEW OF THE LANGUAGE OF KNOWLEDGE

This point of view, with a nonessential modification which we shall consider later, has been given expression most recently by Quine in his "Two Dogmas of Empiricism".[1] He writes :

> The totality of our so-called knowledge or beliefs, from the most casual matters of geography and history to the profoundest laws of atomic physics or even of pure mathematics and logic, is a man-made fabric which impinges on experience only along the edges. Or, to change the figure, total science is like a field of force whose boundary conditions are experience. A conflict with experience at the periphery occasions readjustments in the interior of the field. Truth values have to be redistributed over some of our statements. Reëvaluation of some statements entails reëvaluation of others, because of their logical interconnections — the logical laws being in turn simply certain further statements of the system, certain further elements of the field. Having reëvaluated one statement we must reëvaluate some other, which may be statements logically connected with the first or may be the statements of logical connections themselves. But the total field is so underdetermined by its boundary conditions, experience, that there is much latitude of choice as to what statements to reëvaluate in the light of any single contrary experience. No particular experiences are linked with any particular statements in the interior of the field, except indirectly through considerations of equilibrium affecting the field as a whole.[2]

As we noted above, the lexicographer's problem is the providing, by a practical nonintuitive procedure making no reference to extra-linguistic context, of a dictionary entry for each word in our language. Since much of the literature relevant to the lexicographer's problem is in terms of the analytic-synthetic distinction rather than in terms of dictionary entries, let us characterize the lexicographer's problem in terms of the analytic-synthetic distinction. In the context of lexicography, for each word there are relations between the given word and other expressions which hold contingently upon experience (synthetic relations), and there

---

[1]   W.V. Quine, "Two Dogmas of Empiricism", *From a Logical Point of View* (New York : Harper and Row, 1953).
[2]   *Ibid.*, pp. 42-43.

are relations which hold regardless of experience (analytic relations). The problem of lexicography in terms of the analytic-synthetic distinction is the following : For a given true statement,
by a practical nonintuitive procedure making no reference to
extra-linguistic context, determine whether the statement is analytic (true regardless of experience) or synthetic (contingent upon
experience).

Now the incompatibility of Quine's point of view concerning
our system of knowledge with the solution of the lexicographer's
problem should be evident. If this point of view concerning our
system of knowledge is correct it surely would be impossible to
decide, nonintuitively and without reference to context, whether
a given statement was analytic or synthetic. For the lexicographer
attempting to construct a dictionary, an analytic statement is a
statement which fluent speakers would hold on to no matter what.
An analytic statement is a statement which is not subject to revision in the light of experience. Now if the above stated point of
view concerning our organization of knowledge is correct, any
statement in our system of beliefs, regardless of how close to the
'periphery', could be taken as analytic if we were willing to make
the necessary accomodations elsewhere in the system. Similarly,
any statement in our system of beliefs, regardless of how close
to the 'core', could be taken as synthetic.

Perhaps at this point we should obviate a possible misunderstanding of our use of 'analytic statement'. We do not mean by
'analytic statement' a statement which on a particular occasion
and for a particular purpose is used definitionally. To deny that
we can make a list of statements which, on a particular occasion
and for a particular purpose, are used as definitions or which
follow from such definitions would be absurd. We must keep in
mind that we are trying to construct a dictionary which will be
good for more than one occasion or one particular purpose. We
must keep in mind that our dictionary cannot take into consideration extra-linguistic context. The lexicographer's task determines what we mean by 'analytic statement'. The lexicographer
cannot take as analytic a statement which is used definitionally in

certain contexts. He can only take as analytic a statement which fluent speakers use definitionally and intend to continue to use definitionally regardless of experience.

At this point we should stress that everything we are saying here about the analytic-synthetic distinction must be understood within the context of the lexicographer's problem and more generally within the context of a theory of natural language having all of the restrictions we have placed upon such a theory. We are NOT saying that the analytic-synthetic distinction simply does not exist. We are saying that our intuition of analyticity cannot be duplicated nonintuitively within a theory which precludes considerations of extra-linguistic context. We are saying that the lexicographer, forced to work with a restricted sense of 'analytic statement' cannot possibly construct his dictionary.

Let us for the moment revert to the terminology of dictionary entries. If we accept the point of view offered by Quine, it follows that just as it would be impossible to decide, nonintuitively and without reference to extra-linguistic context, whether a given true statement was a true synthetic statement (a statement contingent upon experience) or an analytic statement (a statement which we would never be willing to give up because of a contrary experience), it would be impossible to decide, nonintuitively and without reference to extra-linguistic context, whether a given equivalence was factually equivalent (equivalent only because the world is as it is) or semantically equivalent (equivalent regardless of what the world is like). Supposedly *bird* and *warmblooded feathered vertebrate* are semantically equivalent while *bird* and *egg-laying biped* are merely factually equivalent, on the ground that we are not prepared to give up the former equivalence, *bird* and *warmblooded feathered vertebrate,* because of a contrary experience, but we are prepared to give up the latter equivalence, *bird* and *egg-laying biped.* However, a contrary experience could be accomodated either by giving up the former equivalence while keeping the latter or by giving up the latter while keeping the former. In fact, because of considerations of systematic simplicity and convenience it very well might be that we would be inclined to give up the so-called semantic equivalence rather than the so-called factual equivalence.

The point that the lexicographer's problem is insoluble must not be confused with the trivial point that no two expressions are ever exactly semantically equivalent. This latter point can be circumvented merely by specifying a significant sense of 'semantic equivalence' which would exclude nonlogical considerations such as psychological and aesthetic associations of expressions. The point that the lexicographer's problem is insoluble is much more significant and not so easily circumvented. It amounts to the following: No matter to what degree we refined the concept of semantic equivalence so long as it remains useful in regard to the job of the lexicographer, we shall not be able to solve the lexicographer's problem.

Somewhat similarly, the point that the lexicographer's problem is insoluble amounts to much more than the trivial point that the boundaries between analytic and synthetic are fuzzy. Fuzzy boundaries would present no real problem. If Quine's view of our system of beliefs is correct, the lexicographer's problem is radically insoluble, as there would be no basis in our total organization of knowledge for nonintuitively drawing up a list of dictionary entries. The solution to the lexicographer's problem depends upon there being statements which we would hold on to no matter what. The solution does not depend upon there being no fuzziness between the analytic and synthetic. To say that there are statements which we would hold on to no matter what and to say that the boundaries between the analytic and synthetic are fuzzy are to say two different things.


## DUHEM'S VIEW OF THE POSTULATES OF PHYSICS


Though Quine has been the most recent advocate of the position presented concerning our system of beliefs, he certainly does not stand alone. In general, theoretical scientists are very hesitant to label, irrespective of context, one pair of expressions 'semantically equivalent' and another 'factually equivalent'. They look upon no set of equivalent expressions as beyond possible revision in the light of experience.

As early as 1906 Pierre Duhem expressed essentially the same point of view concerning our system of beliefs as Quine has recently done. According to Duhem no experiment in physics can ever condemn an isolated hypothesis but only an entire theory.

People generally think that each one of the hypotheses employed in Physics can be taken in isolation, checked by experiment, then when many varied tests have established its validity, given a definitive place in the system of Physics. In reality, this is not the case. Physics is not a machine which lets itself be taken apart; we cannot try each piece in isolation, and in order to adjust it, wait until its solidity has been carefully checked; physical science is a system that must be taken as a whole; it is an organism in which one part cannot be made to function without the parts that are most remote from it being called into play, some more so than others, but all to some degree. If something goes wrong, if some discomfort is felt in the functioning of the organism, the physicist will have to ferret out through its effect on the entire system which organ needs to be remedied or modified without the possibility of isolating this organ and examining it apart.[3]

Let us assume that a physicist decides to test an hypothesis in physics. In order for him to deductively elaborate the hypothesis, in order for him to set up an experiment which will determine whether or not such and such phenomena occur, and in order for him to interpret these results relative to the hypothesis in question, the physicist must make use of a set of systematic principles, a theory, besides the given hypothesis. The prediction that such and such phenomena will occur does not derive solely from the hypothesis in question but from the hypothesis together with a theory. If the predicted phenomena do not occur, the only conclusion which the physicist can draw is that at least one of the many statements in the set of statements, consisting of the hypothesis plus the statements in the supporting theory, is in error.

[3] Pierre Duhem, *Aim and Structure of Physical Theory*, trans. Philip Wiener (Princeton : Princeton University Press, 1953), pp. 187-188.

Duhem considers a specific example from the history of science. We are confronted with two hypotheses concerning the nature of light. According to Newton, Laplace, and Biot, light consists of projectiles; according to Huygens, Young, and Fresnel, light consists of vibrating waves within an ether. According to the projectile hypothesis light travels faster in water than in air; according to the wave hypothesis light travels faster in air than in water. We set up Foucault's apparatus and begin our experiment. If the greenish band of light is to the left of the colorless band it means that light travels faster in water than in air; if the greenish band of light is to right of the colorless one it means that light travels faster in air than in water. We look and note that the greenish band is to the right of the colorless one. Can we conclude categorically that light consists of vibrating waves in an ether ? Certainly not. Foucault's experiment does not decide between two hypotheses, the projectile and wave hypotheses; Foucault's experiment decides, rather, between two theories; namely, between Newton's Optics and Huygens' Optics.

Duhem's systematic view of our system of beliefs causes him to ask whether certain postulates of physical theory are incapable of being refuted by experiment — a question most relevant to our main concern in this section. His answer is, No ! He admits that the physicists of a given epoch usually accept without test, and regard as beyond dispute, certain principles of physics, and that if they are forced to modify their system because of experimental results, they will bring their modifications to bear on statements other than the principles in question. However, he quickly goes on to make clear that physicists are not impelled to act in this manner out of logical necessity. More significantly, he adds that there are times when in the face of contrary experimental results a physicist refuses to hold on to those principles 'declared untouchable by common consent' and instead institutes a reform among such principles. Such a physicist accomplishes a work of genius and initiates a new epoch.

The history of Physics shows us that very often the human mind has been led to overthrow such principles completely, though regarded by common consent for centuries as inviolable axioms, and to rebuild its physical theories on new hypotheses.

Was there, for instance a clearer or more certain principle for thousands of years than this one: In a homogeneous medium, light is propagated in a straight line? ... However, the day came when physicists tired of attributing to some cause of error the diffraction effects observed by Grimaldi, when they resolved to reject the law of the rectilinear propagation of light and to give Optics entirely new foundations; and this bold resolution was the signal of remarkable progress for physical theory.[4]

## PUTNAM'S VIEW OF THE STATEMENTS OF PHYSICS

In a similar vein Hilary Putnam, in his article "The Analytic and the Synthetic",[5] gives an example of the dangers involved in labeling as analytic, irrespective of context, certain expressions of physics. Before relativistic physics the expression 'Kinetic energy is equal to one half the product of mass and velocity squared' ($e = \frac{1}{2} mv^2$) would have been taken as an analytic expression in physics if any expression had been so taken. In fact those who would maintain the analytic-synthetic distinction in science, in so far as it affects the lexicographer's problem, would have said that '$e = \frac{1}{2} mv^2$' is the definition of 'kinetic energy'. With the Einsteinian revolution in physics some of the principles of physics were revised. Some of these principles, such as that the velocity of light cannot be exceeded, certainly would have been listed as synthetic prior to the revolution. More interestingly, some principles which prior to the revolution had been considered to be definitional in character, and hence listed as analytic, were revised in an exactly similar way. In particular, Einstein replaced the principle '$e = \frac{1}{2} mv^2$' by a different and more complicated one. In other words, he replaced the statement which had been con-

---

[4]  *Ibid.*, p. 212.
[5]  Hilary Putnam, "The Analytic and the Synthetic", *Minnesota Studies in the Philosophy of Science*, 3 (1962), pp. 358-397.

sidered the definition of 'kinetic energy' by another statement concerning kinetic energy. Against the contention that 'kinetic energy $= \frac{1}{2} mv^2$' was a definition and that Einstein merely changed the definition Putnam writes:

> What is striking is this: whatever the status of the "energy definition" may have been before Einstein, in revising it, Einstein treated it as just another natural law. There was a whole set of pre-existing physical and mechanical laws which had to be tested for compatibility with the new body of theory. Some stood the test unchanged — others only with some revision. Among the equations that had to be revised (and formal considerations indicated a rather natural way of making the revision, one which was moreover, borne out richly by experiments) was the equation '$e = \frac{1}{2} mv^2$'.[6]

If, in revising a theory, statements listed as analytic are treated no differently from statements listed as synthetic, the analytic-synthetic distinction, as it applies to the lexicographer's problem, hardly seems to be a genuine distinction in science. With James we maintain, a difference to be a difference must make a difference.

Conventionality is not a "lingering trait" of those statements introduced by stipulation at the frontiers of science. Though the principle '$e = \frac{1}{2} mv^2$' may have been introduced as a stipulation and though the Newtonian law of gravity may have been determined experimentally by observing the known satellite systems and the solar system, these two formulas came to be used in the same way. Before Einstein both were considered not to be refutable by any isolated experiment. With the Einsteinian revolution both were abandoned. It appears that the closer we look at the analytic-synthetic distinction in science, as it applies to the lexicographer's problem, the more untenable it becomes.

We want to emphasize that we are not denying that, in science on a given occasion and for a given reason, a statement may be used definitionally. We are saying that we are not forced to continue to use a statement definitionally just because it has been

---

[6]  *Ibid.*, p. 371.

so used on other occasions. We repeat : The sense of 'analytic statement' which is forced upon the lexicographer because of the nature of his work, is that in which an analytic statement is one which would be held on to no matter what. The lexicographer cannot make use of a notion of analytic statement which is context dependent.

Both Duhem and Putnam make their comments concerning the analytic-synthetic distinction, as it applies to the lexicographer's problem, in the context of science. Though there are some differences between the language of science and natural language, the problem of the analytic-synthetic distinction, in so far as it affects the lexicographer, is the same for both the language of science and natural language.

## IN DEFENSE

Hofstadter, in his article "The Myth of the Whole: A consideration of Quine's View of Knowledge",[7] suggests that our body of knowledge, rather than consisting of a single unified system of statements, consists of a number of independent systems of statements. In other words, he suggests that not every statement in our body of knowledge is related to every other statement, but rather that there are various independent groups of interrelated statements. He writes :

In what way, for instance, does my discovery that I have forgotten whether I boarded the train at 12:12 or 12:13 p.m. affect the sunspot theory of economic crises? Is it not a *dogma* to suppose that the whole of the language of knowledge is involved in every cognitive decision.[8]

Hofstadter's attack upon Quine's holistic view of knowledge is irrelevant to the problem of lexicography. Regardless of whether our body of knowledge consists of a single unified system of

[7] A. Hofstadter, "The Myth of the Whole : An Examination of Quine's View of Knowledge", *Journal of Philosophy*, 51 (1954), pp. 397-417.
[8] *Ibid.*, p. 408.

statements or a number of independent systems of statements, so long as within the language of knowledge there are some systems of interrelated statements, every point we have made and shall make concerning the problem of synonymy holds. For our points depend upon there being system and not upon there being one system. It must be remembered that the significant differences in our dispute with the structural linguists is that between system and the absence of system and not between holism and the alternative suggested by Hofstadter. The point of view concerning the nature of language and knowledge we commit ourselves to is that point of view expressed by Quine, Duhem, and Putnam minus the holism involved in their view. Further we attach no metaphysical significance to the view we take. In taking this view we claim nothing which is not relevant to some practical problem regarding language.

The reader may recall that we said in our general remarks about semantic theories that in those cases in which fluent speakers cannot decide concerning semantic interpretations we are ready to let the theory itself decide. A serious problem arises here. To let a theory stipulate as to the analytic and synthetic would be acceptable if the analytic-synthetic distinction were a vague one which needed to be made more definite or clear-cut. The trouble with the analytic-synthetic distinction as understood by the lexicographer is not that it is vague. Fluent speakers often cannot decide whether a given statement is analytic or synthetic, not because the distinction is vague, but because the statement is 'analytic' according to one conceptual schema but 'synthetic' according to another. (By the use of the term 'conceptual schema' we are not trying to introduce into our discussion such troublesome things as concepts, intensions or ideas. By 'conceptual schema' we mean nothing more than 'system of definitions'. When we say that there may be more than one conceptual schema for organizing our body of knowledge we mean that there may be more than one set of interrelated definitions for organizing our body of knowledge.) In such a case there is no room for stipulation. In natural language we have at our disposal a great number of intuitive 'dictionaries' — each corresponding to a different conceptual schema. The fluidity due to the different conceptual schemata is a desirable feature of language and not something to be done away with. We do not want a semantic theory to decide between analytic and synthetic in those cases in which we are undecided simply because we want to stay undecided. And we want to stay undecided simply because we do not want to be bound by a single conceptual schema.

A semantic theory making use of a single dictionary would have the following kind of unacceptable results. If *bird* is defined by the dictionary as *warm-blooded feathered vertebrate,* the sequence *Here is a featherless bird* would not be generated by the theory as a meaningful sentence. On the other hand, *Here is a four-legged bird* would be generated by the theory as a meaningful sentence. This, however, might not be a correct rendering of our language in the light of certain future experiences concerning strange birds. We might want to be able to say *Here is a featherless bird* but not *Here is a four-legged bird.*

In natural language we change from 'dictionary' to 'dictionary' and usually are not even sure which 'dictionary' we are using. Sometimes when we use different 'dictionaries' at the same time we arrive at contradictions. When things get difficult with one we drop it and pick up another. This is both the salvation and damnation of natural language. We have many 'dictionaries' to work with. This makes our language exceedingly flexible but at the same time inaccurate, imprecise, and above all incapable of formalization. To formalize natural language is to throw out all the 'dictionaries' but one; however, this would amount to making natural language into something it is not.

We have argued that the point of view concerning our system of beliefs to which we have committed ourselves is incompatible with the solution of the lexicographer's problem. Grice and Strawson at times seem to claim that there is no such incompatibility. Let us briefly look into this matter. Quine argues that it is a mistake to think that an isolated statement can be confirmed or disconfirmed by experience. Yet precisely on such a mistaken belief, Quine continues, rests the following criterion of statement synonymy : Two statements are synonymous if and only if any experience tending to confirm or disconfirm, one would also tend to confirm or disconfirm, respectively, the other. This proposed criterion, Quine argues, must be rejected as it is based upon a theory of verification which is manifestly false.

Grice and Strawson argue against Quine that the rejection of the verification theory holding that isolated statements can be confirmed or disconfirmed does not force us to reject the above suggested criterion for statement synonymy but only to modify it. They write :

Quine does not deny that individual statements are regarded as confirmed or disconfirmed, are in fact rejected or accepted, in the light of experience. He denies only that these relations between single statements and experience hold independently of our attitudes to *other* statements. He means that experience can confirm or disconfirm an individual statement, only given certain assumptions about the truth or falsity of other statements... . This view, however, requires only a slight modification of the definition of statement-synonymy in terms of confirmation and disconfirmation. All we have to say now is that two statements are synonymous if and only if any experience which, *on certain assumptions about the truth-values of other statements*, confirm or disconfirm one of the pair, also, *on the same assumptions*, confirm or disconfirm the other to the same degree... . So Quine's views are not only consistent with, but even suggest an amended account of statement synonymy along these lines.[9]

Grice and Strawson here seem to be trying to give a formal nonintuitive criterion for statement synonymy — one which supposedly could be used by lexicographers. They thus are not just dealing with the problem of statement synonymy on an intuitive basis. Grice and Strawson's modified criterion for statement synonymy amounts to no more than a criterion for the equivalence of two systems of statements. (A system of statements need not include every statement in our entire body of knowledge. Our entire body of knowledge may consist of a number of independent

⁹ H.P. Grice and P.F. Strawson, "In Defense of Dogma", *Philosophical Review*, LXV (1956), p. 156.

systems of statements. We want to emphasize that in our criticism of Grice and Strawson's criterion for the synonymy of statements, all that we are required to show is that their criterion is not one for isolated statements. Whether their criterion is one for the equivalence of entire languages or for the equivalence of portions of languages [subsystems of languages], our criticism holds.) Unfortunately, however, the notion of statement synonymy which could be of use to the lexicographer is one between isolated expressions and not one between systems of expressions. The reason for this is that lexicographers require a single dictionary for their theory. If they worked with a notion of synonymy between systems of statements they would come up with a number of dictionaries (each inadequate by itself) instead of a single adequate dictionary.

In order to substantiate the point that Grice and Strawson's criterion is not one for isolated statements but only one for systems of statements, we need only turn to he practical work of the lexicographer. If he makes use of Grice and Strawson's modified criterion for statement synonymy his entries will have to be of the following kind : Statement A is synonymous with statement B on the assumption that _____ . And he will have to fill in the blank with a list of true statements. This list of true statements must itself presuppose a statement of the logical and semantical relations (including synonymy) among the statements in the system. To neglect the logical and semantical relations among the statements would be an invitation to contradiction. So we see that each entry of a pair of synonymous statements will implicitly include every other entry in the system. The only happy note for the lexicographer in such a case is that if for a given system he makes explicit every consideration involved in making his first entry, he will not have to go beyond his first entry. The most that a lexicographer could do using Grice and Strawson's criterion for statement synonymy is to state that a given system was, in some sense, synonymous with another. But this certainly would be of little help to the lexicographer attempting to construct a single dictionary which he can use in constructing a unified theory of language.

Quine states in his "Two Dogmas of Empiricism" that it is a mistake to think that there is a class of statements which are in principle immune from revision in the light of experience. And, he continues, it is this mistaken belief which must be held by those who maintain the distinction between the analytic and synthetic. Grice and Strawson counter that acceptance of the position that no statement is, in principle, immune from revision is quite compatible with holding to the distinction between the analytic and synthetic. They write :

Only, the adherent of *this* distinction must also insist on another; on the distinction between that kind of giving up which consists in merely admitting falsity, and that kind of giving up which involves changing or dropping a concept or set of concepts. Any form of words at one time held to express something true may, no doubt at another time come to be held to express something false. But it is not only philosophers who would distinguish between the case where this happens as the result of a change of opinion solely as to matters of fact, and the case where this happens at least partly as a result of a shift in the sense of the words. Where such a shift in the sense of the words is a necessary condition of the change in truth-value, then the adherent of the distinction will say that the form of words in question changes from expressing an analytic statement to expressing a synthetic statement... . And if we can make sense of this idea [conceptual revision], then we can perfectly well preserve the distinction between the analytic and the synthetic, while conceding to Quine the revisability-in-principle of everything we say.[10]

With this argument of Grice and Strawson we have no quarrel, since they obviously are dealing with the analytic-synthetic distinction on an intuitive level. However, it would be wrong to think that this argument has any bearing upon the lexicographer's problem. Involved in this argument is the position that a reading of a sentence can express an 'analytic statement' at one time and a 'synthetic statement' at another time. In our introductory chapter we made it quite clear that we would not use 'statement' in this sense, that is, in the sense in which a single reading of a sentence

[10]    *Ibid.*, p. 157.

can express two different 'statements'. We pointed out that we would not use 'statement' in this sense because the lexicographer, not being able to handle extra-linguistic context, cannot make use of such a sense of 'statement' in his practical work. A lexicographer cannot manipulate a 'statement' which is not completely determined by a reading of a sentence. He requires a notion of analyticity which is context-free. He, presented which a given statement, wants to know whether it is revisable or not, not whether it could be used definitionally on some occasions and factually on others. The lexicographer wants to distinguish between ordinary revisable statements and statements having the privileged status of holding regardless of experience.

# X

## DIFFICULTIES IN LEXICOGRAPHY

### A PRACTICAL NONINTUITIVE PROCEDURE

In "Two Dogmas of Empiricism"[1] Quine claims to have shown that the analytic-synthetic distinction simply does not exist. He writes :

> But, for all its a priori reasonableness, a boundary between analytic and synthetic statements simply has not been drawn. That there is such a distinction to be drawn at all is an unempirical dogma of empiricists, a metaphysical article of faith.[2]

However, what Quine claims to have shown and what he in fact has shown are two different things. He shows that philosophers and logicians have failed to provide a practical nonintuitive procedure for deciding, irrespective of extra-linguistic context, whether a given statement is analytic or synthetic. Further, he shows that there are good reasons for believing that such a nonintuitive procedure cannot be provided. Everything he does establish is clearly in the realm of practical nonintuitive criteria.

In this book we are interested in whether or not it is possible to provide a practical nonintuitive procedure for deciding, irrespective of extra-linguistic context, whether a given statement is analytic or synthetic (the question to which Quine in fact addresses himself) and we definitely are not interested in whether or

---

[1] W.V. Quine, "Two Dogmas of Empiricism", *From a Logical Point of View* (New York : Harper, 1963), pp. 20-46.
[2] *Ibid.*, p. 37.

not the analytic-synthetic distinction exists in some form or other (the question to which Quine claims to address himself). In other words, the problem which Quine in fact tackles is the same as the problem we are concerned with here — roughly, the possibility of solving the lexicographer's problem. Therefore to defend what we claim Quine has shown (though not what he claims he has shown) is to defend our position concerning the problem of lexicography.

It appears to us that critics of Quine, in their efforts to show that he has failed to provide good reasons for believing that the analytic-synthetic distinction simply does not exist, have often overlooked what he has in fact gone a long way toward establishing. Further, the importance, especially to lexicography, of what he has gone a long way toward showing — that a practical nonintuitive procedure for deciding, irrespective of extra-linguistic context, whether a given statement is analytic or synthetic cannot be provided — has often been overlooked. Of even greater significance is the fact that many of the arguments offered against Quine's "Two Dogmas of Empiricism" are taken as valid against both what Quine claims to have shown in this article and what we are claiming he has in fact shown. (It has been my experience that when I have made the claim that it is not possible to provide a practical nonintuitive procedure for distinguishing, irrespective of extra-linguistic context, between analytic statements and synthetic statements, I have been referred to those arguments in the literature against Quine's "Two Dogmas of Empiricism"). In what follows we shall consider a number of these arguments. Though they all may be valid against what Quine claims to have shown, we shall not examine them from that point of view. We only want to show that these arguments are not valid against the position that the practical nonintuitive procedure we are concerned with does not and cannot exist. We obviate here any criticism of our efforts to the effect that Quine's critic is not directing his attack against the position we are defending. If we can successfully defend the position that a practical nonintuitive procedure for deciding, irrespective of extra-linguistic context,

whether a given statement is analytic or synthetic cannot be provided, then we shall have made a most important point concerning
the lexicographer's problem.

## IN DEFENSE

Grice and Strawson, in their article "In Defense of Dogma",[3]
offer a number of arguments against Quine's "Two Dogmas of
Empiricism". Let us begin by considering the following argument.
To say that two expressions are synonymous in Quine's sense
corresponds roughly to saying that one expression means the
same as the other. Therefore Quine is claiming that the distinction
we suppose ourselves to be making by the use of the expressions
'means the same as' and 'does not mean the same as' does not
exist. Grice and Strawson continue :

> Yet the denial that the distinction (taken as different from the distinction
> between the coextensional and the non-coextensional) really exists, is
> extremely paradoxical... . It involves saying that it is always senseless
> or absurd to make a statement of the form "Predicates x and y in fact
> apply to the same objects, but do not have the same meaning". But the
> paradox is more evident than this. For we frequently talk of the presence
> or absence of relations of synonymy between kinds of expressions —
> e.g., conjunctions, particles of many kinds, whole sentences — where
> there does not appear to be any obvious substitute for the ordinary
> notion of synonymy, in the way in which coextensionality is said to be
> a substitute for synonymy of predicates. Is all such talk meaningless?
> Is all talk of correct or incorrect *translation* of sentences of one language
> into sentences of another meaningless? It is hard to believe that it is.[4]

The above argument of Grice and Strawson — which amounts
to a plea to our semantic intuition — may hold against what
Quine claims to have shown but it does not hold against what we
claim he has shown. We do speak of synonymous expressions;
we do say such things as *unicorn* and *centaur* apply to the same

---

[3] H.P. Grice and P.F. Strawson, "In Defense of Dogma", *Philosophical
Review*, LXV (1955), pp. 141-158.
[4] *Ibid.*, pp. 145-146.

things but do not have the same meaning; and we do translate one sentence into another. However, the fact remains that the lexicographer, who is looking for a practical nonintuitive procedure for distinguishing between semantic equivalence and factual equivalence, is not helped by these intuitive considerations. For the lexicographer, who has a very down to earth job to do, all of this intuitive talk about synonymy is of no help whatsoever.

A second argument offered by Grice and Strawson is the following: Quine argues that to adequately classify or to make "satisfactory sense" of such expressions as 'synonymy', 'analyticity', 'logical possibility' — expressions all of which belong to a family circle of interdefinable expressions — would involve two things. It would involve specifying some feature common and peculiar to all cases to which the expression applied while at the same time not making use of any yet undefined expression in the family circle. Grice and Strawson argue that though the expressions may not be capable of explanation in this strict sense demanded by Quine, they can be explained in less formal ways. They write :

Let us suppose we are trying to explain to someone the notion of *logical impossibility* (a member of the family which Quine presumably regards as no clearer than any of the others) and we decide to do it by bringing out the contrast between logical and natural (or causal) impossibility. We might take as our examples the logical impossibility of a child of three's being an adult, and the natural impossibility of a child of three's understanding Russell's Theory of Types. We might instruct our pupil to imagine two conversations one of which begins by someone (X) making the claim:

    (1)  "My neighbor's three-year-old child understands Russell's Theory of Types,"
and the other of which begins by someone (Y) making the claim:

    (1 ')  "My neighbor's three-year-old child is an adult... ."
We might say that in both cases we would tend to begin by supposing that the other speaker was using words in a figurative or unusual or restricted way; but in the face of his repeated claim to be speaking literally, it would be appropriate in the first case to say that we did not believe him and in the second case to say that we did not understand him.[5]

[5]  *Ibid.*, pp. 150-151.

Thus Grice and Strawson conclude that since this informal type of explanation is available, Quine's argument breaks down.

It should be evident that Grice and Strawson's "less formal way" of explaining logical impossibility is of absolutely no value to the lexicographer. The lexicographer is quite familiar with the intuitive distinctions between logical impossibility and natural impossibility; he in fact uses these notions correctly, relying upon his intuitive understanding of them. His task, however, consists in explaining in a formal nonintuitive way our abilities to use correctly the expressions 'logical impossibility' and 'natural impossibility'. In other words his task is to render in a nonintuitive manner a skill which we perform intuitively. It should be obvious that the "less formal way" of explaining our intuitive uses of 'logical impossibility', offered by Grice and Strawson, relies upon our intuition of language — the very thing we are attempting to explain.

A third argument offered by Grice and Strawson is the following:

If talk of sentence-synonymy is meaningless, then it seems that talk of sentences having meaning at all must be meaningless too. For if it made sense to talk of a sentence having meaning, or meaning something, then presumably it would make sense to ask "What does it mean?" of a sentence,... then sentence-synonymy could be roughly defined as follows: Two sentences are synonymous if and only if any true answer to the question "What does it mean?" asked of one of them, is a true answer to the same question asked of the other. We do not, of course, claim any clarifying power for this definition. We want only to point out that if we are to give up the notion of sentence-synonymy as senseless, we must give up the notion of sentence significance (of a sentence having meaning) as senseless too.[6]

This argument is clearly fallacious. By rejecting the notion of sentence-synonymy it follows that we must reject the notion of 'the meaning of a sentence', but certainly it does not follow that we must reject the notion of a sentence's having meaning — sentence significance. There is all the difference in the world between

---

[6]  *Ibid.*, p. 146.

knowing that a sentence is meaningful and 'knowing the meaning of a sentence'. I may know that a given utterance in a foreign language has meaning by the way fluent speakers respond to the utterance, yet I may not know the meaning of the utterance. In my own language I may know that a given utterance is meaningful without knowing something called 'its meaning' which I can compare with some other meaning. Let us say that I know the utterance *Hello Joe* is meaningful. Then presumably I would 'know its meaning' in the sense that I would know how to employ the utterance. However, to 'know its meaning' in this sense is not the same as to know something called 'its meaning' which I can compare to some other meaning in order to determine whether or not *Hello Joe* is synonymous with another utterance. Grice and Strawson jump from the notion of knowing the meaning (in the first sense) of a sentence to the notion of knowing the meaning (in the second sense) of a sentence. If we know the meanings (in the second sense) of two sentences we can determine whether or not the two sentences are synonymous merely by comparing the two meanings. However, if we know that two sentences each have meaning, or are significant, we have no solution to the synonymy problem concerning them, since we have no meanings to compare.

Putnam, in his article "The Analytic and the Synthetic"[7] states that though he believes the analytic-synthetic distinction is greatly overworked by philosophers, he cannot accept "Quine's thesis — the thesis that the distinction which certainly seems to exist does not in fact exist at all". Putnam flatly rejects "the idea that every statement is either analytic or synthetic [even allowing for borderline cases]; the idea that all logical truths are analytic; the idea that all analytic truth derives its necessity from "linguistic convention", but he unequivocally maintains: "There are analytic statements : 'All bachelors are unmarried' is one of them".[8] He

[7]   H. Putnam, "The Analytic and the Synthetic", *Minnesota Studies in the Philosophy of Science*, 3 (1962), pp. 358-397.
[8]   *Ibid.*, p. 361.

offers one main argument against Quine, an argument in which he attempts to provide Quine with suitable criteria for analytic statement. He writes :

In short, I shall present criteria which are intended to show what is unique or different about certain analytic statements. Such criteria do not constitute a definition but one might obtain a definition, of a rough and ready sort, from them: an analytic statement is a statement which satisfies the criteria to be presented, or a consequence of such statements, or a statement which comes pretty close to satisfying the criteria, or a consequence of such statements.[9]

As Putnam goes on to explain, the criteria he offers strictly speaking are not criteria for an analytic statement, but rather are criteria for a "fundamental subset of the totality of analytic statements in the natural language" — the so-called analytic definitions. An example of an analytic definition is : 'Someone is a bachelor if and only if he is an unmarried man'. An analytic statement, then, would be a statement which either satisfies his criteria or is a consequence of a statement which satisfies his criteria. An example of a statement which is analytic but not an analytic definition is : 'Someone is a bachelor only if he is a man'.

The criteria offered for 'analytic definition' by Putnam are the following :

(1)     The statement has the form "Something (Someone) is an $A$ if and only if it (he, she) is a $B$," where $A$ is a single word.

(2)     The statement holds without exception, and provides us with a criterion for something's being the sort of thing to which the term $A$ applies.

(3)     The criterion is the only one that is generally accepted and employed in connection with the term.

(4)     The term $A$ is not a "law-cluster [10] word".[11]

Concerning criterion (1) Putnam comments that it, by itself, is not enough to distinguish between analytic definition and natural law. Concerning criteria (2) and (3) he writes :

[9]     *Ibid.*, p. 392.
[10]     A law-cluster concept is one which is determined by a cluster of laws. The energy concept in physics is a law-cluster concept.
[11]     *Ibid.*, pp. 392-393.

A statement of the form "Something is an *A* if and only if it is a *B*" provides a criterion for something's being a thing to which the term *A* applies if people can and do determine whether or not something is an *A* by first finding out whether or not it is a *B*. For instance, the only generally accepted method for determining whether or not someone is a bachelor, other than putting the question itself, is to find out whether or not the person is married and whether or not he is an adult male.[12]

He goes on to explain what he means by the word 'criterion' in (2) and (3). "... the 'criteria' I am speaking of are necessary and sufficient conditions for something's being an *A*; and ... by mean of them [the criteria] people can and do determine that something is an *A*."[13] Let us see how Putnam's argument fares against what we claim Quine has in fact established.

Criterion (4) is stated negatively. We concede to Putnam that if the term *A* is a law-cluster word, then a statement satisfying criterion (1) is not an analytic definition. [We are interested in whether or not Putnam's criteria can provide us with analytic statements, not in whether or not his criteria can fail to do so.) With criterion (1) we have no quarrel : it is a simple matter to determine whether or not a given statement has the form specified. In the discussion which follows, let us consider the following statements [all of which have the form specified by criterion (1)] : *Something is a man if and only if it is a rational animal, Something is a man if and only if it is a featherless biped, Something is a man if and only if it is a rational animal or a unicorn.*

The first part of criterion (2), "The statement holds without exception", is not required since if the second part of criterion (2), "the statement provides us with a criterion for something's being the sort of thing to which the term *A* applies", holds, the first part will hold necessarily. Criteria (2) and (3) might better be combined into the following : The statement provides us with the one and only criterion which is generally accepted for something's being the sort of thing to which the term *A* applies. Putnam, by speaking of a criterion in (2) and of a generally accepted criterion in (3), seems to unnecessarily complicate things. Why must we even consider 'criteria' which are not generally accepted ?

Now we come to the crux of our argument. How do we determine whether or not a given statement, satisfying the form specified in (1), provides us with the generally accepted criterion for something's being the sort of thing to which the term *A* applies ? Given *Something is a man if and only if it is a rational animal* how do we determine whether or not being a rational animal is the generally accepted criterion for something's being a man ? We might ask ourselves 'Is being a rational animal the generally accepted criterion for something's being a man ?', but this clearly would be an appeal to our linguistic intuition. We might just as well ask ourselves if the statement *something is a man if and only if it is a rational animal* is analytic. We might make a statistical investigation, asking a large number of fluent speakers individually 'Is being a rational animal your criterion for something's being a man ?'. Then if speakers generally answered 'yes' we would conclude that being a rational animal was the generally accepted criterion for something's being a man. But in this case we would be appealing to the linguistic intuition of the individual speakers. We might just as well ask each speaker in turn if he considered the statement *Something is a man if and only if it is a rational animal* to be true by definition. Appealing to the linguistic intuition of the investigator or of a group of fluent speakers surely cannot be part of a practical nonintuitive criterion for analytic statement. A criterion for analyticity must be of such a nature that it can decide concerning a totally novel statement without presenting the given statement to a fluent speaker for comment. We therefore must try to find a way, without appealing to linguistic intuition, for determining whether or not being a rational animal is the generally accepted criterion for something's being a man.

Following the custom of anthropologists, we might point to a rational animal and ascertain whether or not a fluent speaker would assent to the utterance *man*. If most speakers assented to *man* when a rational animal was pointed out, but dissented from *man* when something other than a rational animal was pointed out, we might conclude that something's being a rational animal was the generally accepted criterion for something's being a man. Though such a test would be behavioristic (and thus among other things practical and nonintuitive) it would not do the job. Even if every fluent speaker assented to *man* if and only if a rational animal was pointed out, we could not know that something's being a rational animal was the generally accepted criterion for something's being a man. Anytime a rational animal was pointed out, so also would a featherless biped be pointed out; anytime a rational animal was not pointed out, so also a featherless biped would not be pointed out. Likewise, a rational animal would be pointed out if and only if a rational animal or a unicorn was pointed out. Though all speakers were to assent to *man* if and only if a rational animal was pointed out, we could not know that their criterion for something's being a man was not something's being a featherless biped or something's being a rational animal or a unicorn.

Putman goes on to ask on what basis we are to reject, as not an analytic definition, the statement *Someone is a bachelor if and only if he is either an unmarried man or a unicorn.* To this he answers :

... people do not ascertain that someone is a bachelor by first finding out that he is either an unmarried man or a unicorn... . People (other than formal logicians) would certainly deny that they ascertain that someone is a bachelor by first finding out that he is either unmarried or a unicorn.[14]

In light of our comments above, the obvious question is : How do you know this ? We have shown that we cannot know this without appealing to our linguistic intuition.

In "Analytic Sentences"[15] Benson Mates offers some arguments against Quine's "Two Dogmas of Empiricism". Let us see how

---

[14]  *Ibid.*, p. 394.
[15]  B. Mates, "Analytic Sentences", *Philosophical Review*, 60 (1951), pp. 525-534.

Mates's arguments fare against what we claim Quine has in fact established. Mates reminds us that, as has been observed from Aristotle to Russell, in order to better understand a term it is not necessary to define the term by means of terms we understand. Circular definitions often contribute to understanding, he notes, and definitions of the type rejected by Quine as being circular, state 'interesting semantical relationships' which add to our understanding.

Quine would not deny that circular definitions may add to our understanding. In fact he, more than anyone else, has spelled out the interconnections between such terms as 'analytic', 'synonymous', 'contradictory', etc. Such an understanding, however, is of formal relations among concepts. Unfortunately this is not the kind of understanding which a lexicographer can make use of — at least at the start of his investigation. Circular definitions are of no use when one has the practical task of actually enumerating the articles which are circularly defined. We may define 'battle-axe' in terms of 'hatchet' and 'hatchet' in terms of 'axe', and 'axe' in terms of 'battle-axe', but unless we are given an independent practical criterion for one of these three items, we shall not be able to form a pile of battle-axes. Likewise, we may define 'synonymy' in terms of 'analyticity', 'analyticity' in terms of 'contradiction', and 'contradiction' in terms of 'synonymy', but unless we are given an independent practical criterion for one of these three notions, we shall not be able to compile a list of analytic sentences. Though one may be able to 'understand' — in some sense of 'understand' — a term without being able to decide whether or not given cases fall under it, this certainly is not the kind of understanding which is required in the construction of a theory of natural language.

Mates notes that Quine requires of an adequate definition of 'analytic' that the *definiens* be understood better than the *definiendum*. (Actually, according to what White tells us about Quine's requirements, Quine makes an even stronger demand: He requires that the *definiens* be in behavioristic terms.) Regarding this requirement Mates writes: "It may easily happen that the conditions of adequacy for a definition are so strong that no adequate definition is possible."[16]

The requirement that the *definiens* be understood better than the *definiendum,* as well as the requirement that the *definiens* be in behavioristic terms, is not a capricious requirement but is dictated by the job that the lexicographer has to do. Any weaker requirement upon the definition of 'analytic' would preclude the lexicographer from constructing his dictionary. It may very well be that the requirements upon the definition of 'analytic' are so strong as to make a definition impossible — in fact this is what we in general are arguing — but in the light of the lexicographer's problem, this can be no reason for making the requirement weaker. The requirements are set by the task before us, not by what is available in terms of definitions. So long as we are concerned with the problem of lexicography, his demands upon the definition of 'analytic' are not exorbitant.

Mates claims that is seems possible "to devise a fairly reliable empirical criterion for determining whether a given person holds a given sentence as analytic." (We assume that Mates means 'reading of a sentence' or 'statement' by 'sentence'.) The empirical test would ascertain whether or not a given speaker had a certain attitude toward a given true statement, and upon this basis the statement would be declared analytic or synthetic. The particular empirical test which Mates sketches seems to boil down to asking the speaker whether or not he would claim the given statement to be true no matter what. If the speaker answers that he would claim the statement to be true no matter what, the statement would be declared analytic for him. (Supposedly if a given statement is declared analytic for most speakers then it would be declared analytic in the language.) Let us look into this test.

Mates's 'empirical criterion' unfortunately is not nonintuitive. When we ask a speaker if he would hold on to a given statement no matter what we are appealing to his intuition of language. The lexicographer in seeking a nonintuitive criterion for analyti-

[16]  *Ibid.,* p. 529.

city in seeking to explicate this very same intuition of language. He, therefore, cannot appeal to it in his criterion.

Though Mates does not do so, it might be argued that in order to determine whether or not a given statement is analytic for a speaker, we need not ask him to make meta-linguistic comments about the given statement. It might be suggested that we just watch his behavior concerning the given statement; if he would hold on to the given statement no matter what, then the given statement would be analytic for him. Such a suggestion would be of little use to the lexicographer. We can determine, by watching a speaker's behavior, whether or not a given statement is held on to, but surely we cannot determine, by watching a speaker's behavior whether or not a given statement WOULD be held on to no matter what. There is just no practical nonintuitive way for determining the intention of a speaker toward a given statement.

Let us next consider an argument offered by Hofstadter against Quine's "Two Dogmas of Empiricism". Again we shall consider this argument from the lexicographer's point of view. Hofstadter argues :

... the analytic-synthetic distinction breaks down just to the degree to which the pragmatic function of precision and clearness in communication and prediction breaks down, and conversely. ... It is pragmatically necessary to make language more determinate in application and inference. But if we do this we make it more possible to attribute to particular sentences the properties of being analytic or synthetic.[17]

A statement may not be 'sufficiently definite or clear-cut' to be decidably analytic or synthetic. However, scientists, by achieving greater definiteness, approach a situation in which the given statement becomes more decidable regarding the analytic-synthetic distinction. Hofstadter illustrates this in the following manner :

For instance, given a shade of color in the spectrum somewhere between definite orange and definite red, the statement "An object having that

[17] A. Hofstadter, "The Myth of the Whole : An Examination of Quine's View of Knowledge", *Journal of Philosophy*, 51 (1954), p. 412.

shade of color is either red or non-red" is indeterminate in this way. We cannot say it is analytic, nor can we say it is non-analytic. We do not know what to say because the statement is defective. The terms "red" and "non-red" are not sharp enough to put the given shade under the one or under the other. Or, put otherwise, our "semantical rules" for the two terms are defective in not allowing decisions to be made regarding the applicability of the terms in all circumstances. This is why color-scientists will substitute color-numbers, wave lengths, or other metrical terms for the ordinary color-terms. They wish to achieve greater definiteness of meaning, more universal possibility of decision, i.e., they wish to get closer to a situation in which a statement such as "This shade is either A or non-A" becomes analytic.[18]

Hofstadter concerns himself with the indefiniteness of statements and terms. However, that a nonintuitive criterion for analyticity cannot be provided does not depend upon the vagueness of natural language — the indefinite reference of terms — but rather upon the loose and indeterminate structure of natural language. Making natural language more definite and precise would not help the lexicographer seeking a nonintuitive criterion for analyticity. The impossibility of such a criterion does not depend upon the vagueness of terms such as *bird* but rather upon relations between expressions such as *bird*, *egg-laying biped*, and *warmblooded feathered vertebrate*. Even if we were absolutely definite about the extension of *bird* we still would be in doubt about the relation of *bird* to *egg-laying biped* and *warmblooded feathered vertebrate*.

Hofstadter's further point that there are a great many statements which Quine would hardly deny to be analytic, clearly is not relevant to the lexicographer's problem as we are concerned with here.

# XI

## SKINNER'S FUNCTIONAL ANALYSIS

Our survey of language analyses which might possibly be construed as attempts to provide a descriptive theory of natural language would be incomplete if we did not consider those efforts of behavioristic psychologists to account for linguistic behavior in terms of such experimental notions as stimulus, response, reinforcement, etc. We have, of course, in mind principally the work along these lines by B.F. Skinner as presented in his book *Verbal Behavior.*[1]

The reason that we did not include Skinner's treatment of verbal behavior in our earlier discussions concerning the problems of grammar and semantics is that Skinner's approach to such problems is radically different from any we have examined thus far. The fact that most of the attempts, we examined, at solving the problems of semantics involve behavioristic controls of some sort, should not mislead one into thinking that Ziff, Katz and Fodor, etc., are trying to do the same thing as Skinner. Ziff, Katz and Fodor, etc. are attempting to provide behavioristic criteria for certain semantic notions such as synonymy and analyticity — a rather modest goal compared to Skinner's. On the other hand, Skinner, as we shall elaborate below, is attempting to construct a theory which would actually predict the verbal behavior of people. Whereas the former are attempting to construct a theory which would predict what could — and I stress 'could' — be said correctly, Skinner is attempting to construct a theory

[1] B.F. Skinner, *Verbal Behavior* (New York : Appleton-Century-Crofts, 1957).

which would predict what actually is — and I stress 'is' — said by people. The former group of linguists would want to say something like : A fluent speaker of English might say 'Today is a fine day'. They would mean by this that the utterance *Today is a fine day* is a meaningful English sentence. Skinner would want to say something like the following : This man standing before me will now say *Today is a fine day*. There could hardly be a greater difference between these two approaches to language theory.

By way of introduction to his main concern in this book, Skinner tells us that man (as well as other species), by means of his behavior, alters his environment. Sometimes his behavior alters the environment through purely mechanical action; at other times the altering mechanism is more complex. The latter is the case with verbal behavior.

Much of the time, however, a man acts only indirectly upon the environment from which the ultimate consequences of his behavior emerge. His first effect is upon other men. Instead of going to a drinking fountain, a thirsty man may simply "ask for a glass of water" — that is, may engage in behavior which produces a certain pattern of sounds which in turn induces someone to bring him a glass of water. The sounds themselves are easy to describe in physical terms, but the glass of water reaches the speaker only as the result of a complex series of events including the behavior of a listener. The ultimate consequence, the receipt of water, bears no useful geometrical or mechanical relation to the form of the behavior of "asking for water". Indeed, it is a characteristic of such behavior that it is impotent against the physical world. Rarely do we shout down the walls of a Jericho or successfully command the sun to stop or the waves to be still. Names do not break bones. The consequences of such behavior are mediated by a train of events no less physical or inevitable than direct mechanical action, but clearly more difficult to describe.[2]

## FUNCTIONAL ANALYSIS

Skinner's main concern in his above mentioned book is the providing of a 'functional analysis' of verbal behavior. A func-

---

[2]  *Ibid.*, pp. 1-2.

tional analysis of verbal behavior, according to Skinner, amounts to identifying the variables which control verbal behavior and showing how they interact in the producing of particular verbal responses. He places rather severe limitations upon the nature of the variables which he will make use of; the variables are to be described only by means of those rather simple notions developed with animal experimentation, such as stimulus, response, reinforcement, etc. The attempt at the explication of verbal behavior in terms of such few and simple notions, if successful, surely would be one of the milestones of science. Let us, in order to make Skinner's goal perfectly clear, state it in less technical terms. Skinner in *Verbal Behavior* hopes to provide a mechanism which would both predict verbal behavior by our observing the physical environment of the speaker, and control verbal behavior by our manipulating this environment. In other words, he hopes to determine the causal factors of verbal behavior. In order to provide the reader with documentation regarding the ambitious goals (both immediate and remote) of a functional analysis of verbal behavior as conceived by Skinner, we quote the following :

The extent to which we understand verbal behavior in a "causal" analysis is to be assessed from the extent to which we can predict the occurrence of specific instances and, eventually, from the extent to which we can produce or control such behavior by altering the conditions under which it occurs. In representing such a goal it is helpful to keep certain specific engineering tasks in mind. How can the teacher establish the specific verbal repertoires which are the principal end-products of education? How can the therapist uncover latent verbal behavior in a therapeutic interview? How can the writer evoke his own verbal behavior in the act of composition? How can the scientist, mathematician, or logician manipulate his verbal behavior in productive thinking? Practical problems of this sort are, of course, endless. To solve them is not the immediate goal of a scientific analysis, but they underline the kinds of processes and relationships which such an analysis must consider.[3]

Skinner assures us that he is not unaware of the ambitiousness

---

[3]  *Ibid.*, p. 3.

of his goal, and he then goes on to give the reason for his optimism regarding the reaching of this goal.

It would be foolish to underestimate the difficulty of this subject matter, but recent advances in the analysis of behavior permit us to approach it with a certain optimism. New experimental techniques and fresh formulations have revealed a new level of order and precision. The basic processes and relations which give verbal behavior its special characteristics are now fairly well understood. Much of the experimental work responsible for this advance has been carried out on other species, but the results have proved to be surprisingly free of species restrictions. Recent work has shown that the methods can be extended to human behavior without serious modification.[4]

Probably the most astonishing feature of the task Skinner sets for himself is the restriction upon the variables which control verbal behavior to external factors exclusively. One would think that prediction of the verbal behavior of a human being would require, not only knowledge about the external environment in the situation of verbal behavior, but also knowledge about the particular human being. For example, one would think that in predicting the verbal behavior of MacArthur when he, in reviewing General Yamashita's case, said : "It is not easy for me to pass penal judgement upon a defeated adversary in a major military campaign" one would have to know something about MacArthur and not just such external factors as present stimulation, history of reinforcement, etc. Yet Skinner repeatedly claims to have shown that the speaker's contribution in verbal behavior is trivial and that prediction of the details of verbal behavior depends overwhelmingly upon those simple external factors isolated in animal experimentation.

Skinner's efforts at functional analyses in *Verbal Behavior* received a crushing criticism in Noam Chomsky's review[5] of this book. According to Chomsky, the force of Skinner's argument lies in the "enormous wealth and range of examples for which he

[4]  *Ibid.*
[5]  Noam Chomsky, "Review of Verbal Behavior", *Language*, (1959), pp. 26-58. We quote from this review by kind permission of the author and the Linguistic Society of America.

proposes a functional analysis." Chomsky reviews these examples in detail, showing time and time again how Skinner has completely failed in his thesis. Chomsky's general attitude and criticism toward Skinner's efforts are expressed in the following quotation :

Careful study of this book (and of the research on which it draws) reveals, however, that these astonishing claims are far from justified. It indicates, furthermore, that the insights that have been achieved in the laboratories of the reinforcement theorists, though quite genuine, can be applied to complex human behavior only in the most gross and superficial way, and that speculative attempts to discuss linguistic behavior in these terms alone omit from consideration factors of fundamental importance that are, no doubt, amenable to scientific study, although their specific character cannot at present be precisely formulated.[6]

Chomsky provides many devastatingly critical reviews of Skinner's individual functional analyses. We shall include a small sample of these reviews; we shall concentrate on those which are most germane to this investigation. Before we begin, however, we must note a few definitions which are essential to the understanding of Skinner's presentation. We shall not bother to define such common psychological notions as stimulus, response, reinforcement, etc. Responses are divided into two categories. Respondents are purely reflex responses elicited by way of particular stimuli. Operants, on the other hand, are responses for which no obvious stimulus can be found. A mand is "a verbal operant in which the response is reinforced by a characteristic consequence and is therefore under the functional control of relevant conditions of deprivation or aversive stimulation." Mands include questions and commands. A tact is "a verbal operant in which a response of given form is evoked (or at least strengthened) by a particular object or event or property of object or event." An autoclitic is an operant which is a response to already given responses or to potential verbal behavior. Autoclitics are involved in assertion, negation, quantification, the construction of sentences, etc.

---

[6]   *Ibid.*, p. 28.

According to Chomsky, the basic mistake made by Skinner repeatedly in his analyses is the following: Such notions as stimulus, response, reinforcement, etc. are relatively well-defined in animal experimentation. Skinner thus uses these notions as evidence of the scientific nature of his work covering verbal behavior. However, the terms 'stimulus', 'response', etc., as applied to animal experimentation, turn out to be mere homonyms of the terms 'stimulus', 'response', etc., as applied to verbal behavior. If such terms are taken literally — that is, as defined in animal experimentation — Skinner's analyses cover hardly any aspect of verbal behavior; if such terms are taken metaphorically — so as to be descriptive of verbal behavior — Skinner's analyses are just not scientific.

## STIMULUS CONTROL

Now let us look at the specific examples of Skinner's analysis. The response to a painting with the tact *Dutch* would be an example of stimulus control. The tact (response) is "under the control of extremely subtle properties", according to Skinner. Now, we realize that there could be many different responses to a painting, some of which might be : *Clashes with the wallpaper, Hanging too low, Beautiful, What's for dinner ?*. Skinner would say that each response is under the control of a different stimulus property of the painting. Chomsky points out that since properties are "free for the asking" we can account for any number of responses by identifying the controlling stimulus, however, the term 'stimulus' has lost all its scientific objectivity.

Stimuli are no longer part of the outside physical world; they are driven back into the organism. We identify the stimulus when we hear the response. It is clear from such examples, which abound, that the talk of 'stimulus control' simply disguises a complete retreat to mentalistic psychology. We cannot predict verbal behavior in terms of the stimuli in the speaker's environment, since we do not know what the current stimuli are until he responds. Furthermore, since we cannot control the property of a physical object to which an individual will respond, except in highly artificial cases, Skinner's claim that his system, as opposed to the traditional one, permits the practical control of verbal behavior is quite false.[7]

Another example of stimulus control given by Skinner is more directly relevant to other sections of this study. A proper noun is a response "under the control of a specific person or thing". Chomsky simply points out that he has used the proper nouns *Eisenhower* and *Moscow* yet he has never been 'stimulated' by the corresponding objects. Skinner claims that a stimulus controls a response in the sense that the presence of the stimulus increases the probability of the response. Chomsky points out that it just isn't true that the probability of a speaker's producing a full name is increased when the bearer of the name is in the presence of the speaker. Further, what about one's own name? Concerning the general problem of reference Skinner writes:

But how a word "stands for" a thing or "means" what the speaker intends to say or "communicates" some condition of a thing to a listener has never been satisfactorily established. The notion of the verbal operant brings such relations within the scope of the methods of natural science. How a stimulus or some property of a stimulus acquires control over a given form of response is now fairly well understood. The form of a response is shaped by the contingencies prevailing in a verbal community. A given form is brought under stimulus control through the differential reinforcement of our three-term contingency. The result is simply the probability that the speaker will emit a response of a given form in the presence of a stimulus having specific properties under certain broad conditions of deprivation or aversive stimulation. So far as the speaker is concerned, this is the relation of reference or meaning.[8]

If we take the above terms 'presence', 'stimulus', and 'probability' literally, Skinner's claim is just untrue; if we take them metaphorically, his claim is far from scientific. In fact the phrase 'under the control' turns out to be just a misleading paraphrase of such vacuous traditional terms as 'denote' or 'designate'. So long as 'control' has surrendered all of its scientific objectivity,

[7]  *Ibid.*, p. 32.
[8]  Skinner, *op. cit.*, pp. 114-115.

it doesn't matter much whether we say '*Moscow* designates Moscow' or '*Moscow* is under the control of Moscow'.

Skinner tells us that a person plays what music he likes because he finds it reinforcing to do so, that a person says what he likes because he finds it reinforcing to do so, and that an author writes books because he is reinforced by what he hopes will be the ultimate behavior of his reader. It is obvious that 'reinforce' does not have the meaning it has in animal experimentation. Saying '*X* is reinforced by *Y*' introduces no scientific objectivity over '*X* wants *Y*', '*X* likes *Y*', '*X* wishes that *Y* were the case', etc. In fact, '*X* is reinforced by *Y*' blurs certain distinctions which are provided by the more traditional formulations. Concerning Skinner's distortion of such scientific notions as stimulus and reinforcement, Chomsky writes:

What has been hoped for from the psychologist is some indication how the casual and informal description of everyday behavior in popular vocabulary can be explained or clarified in terms of the notions developed in careful experiment and observation, or perhaps replaced in terms of a better scheme. A mere terminological revision, in which a term borrowed from the laboratory is used with the full vagueness of the ordinary vocabulary, is of no conceivable interest.[9]

Skinner claims his analysis of mands provides a scientifically objective basis for the traditional classification into requests, commands, prayers, etc. Whereas the traditional classification is in terms of the intention of the speaker, Skinner claims that he can explain the traditional classification in terms of the reinforcing behavior of the listener. A question is a mand which specifies verbal action. We can in turn classify a question as request, command, or prayer according to the behavior of the listener. A question is a request if the "listener is independently motivated to reinforce the speaker", a question is a command if "the listener's behavior is ... reinforced by reducing a threat", a question is a prayer if it "promotes reinforcement by generating an emotional disposition". Chomsky points out that *Please pass the salt*

⁹ Chomsky, *op. cit.* p. 38.

is a request even if the listener does not happen to be motivated to fulfill it. An utterance does not cease to be a command just because it is not complied with. A question does not become a command just because the listener feels threatened. If Skinner is using the terms 'request', 'command', and 'prayer' in any sense like these terms have in ordinary language, his analysis is a complete failure. He surely has not shown that he can explain the traditional classification of such terms as request, command, etc., which is in terms of the intention of the speaker, solely in terms of the behavior or disposition of the listener. The problem of intentionality is not that simple.

## GRAMMATICAL SENTENCE

Now we come to an example of Skinner's analysis the subject of which we have dealt with extensively in previous chapters. Skinner claims that a sentence is a set of key responses on a skeletal frame. If we are considering the fact that a dog jumped through a hoop, the responses to that situation are *dog, jumps, through,* and *hoop.* These responses are qualified by autoclitics is evidence supporting the claim that the 'key responses' are then added by means of a process called composition. The result is a grammatical sentence. Chomsky, after pointing out that there is evidence supporting the claim that the 'key responses' are chosen only after the grammatical frames, states a few linguistic facts which Skinner's analysis of sentencehood does not account for. (A grammatical frame is a sentence frame whose constituents have grammatical significance. For example, the sequences *Iggle squiggs trazed wombly* and *Little pigs wallowed happily* both have the grammatical frame '_____ _____s _____ed _____ly'. This sentence frame is of grammatical significance since it is capable of indicating subject, verb, and adverb.) Such shortcomings of Skinner's analysis do not merely indicate minor imperfections in his analysis, but rather because of their fundamental nature, demonstrate that Skinner's analysis is radically inadequate. *Sheep provide wool* does not have a frame yet no other arrangement of these words constitute a grammatical sentence. Of the two sequences *furiously sleep ideas green colorless* and *friendly young dogs seem harmless,* both having the same frame, only the second is a grammatical sentence. *Struggling artists can be a nuisance* and *Marking papers can be a nuisance* have the same frame yet they differ in sentence structure as is evident if we replace *can be* by *is* in both sentences. Skinner's analysis of sentencehood is based upon the assumption that sentence structure consists merely of the insertion of lexical items in grammatical frames. The above stated difficulties, as well as certain things we have said in previous chapters, begin to show the failings of such an assumption.


CHOMSKY'S CONCLUSIONS


Chomsky's conclusions concerning Skinner's attempts at functional analysis — functional analysis as defined by Skinner — amount to the following points. First, if we take Skinner's fundamental terms, such as 'stimulus', 'response', 'reinforcement' literally, his analysis covers practically no aspect of verbal behavior; if we take his fundamental terms metaphorically, his analysis is even less adequate than the traditional formulations. Second, any attempt to account for the verbal behavior of speakers which is not grounded in a prior understanding of the nature of grammar is doomed to failure. Third, the attempt to account for the verbal behavior of speakers solely in terms of external factors — that is, totally neglecting the contribution of the speaker — is overly ambitious and doomed to failure. Concerning the third point, Chomsky writes :

Since Skinner limits himself to such a small set of terms for paraphrase, many important distinctions are obscured. I think that this analysis [Chomsky's analysis] supports the view ... that elimination of the independent contribution of the speaker and learner ... can be achieved only at the cost of eliminating all significance from the descriptive system, which then operates at a level so gross and crude that no answers are suggested to the most elementary questions. The questions to which Skinner has addressed his speculations are hopelessly premature. It is futile to inquire into the causation of verbal behavior until much more is know about the specific character of this behavior.... [10]

The magnitude of the failure of this attempt to account for verbal behavior serves as a kind of measure of the importance of the factors omitted from consideration, and an indication of how little is really known about this remarkably complex phenomenon.[11]

As we said at the beginning of this section, there is reason to believe that after such a scathing review by Chomsky of Skinner's *Verbal Behavior,* the movement in behavioristic psychology to account for verbal behavior along the lines of Skinner, will no longer be taken seriously.

[10]   *Ibid.,* pp. 54-55.
[11]   *Ibid.,* p. 28.

# XII

## CONCLUSION

Our explicitly stated goals in this book were to ascertain to what
extent so-called theories of natural language represent attempts
to provide genuine scientific theories of natural language, and,
for those theories representing such attempts, to critically evaluate
the progress made and difficulties encountered in their construction. At the very outset we made it clear what we mean by 'a
scientific theory of natural language'. We stated the goals of such
a theory and clearly excluded matters of extra-linguistic setting
from consideration. From the goals we set for a scientific theory
of natural language we determined the essential features of such
a theory, some of which are the following: A theory of natural
language is a descriptive, predictive, and falsifiable device. A
theory of natural language is a formal nonintuitive device. The
empirical controls placed upon such a theory are found in the
actual verbal behavior of fluent speakers.

The candidates for scientific theories of natural language which
we examined were those 'language theories' offered by ordinary-
language philosophers, ideal-language philosophers, behavioristic
psychologists (specifically Skinner's functional analysis of verbal
behavior), and descriptive linguists. Concerning the work of ordinary-language philosophers, our conclusions were the following:
They have not provided us with any part of a theory of natural
language. Though they have touched upon matters which are
relevant to the dictionary component of a theory of natural language, they have not supplied us with a method for assigning even
the simplest semantic properties to expressions of natural lan-

guage. We took Wittgenstein, Austin, and Ryle as representatives of ordinary-language philosophers. In our analysis of the relevant material concerning these philosophers we were as sympathetic as possible in interpreting their intentions and contributions toward a theory of natural language. Nevertheless we found no contribution and little intention.

Concerning Wittgenstein we noted any of his comments which might be construed as relevant to the construction of a theory of natural language. We found that he shares a number of views concerning natural language with those advocating the construction of a theory of natural language. However we went on to show that though he uses expressions such as 'rules of grammar' and 'language game', he does not advocate the construction of a systematic theory of natural language.

Although Austin leaves open the possibility that someday a comprehensive science of language will absorb a certain portion of what now is considered philosophy and though he has doubts about there being an ultimate boundary between the logical grammar of the philosopher and the grammar of the linguist, it is clear that he neither gives us a theory of natural language nor is entirely sympathetic with the construction of such a theory. His method of ordinary-language philosophy may be characterized as piecemeal and intuitive while the kind of theory we are concerned with in this investigation may be charaterized as comprehensive and nonintuitive.

Ryle, more so than Wittgenstein or Austin, might be interpreted as calling for the construction of a theory of natural language. His distinction between use and usage, his reference to rules of logic, categories, and category-mistakes all might be interpreted as indicating that he is attempting to provide the basis for a genuine theory of natural language. Ryle, however, does not provide us with such a basis. His method for showing that two expressions differ in category has the effect of relegating every word to a different category. His general discussion concerning categories and category-mistakes proves totally unilluminating for our purposes. His single example of a rule of grammar proves totally inadequate as a rule which might play a part in a theory of natural language. We conclude that ordinary-language philosophers have not contributed to the construction of a theory of natural language.

Concerning the work of ideal-language philosophers our conclusions were the following: Ideal languages, with their formal syntax and semantics, fail as descriptive devices. They hardly resemble natural language and the concepts of formal semantics have little relation to our intuitive understanding of such semantic notions as synonymy and analyticity. The inability of ideal-language philosophers to describe in detail the complexities of natural language does not necessarily mean that natural language is highly unsystematic. In fact the progress made by linguists in grammar indicates that natural language is much more systematic than ideal-language philosophers thought. Ideal-language philosophers, by stressing the unsystematic aspect of natural language and the ideal nature of their theories, have failed to make their theories answerable to the details of natural language. Consequently, they have provided us with arbitrarily constructed ideal languages having little resemblance to natural language. As for the matter of empirical controls upon the semantic theories of ideal-language philosophers, we find an absence of correspondence rules connecting the abstract terms of the theory with empirical procedures. The key semantic concepts such as synonymy and analyticity are not linked to any procedures rooted in natural language. The key semantic concepts are left as unanalyzed primitives. Further, because of the lack of empirical controls upon the theories of ideal-language philosophers there is no way of evaluating between competing theories except by the standards of consistency and elegance — inadequate standards for a descriptive theory. Lastly, all attempts by ideal-language philosophers to link the primitive notions of their theories of formal semantics with empirical procedures relating to natural language have failed.

Concerning Skinner's functional analysis of verbal behavior, we merely passed on Chomsky's criticism. We thought that this was more than sufficient for dealing with Skinner's approach.

We only included the chapter on Skinner's functional analysis in order to make our survey complete. Let us here sum up Skinner's position and Chomsky's criticism.

According to Skinner a functional analysis of verbal behavior amounts to identifying the variables controlling verbal behavior and showing how they interact to produce particular verbal responses. Furthermore, Skinner proposes to describe his variables only by means of the simple notions developed with animal experimentation, such as stimulus, response, etc. Chomsky shows that the terms 'stimulus', 'response', etc. as applied to animal experimentation are mere homonyms of the terms 'stimulus', 'response', etc. as applied to verbal behavior. If such terms are taken literally Skinner's analysis covers hardly any aspect of verbal behavior; if they are taken metaphorically his analysis is not scientific.

Thus in our search for an adequate theory of natural language we are left with the work of descriptive linguists. Descriptive linguists not only have sought to construct a scientific theory of natural language but have actually succeeded in constructing portions of such a theory. We have shown how, in their work, descriptive linguists have sought to meet the basic requirements of a scientific theory. They have sought to construct a device which is descriptive, predictive, falsifiable, and grounded in empirical matters. They have insisted on a device which is formal and nonintuitive so as to save it from vacuity. We have noted some of their achievements in phonology and morphology. In noting these achievements, we took pains to distinguish between the traditional intuitive explanations in terms of meaning and the nonintuitive explanations. This was done in order to make quite clear and unambiguous what is meant by 'a formal nonintuitive theory of natural language' as well as to indicate some of the achievements of descriptive linguists. Further, by stressing the elimination of matters of meaning in phonology and morphology, we were setting the stage for our criticism of descriptive linguists' optimism concerning semantics.

Because of the success descriptive linguists have had in phonology and morphology, and especially in grammar, some of them have become optimistic concerning the construction of a complete theory of natural language, including a formal nonintuitive semantic component. Concerning this optimism we made the following points : The success descriptive linguists have had in phonology and morphology is reason for optimism concerning the completion of their syntactic task but cannot be considered reason for optimism concerning the completion of their semantic task. The success they have had in phonology and morphology, including grammar, is to a large extent due to the elimination of explication in terms of semantics. We showed in some detail how the characterization of such linguistic notions as phonemic distinctness, morphemic distinctness, and grammatical sequence in terms of semantics only brought chaos and confusion into phonology and morphology. Real progress in these two fields was made possible only after they were freed from dependence upon semantic matters. This progress, rather than being reason for optimism concerning the solution of the semantic problems of a theory of natural language, might be considered reason for reaffirming the belief that the real difficulties in language theory only begin with semantics.

In semantics we noted that all practical questions of meaning can be reduced to questions of the sameness of meaning. That is, we noted that lexicography only calls for associating synonymous expressions rather than discovering the 'absolute meaning' of expressions — whatever that may be. However, even the problem of synonymy, the most elementary part of a semantic theory, resisted solution. All attempts to solve this problem in terms of definition, extension, interchangeability, stimulus meaning, etc. proved unfruitful.

Most of our criticisms of attempts do deal with the problem of synonymy can be found in the recent literature. Yet we have not merely collected arguments. All too often arguments against proposals for solving the problem of synonymy have been advanced in ambiguous contexts. Sometimes such arguments have been advanced when intuitive questions of synonymy were being considered rather than the nonintuitive questions relevant to the lexicographer's problem. Many times it has not been clear just what the problem was. We have placed these arguments clearly within the lexicographer's problem and have gone on to show that in such a setting they are valid regardless of how they fare in other settings. Criticism of attempts to solve the intuitive problem of synonymy is one thing; criticism of attempts to solve the nonintuitive problem of synonymy is another. Directing the criticism against the proper object is as important as the criticism itself. Much of the misunderstanding concerning the problem of synonymy is the result of the lack of definition of the problem.

We were left with two major efforts to solve the lexicographer's problem : Katz and Fodor's semantic theory and Ziff's semantic analysis. We have seen that Katz and Fodor's semantic theory and Katz's explication of analyticity hinge upon the adequacy of their solution to the dictionary problem. Not only have they not provided us with a discovery procedure for dictionary entries, but they have not even provided us with an adequate evaluation procedure for competing dictionary entries or competing dictionaries. Regarding Katz and Fodor's normal form for dictionary entries, we showed that unless every last bit of lexical information, both explicit and implicit, found in the terminal distinguishers is parceled out to individual semantic markers (a job which would make the theory impractical) there will be sentences which the theory finds ambiguous but a fluent speaker does not.

Ziff's attempted solution of the lexicographer's problem proved totally inadequate. Ziff's principle of conventionality is an essential part of his semantic theory, since with it he hopes to eliminate irrelevant conditions associated with utterances and thus make his theory workable. Yet this principle proves to be incapable of eliminating a single irrelevant condition without also eliminating relevant conditions. Ziff's principle of composition cannot be applied without appealing to the linguistic intuition of the investigator and thus cannot qualify as part of a nonintuitive semantic theory. Lastly, we have shown that no semantic theory based

upon correlations between utterances and conditions generally occurring when the utterances are made, can distinguish between
semantic equivalences and factual equivalences.

Because of the many failures to solve the lexicographer's problem, we sought to determine whether or not there was some characteristic of the structure of natural language which precluded the
solution of this problem. We found that if a certain view concerning our language of knowledge (a part of natural language)
is correct then the lexicographer's problem is insoluble. If the
language of knowledge consists of a system or systems (not necessarily one all-embracing system) in which no single statement can
be said to be true or false in isolation from other statements in
its system, then the lexicographer's problem is insoluble. Though
this view of our language of knowledge is usually combined with
a holistic conception of knowledge, it need not be. The insolubility of the lexicographer's problem does not depend upon a
holistic view of knowledge; it depends upon a systematic view.
It should be evident that any argument attacking the holistic view
of knowledge and not the systematic view is irrelevant to our
thesis.

Thus in Chapter VI through Chapter VIII we showed that the
lexicographer's problem, as we understand it, has not been solved.
In Chapters IX and X we showed that, due to the systematic
nature of the language of knowledge, the lexicographer's problem
is insoluble. In defending this latter point, we distinguished between what Quine claims to establish in "Two Dogmas of Empiricism"[1] and what he in fact establishes. He claims to establish
that the analytic-synthetic distinction simply does not exist. He
in fact establishes that philosophers and logicians have failed to
provide a practical nonintuitive procedure for deciding, irrespective of extra-linguistic context, whether a given statement is analytic or synthetic. Further, he gives good reasons for believing
that such a nonintuitive procedure cannot be provided. In other
words the problem which Quine in fact deals with is the same
as the problem we are concerned with — roughly, the possibility

[1] W.V. Quine, "Two Dogmas of Empiricism", *From a Logical Point of View* (New York : Harper, 1963), pp. 20-46.

of solving the lexicographer's problem. To defend what we claim Quine has established (as distinct from what he claims to have established) is to defend our own position concerning the problem of lexicography. We showed that none of the many arguments we examined regardless of their intent was valid against what we claim Quine in fact establishes.

At this point we are prepared to summarize our answers to the questions we posed at the beginning of this book. The 'theories of language' offered by ordinary-language philosophers and ideal-language philosophers, regardless of how these 'theories' were intended, do not qualify as descriptive theories of natural language. Skinner's functional analysis of verbal behavior, though couched in the terminology of behavioristic psychology, so distorts its basic terms that it completely fails in its highly overambitious task. Descriptive linguists, alone, have succeeded in giving us portions of a descriptive theory of natural language. Their work in phonology and morphology is most impressive. However, the success in phonology and morphology was made only after explication in terms of semantics was eliminated. All attempts to solve the problem of lexicography have failed. Due to the systematic nature of the language of knowledge, the lexicographer's problem, as we understand it, is insoluble. Thus, the construction of a descriptive theory of natural language, along the lines we have indicated, is impossible.

# BIBLIOGRAPHY

## BOOKS

Austin, J.L.
1961   *Philosophical Papers.* Edited by J.O. Urmson and G.J. Warnock (Oxford : Clarendon Press).
Black, Max.
1949   *Language and Philosophy* (Ithaca : Cornell University Press).
1954   *Problems of Analysis* (Ithaca : Cornell University Press).
Bloomfield, L.
1933   *Language* (New York : Holt).
Carnap, R.
1937   *The Logical Syntax of Language* (New York : Harcourt, Brace and Co.).
1942   *Introduction to Semantics* (Cambridge : Harvard University Press).
1947   *Meaning and Necessity* (Chicago : University of Chicago Press).
Caton, C.E. (ed.)
1963   *Philosophy and Ordinary Language* (Urbana : University of Illinois Press).
Chomsky, N.
1957   *Syntactic Structures* (The Hague : Mouton and Co.).
Church, A.
1956   *An Introduction to Mathematical Logic* (Princeton : Princeton University Press).
Cohen, M. and Nagel, E.
1934   *An Introduction to Logic and Scientific Method* (New York : Harcourt).
Dewey, J.
1939   *Logic : The Theory of Inquiry* (New York : Holt).
Duhem, P.
1953   *Aim and Structure of Physical Theory.* Translated by Philip Wiener (Princeton : Princeton University Press).
Feigl, H. and Brodbeck, M. (eds.)
1953   *Readings in the Philosophy of Science* (New York : Appleton-Century-Crofts).

Feigl, H. and Sellars, W. (eds.)
1949  *Readings in Philosophical Analysis* (New York : Appleton-Century-Crofts).
Flew, A. (ed.)
1951  *Logic and Language*, First Series (Oxford : Blackwell).
1953  *Logic and Language*, Second Series (Oxford : Blackwell).
Fodor, J. and Katz, J. (eds.)
1963  *The Structure of Language* (Englewood Cliffs : Prentice-Hall).
Gleason, H.A.
1961  *An Introduction to Descriptive Linguistics* (New York : Holt).
Goodman, N.
1951  *The Structure of Appearance* (Cambridge : Harvard University Press).
Harris, Z.
1951  *Methods in Structural Linguistics* (Chicago : University of Chicago Press).
Hempel, C.
1952  *Fundamentals of Concept Formation in the Empirical Sciences* (= *International Encyclopedia of Unified Science*, Vol. II, No. 7) (Chicago : Chicago University Press).
Hilbert, D. and Ackermann, W.
1950  *Principles of Mathematical Logic* (New York : Chelsea).
Hockett, C.F.
1958  *A Course in Modern Linguistics* (New York : Macmillan).
Linsky, L. (ed.)
1952  *Semantics and the Philosophy of Language* (Urbana : University of Illinois Press).
Macdonald, M. (ed.)
1954  *Philosophy and Analysis* (Oxford : Blackwell).
Martin, R.
1958  *Truth and Denotation* (Chicago : University of Chicago Press).
Mises, R. von
1951  *Positivism : A Study in Human Understanding* (Cambridge : Harvard University Press).
Morris, C.E.
1938  *Foundations of the Theory of Signs* (= *International Encyclopedia of Unified Science* Vol. I, No. 2) (Chicago : University of Chicago Press).
Nagel, E.
1961  *The Structure of Science* (New York : Harcourt).
Northrop, F.
1947  *The Logic of the Sciences and the Humanities* (New York : Macmillan).
Passmore, J.
1957  *A Hundred Years of Philosophy* (London : Duckworth).
Quine, W.V.
1952  *Mathematical Logic* (Cambridge : Harvard University Press).

1953    *From a Logical Point of View* (New York : Harper and Row).
1960    *Word and Object* (Cambridge : M.I.T. Press).
Ryle, G.
1949    *The Concept of Mind* (London : Hutchinson).
1954    *Dilemmas* (Cambridge : Cambridge University Press).
Saporta, S. (ed.)
1961    *Psycholinguistics* (New York : Holt).
Skinner, B.F.
1957    *Verbal Behavior* (New York : Appleton-Century-Crofts).
Strawson, P.F.
1952    *Introduction to Logical Theory* (London : Methuen).
Trager, G. and Smith, H.
1957    *An Outline of English Structure* (Washington : American Council of Learned Societies).
Urmson, J.
1956    *Philosophical Analysis* (Oxford : Clarendon Press).
Warnock, G.
1958    *English Philosophy Since 1900* (London : Oxford University Press).
Wittgenstein, L.
1953    *Philosophical Investigations.* Translated by G. Anscombe (Oxford : Blackwell).
Ziff, P.
1960    *Semantic Analysis* (Ithaca : Cornell University Press).


ARTICLES


Alston, W.
1962    "Ziff's *Semantic Analysis*", *Journal of Philosophy*.
Anscombe, G.
1963    "Review of *Semantic Analysis*", *Mind* (April).
Austin, J.L.
1961    "Ifs and Cans", *Philosophical Papers*, edited by Urmson and Warnock (Oxford : Oxford University Press).
1964    "A Plea for Excuses", *Ordinary Language*, edited by V.C. Chappell (Chicago : University of Chicago Press).
Baier, K.
1951    "The Ordinary Use of Words", *Proceedings of the Aristotelian Society*, Vol. LII (1951-1952), pp. 47-70.
Bar-Hillel, Y.
1946    "Analysis of 'Correct' Language", *Mind*.
Carnap, R.
1947    "Meaning and Synonymy in Natural Languages", *Meaning and Necessity* (Chicago : University of Chicago Press).
1964    "Foundations of Logic and Mathematics", *The Structure of*

*Language*, ed. J. Fodor and J. Katz (Englewood Cliffs : Prentice-Hall) pp. 419-436.

Cavell, S.
1964 "Must We Mean What We Say ?" *Ordinary Language*, ed. V.C. Chappell (Chicago : University of Chicago Press).

Chisholm, R.
1951 "Philosophers and Ordinary Language", *Philosophical Review*, LX, pp. 317-328.

Chomsky, N.
1959 "Review of Skinner's *Verbal Behavior*", *Language*, 35, pp. 26-58.

Church, A.
1943 "Carnap's *Introduction to Semantics*", *Philosophical Review*, 52, pp. 298-304.
1951 "The Need for Abstract Entities in Semantic Analysis", *Proceedings of the American Academy of Arts and Sciences*, 80, pp. 100-112.

Fodor, J.
1960 "What Do You Mean ?" *Journal of Philosophy* (July).

Fodor, J. and Katz, J.
1963 "The Availability of What We Say", *Philosophical Review*, LXXII, pp. 57-71.

Goodman, N.
1949 "On Likeness of Meaning", *Analysis*, 10, pp. 1-7.
1953 "On Some Differences about Meaning", *Analysis*, 13.

Grice, H.P. and Strawson, P.F.
1958 "In Defense of Dogma", *Philosophical Review*, LXVII, pp. 52-75.

Hofstadter, A.
1954 "The Myth of the Whole : An Examination of Quine's View of Knowledge", *Journal of Philosophy*, 51.

Katz, J.
1963 "Analyticity and Contradiction in Natural Language", *The Structure of Language*, ed. Fodor and Katz (Englewood Cliffs : Prentice-Hall).
1962 "Review of *Semantic Analysis*", *Language* (January-March).

Katz, J. and Fodor J.
1962 "What's Wrong with the Philosophy of Language ?" *Inquiry*, V, pp. 197-237.
1963 "The Structure of a Semantic Theory", *The Structure of Language*, ed. Fodor and Katz (Englewood Cliffs : Prentice-Hall).

Kemeny, J.
1963 "Analyticity versus Fuzziness", *Synthese* (March).

Malcolm, N.
1951 "Philosophy and Ordinary Language", *Philosophical Review*, LX, pp. 329-340.
1964 "Moore and Ordinary Language", *Ordinary Language*, ed. V.C. Chappell (Chicago : University of Chicago Press).

Martin, R.
1952 "On 'Analytic' ", *Philosophical Studies*, 3, pp. 42-47.
Mates, B.
1951 "Analytic Sentences", *Philosophical Review*, 60, pp. 525-534.
1952 "Synonymity", *Semantics and the Philosophy of Language,* ed. L. Linsky (Urbana : University of Illinois Press).
1964 "On the Verification of Statements about Ordinary Language", *Ordinary Language*, ed. V.C. Chappell (Chicago : University of Chicago Press).
Nagel, E.
1956 "Symbolism and Science", *Logic without Metaphysics* (Glencoe : Free Press), pp. 103-141.
Putnam, H.
1962 "The Analytic and the Synthetic", *Minnesota Studies in the Philosophy of Science*, 3, pp. 358-397.
Quine, W.V.
1953a "Two Dogmas of Empiricism", *From a Logical Point of View* (New York : Harper and Row).
1953b "Mr. Strawson on Logical Theory", *Mind*, LXII.
1953c "The Problem of Meaning in "Linguistics", *From a Logical Point of View* (New York : Harper and Row).
Rogers, R.
1963 "A Survey of Formal Semantics", *Synthese* (March).
Ryle, G.
1937 "Categories", *Proceedings of the Aristotelian Society.*
1964 "Ordinary Language", *Ordinary Language*, ed. V.C. Chappell (Chicago : University of Chicago Press).
Smart, J.J.C.
1937 "A Note on Categories", *British Journal of the Philosophy of Science.*
Strawson, P.F.
1947 "Truth", *Analysis*, IX, pp. 83-97.
Tarski, A.
1952 "The Semantic Conception of Truth", *Semantics and the Philosophy of Language,* ed. L. Linsky (Urbana : University of Illinois Press).
Waismann, F.
1945 "Verifiability", *Proceedings of the Aristotelian Society*, sup., XIX, pp. 119-150.
White, M.
1950 "The Analytic and the Synthetic : An Untenable Dualism", *John Dewey : Philosopher of Science and Freedom*, ed. S. Hook (New York : Dial Press).

# INDEX